What Schools Ban and Why

WHAT SCHOOLS BAN
AND WHY

R. Murray Thomas

PRAEGER

Westport, Connecticut
London

Library of Congress Cataloging-in-Publication Data

Thomas, R. Murray (Robert Murray), 1921–
  What schools ban and why / R. Murray Thomas.
    p. cm.
  Includes bibliographical references and index.
  ISBN: 978-0-313-35298-0 (alk. paper)
    1. School discipline—United States.   2. School management and organization—United
States.   3. Students—Civil rights—United States.   I. Title.
  LB3012.2.T56   2008
  371.5'1—dc22   2008013665

British Library Cataloguing in Publication Data is available.

Library of Congress Catalog Card Number: 2008013665
ISBN: 978-0-313-35298-0

First published in 2008

Praeger Publishers, 88 Post Road West, Westport, CT 06881
An imprint of Greenwood Publishing Group, Inc.
www.praeger.com

Printed in the United States of America

The paper used in this book complies with the
Permanent Paper Standard issued by the National
Information Standards Organization (Z39.48–1984).

10 9 8 7 6 5 4 3 2 1

Contents

Forbidden Environments

As newspaper articles and television newscasts so often demonstrate, many of the conflicts over education in America are about which things to prohibit in schools. The diverse nature of those controversies is illustrated in the following sampling of disputes over what to ban and why.

Books and Periodicals. Mark Twain's novel *The Adventures of Huckleberry Finn* was first censured the year it was published. The *Boston Evening Transcript* on March 17, 1885, reported:

> The Concord [Massachusetts] Public Library committee has decided to exclude Mark Twain's latest book from the library. One member of the committee says that, while he does not wish to call it immoral, he thinks it contains but little humor, and that of a very coarse type. He regards it as the veriest trash. The librarian and the other members of the committee entertain similar views, characterizing it as rough, coarse, and inelegant, dealing with a series of experiences not elevating, the whole book being more suited to the slums that to intelligent, respectable people. (Alward, 2001)

Since that time—well over a century ago—*The Adventures of Huckleberry Finn* has continually been outlawed in some American schools and libraries. It was the fifth most often-banned book over the 1990–2000 decade (American Library Association, 2007). In 2002 it was in the top seven of challenged books for its alleged "racism, insensitivity, and offensive language" (Roberts, 2003).

Computers and Internet Web Sites. MySpace is an Internet service—with nearly 179 million subscribers—that allows friends to keep in touch and meet new people. Persons age fourteen or older can sign up for a MySpace account at no cost, then display whatever information about themselves they wish—interests, hobbies, opinions, educational background, and photos.

In Bloomfield (Michigan), St. –Hugo –of –the Hills Catholic School (kindergarten through grade eight) forbade pupils to use such Internet Web sites as MySpace. According to the school principal, the ban was imposed to protect children from "nasty things" posted on the Internet and from child molesters who search the Internet for potential victims. The ban was also intended to eliminate the "unhealthy competition" among pupils who were bragging about the number of people in their MySpace social network (Witsil, 2007).

Movies, Television, and Photographs. Teachers in the Newburgh (New York) school district were required to fill out a form explaining why a movie shown during class time supplemented the curriculum. The completed form had to be submitted two weeks in advance of the intended screening, and the only films permitted were ones rated PG-13 (parent permission needed for children under age thirteen), PG (parental permission suggested), or G (general—can be viewed by anyone). The regulation would not allow the showing of R-rated films (viewers under age seventeen must be accompanied by a parent or adult guardian).

By outlawing R-rated movies, teachers could no longer use such classroom favorites as the Academy Award-winning *Schindler's List* (life inside a Nazi concentration camp) and *Saving Private Ryan* (the Allied invasion of German-occupied France in 1944)—both highly acclaimed but extremely violent.

One Newburgh high school teacher asked, "Are we not supposed to deal with any of these issues that are generally brought up in R-rated movies?" Another said, "We feel it is our responsibility as educators to view and discuss even the most difficult topics in a safe and honest forum. I think censorship undermines this."

District officials said the new procedure was not intended to censor media or to infringe on teachers' freedoms. Instead, the required forms were a means of holding everyone accountable for appropriate curriculum-based movies (James, 2007).

Garb. A fourteen-year-old honor student at Redwood Middle School in Napa Valley (California) was placed in a detention program called Students With Attitude Problems because she had worn socks embroidered with a figure of Tigger from the Winnie-the-Pooh stories. The punishment was for violating the school's dress code that permitted only solid color clothing without pictures or logos. A lawsuit filed against the school district on behalf of the girl and five other students charged that the school's "unconstitutionally vague, overbroad, and restrictive uniform dress code policy" flouted state law, violated freedom of expression, and wasted teachers and students' time (Bulwa & Egelko, 2007).

> *Food and Drink.* Spurred by the rising rate of obesity among Amer-
> ican youth and the increasing availability of high-calorie, low-
> nutrient products on school grounds, a new report by the Insti-
> tute of Medicine [commissioned by Congress] proposes a set of
> nutritional standards for "competitive" foods and drinks available
> in schools. The standards promote consumption of fruits, vegeta-
> bles, whole grains, and nonfat or low-fat dairy products and limit
> the amount of saturated fat, salt, added sugars, and total calories.
> The standards also restrict the sale of caffeinated items. (Junk food
> ban?, 2007)

Speech. The American Civil Liberties Union (ACLU) filed a lawsuit against the Clark County (Nevada) School District, accusing the school board of failing to ban prayers at graduation ceremonies, thereby allegedly violating the U.S. Constitution's prohibition against public institutions fostering religion. The school board defended its position by citing the cautious wording of the follow-ing policy they had adopted regarding what student speakers said at graduation ceremonies:

> School officials may not mandate or organize prayer at gradua-
> tion or select speakers for such events in a manner that favors
> religious speech such as prayer. Where students or other private
> graduation speakers are selected on the basis of genuinely neutral,
> evenhanded criteria and retain primary control over the content of
> their expression, however, that expression is not attributable to the
> school and, therefore, may not be restricted because of its religious
> (or anti-religious) content. To avoid any mistaken perception that
> a school endorses student or other private speech that is not in

fact attributable to the school, school officials may make appropriate, neutral disclaimers to clarify that such speech is not school sponsored. (Radke, 2003)

However, an ACLU attorney disagreed on the grounds that "A graduation is a ceremony controlled by the school district, and a prayer offered in that context is unconstitutional."

Bullying and Harassment. A ten-year-old boy was hit and choked repeatedly by a bully, leaving the boy with severe bruising on his neck. The bully's mother, in response to complaints about her son's behavior, said her son was having problems at home and that the injured boy was to blame for having provoked her son (Woolf, 2004).

Music. The first amendment to the U.S. Constitution requires that "Congress shall make no law respecting an establishment of religion." This proscription has been interpreted by federal courts to mean that schools, as government-sponsored institutions, should respect the separation of church and state and therefore not promote any religion. As a result, school personnel have been puzzled about what sorts of music can legally be performed during the Christmas season. In the past, most public schools had included Christmas carols that celebrated Jesus' birth. However, in recent decades, such a practice has been challenged as a violation of the Constitution. In response to the challenge, some Arizona schools avoided religious songs by sticking with such selections as *Frosty the Snowman* and *Jingle Bells.* Other schools added tunes unrelated to Christmas so as to offer a culturally balanced program. For instance, Yavapai Elementary in Scottsdale steered clear of religious music by presenting a holiday concert consisting of *It's Beginning To Look a Lot Like Christmas, Santa Claus—You Are Much Too Fat,* a Hanukkah song, a Spanish song, and an African song. The school principal explained, "We don't do *Silent Night,* [because] you have to be real sensitive not to infringe" (Ryman, 2005).

Vandalism. At South San Francisco (California) High School, a planned celebration of *Gay Straight Alliance Week* was marred by racist and homophobic messages scrawled over nearly every wing of the school. The celebration was to include a *Day of Silence* when some students would refrain from chatting in order to demonstrate how gay and lesbian students often have to keep silent about their lives. One student reported: "Nazi symbols on some teachers' doors. There was the Star of David circled and then crossed out. There were a couple of Bible vers[e]s which I found personally offensive. On the side of the gym there was a big hand spray-painted with the middle finger sticking up saying *Day of Silence This*" (Quan, 2007).

Drugs. Four sophomore boys at Evergreen (Colorado) High School appeared to be sick and dizzy early in the school day and thus were transported to the hospital where physicians discovered the four had overdosed on over-the-counter sleeping aids before coming to school that morning (Fong, 2007).

Weapons. Because of the great harm they can do, such devices as firearms, explosives, knives, and the like are outlawed in schools. Punishment for bringing a weapon to school can be rather severe. For example, the *Gun-Safe Schools Act* passed by Congress in 1994 required each state to establish a law ordering local educational agencies to expel from school for a period of not less than one year any student who had brought a weapon to school.

The application of this zero-tolerance legislation is illustrated in the case of three boys who attended Palm Middle School in Lemon Grove (California). The three were confined in juvenile hall on a charge of attempted murder when their plot to kill a teacher was discovered. The intended attack was to be retaliation for the teacher's awarding one of the fourteen-year olds a failing grade for his poor academic performance in her class. That boy and two companions—ages thirteen and fourteen—brought a loaded pistol to school. One planned to distract the teacher so that another could shoot her (Thomas, 2006).

People. Upon pleading guilty to fondling ten girls when he was a teacher at Captain Strong Elementary School in Vancouver (Oregon), a fifty-four-year-old man was dismissed from his teaching position, sent to jail for two months, required to register as a sex offender for ten years, submit to a sexual-deviancy evaluation, and pay court costs (Gilbert, 2005).

Ceremonies and Performances. The superintendent of schools in Fulton (Missouri) cancelled an upcoming performance of the Arthur Miller play *The Crucible* after he received e-mails from three members of the Callaway Christian Church who complained that the recently performed musical *Grease* by the high school drama class had included scenes of drinking, smoking, and kissing. One letter, from a person who had not seen the performance but had heard about it, charged that the musical glorified "immoral behavior veiled behind the excuse of acting out a play." Fearing the same sorts of complaints if *The Crucible* were staged, the superintendent called off that drama's scheduled performance (Schemo, 2006).

Displays. A 1978 Kentucky state statute required all public schools to post the biblical Ten Commandments in every classroom as a guide to pupils about proper behavior. However, the U.S. Supreme Court in 1980 concluded that the statute violated the separation of religion from government that was implied in the U.S. Constitution's first amendment. The justices declared that the Ten Commandments (a) had a religious—not a secular—purpose (b) promoted the Judeo–Christian tradition, and (c) unduly entangled the government with religion. Thus, after 1980 the Ten Commandments could not legally be displayed in public schools (Thomas, 2007, Chapter 10).

THE BOOK'S PURPOSE

As the foregoing examples illustrate, different things can be judged improper for schools, and for various reasons. Proposals to ban things typically generate controversy, with pro-ban enthusiasts pitted against anti-ban advocates in impassioned disputes. The purpose of this book is to examine such controversies. The contents are organized around types of media, with each chapter—2 through 15—dedicated to one of the types illustrated in the sample cases described above, beginning with banned books (Chapter 2) and ending with banned displays (Chapter 15). Chapter 16—A Likely Future—speculates about what may lie ahead for banning things from schools.

A FRAMEWORK FOR INTERPRETING BANS

This book is a compilation of controversies about what is censored in schools. Underlying each controversy are two implied questions: *Why are such things banned? And why do people often disagree about what to ban?* In other words, what thought processes lead people to favor outlawing certain things, and why may one person's mode of thought differ from other person's?

The purpose of the following discussion is to offer a vantage point from which to answer those questions—a vantage point in the form of seven propositions that I believe help account for the ways people think about banning. The propositions are described in this opening chapter so that readers will already understand them when they are mentioned throughout the book.

None of the propositions is a novel, surprising creation. All are so familiar that they may qualify as truisms. So the purpose of reiterating them here is to demonstrate ways in which they may help explain what is banned in schools and why banning is so often controversial.

Proposition 1. People's beliefs and actions result from the interplay between individuals' heredity and environments.

The term *heredity* refers to the collection of genes provided by a person's parents. Genes establish the range of an individual's potential for intellectual, physical, emotional, and social development. Thus, genetic endowment determines what the person potentially *could* become in life. The term *environments* refers to influential daily events that people encounter as they grow up. What a person learns form those events determines the kind of individual the person *will actually become* within the range of his or her genetic potential.

Parents, school personnel, and members of the public try to protect children and youths from environments in which the young might learn harmful things. Such environments can include books, Internet Web sites, movies, music, displays, and more. Protection can take the form of blocking students' opportunities to learn from particular types of environments.

Proposition 2. People's ability to learn from environments changes with age.

From birth through adolescence, the capacity to learn improves at a rapid pace. That capacity can remain high throughout four or five decades of adulthood, then typically declines as old age advances. One kind of learning that is popularly referred to as *mature judgment* or *good sense* or *decision-making ability* is poorly developed among infants and young children but improves in middle childhood and throughout adolescence. Hence, young children are generally more at risk for learning harmful things from their environments than are older children and youths, because the young fail to recognize the potentially damaging results of copying behavior they have witnessed in books, magazines, Internet Web sites, videos, and TV programs.

Because of the age differences in pupils' learning maturity, schools often adopt different media-banning policies for young children than for older ones. More learning environments—books, photographs, ceremonies, and displays—will be banned for primary-grade pupils than for students in middle schools and high schools where youths are expected to have more *mature judgment* or *good sense*.

Proposition 3. Children of the same age level can differ significantly from each other in their genetic endowment, rate of development, and environments.

Among pupils of a particular age, some will readily adopt harmful beliefs in events they witness, while others will not. Some can accurately predict the results to expect from imitating behaviors described in books and movies, whereas others cannot. Therefore, school personnel and parents find it difficult to estimate how a particular story, video, song, or speech might affect students of a given age. Will reading *Huckleberry Finn* enrich twelve-year-olds' understanding of people and of historical times, or will it encourage the young to use coarse language and to deceive and disobey their elders? Will singing *Silent Night* in music class offend students from Jewish, Muslim, or atheist homes and damage faith in their family's traditional beliefs, or will it simply entertain them and broaden their knowledge of different religious traditions? The answer can differ from one student to another.

Consequently, the intellectual, emotional, and social-background differences among students make it difficult for school personnel and parents to judge what should be—and what should not be—banned in schools for students who are the same age.

Proposition 4. Things that people learn can be classified under various types, such types as facts, concepts, generalizations, skills, and more. The type of learning particularly important in this book is that of values.

Values are beliefs people have learned for distinguishing right from wrong, good from bad, and proper from improper. Hence, many people believe it is wrong to have sexual intercourse before marriage. Or they believe it is good to treat people of all ethnic groups in a friendly manner. Or they consider it improper to curse classmates.

Most bans in schools are intended to favor the learning of preferred values by providing students access to experiences that extol those values while blocking access to experiences that promote competing values. Thus, movies that feature people peacefully settling their disagreements may be shown in classrooms, whereas movies filled with violence are prohibited. Students may be assigned to read stories portraying obedience to people in authority as a proper way to act, whereas stories are not assigned that depict resistance to authority as desirable behavior. Songs praising women are performed in music class, whereas songs belittling women are proscribed.

Proposition 5. Because people so often differ from each other in the values they embrace, controversies arise over which values to promote in school—or at least, which values deserve highest priority.

Individuals who particularly cherish the value *freedom of inquiry* often resist the banning of any books, videos, and demonstrations. In contrast, other individuals—who fear that the indiscriminate dissemination of certain events will expose students to harmful values—seek to block students' exposure to books or movies that make ostensibly harmful values appear attractive. Various kinds of behavior may be thought to reflect undesirable values, such behaviors as heroin use, bullying, cheating on tests, using *God damn* and *Jesus Christ almighty* as curse words, sexual harassing, viewing pornographic images, and more. Persons who object to the values those behaviors seem to reflect will try to prevent students from witnessing events depicting the behaviors, even if the banning must sacrifice students' *freedom of inquiry*.

Proposition 6. *People often belong to reference groups whose members are bound together by a common set of values.*

A reference group is a formal or informal organization that a person identifies with and whose agenda the person hopes to advance. The core interests that members share can be religious (Baptist, Hindu, or Muslim), political (Democrat, Republican, or Libertarian), fraternal (Rotary, Elks, Sigma Chi, or Girl Scouts), ethnic (Irish, Mexican, or Jewish), patriotic (Canadian, Norwegian, or Pakistani), or some other kind. Such a group can function as a powerful force in (a) urging bans on school media and events that appear to threaten the group's values and (b) encouraging the school's use of information sources—books, displays, ceremonies, speeches—that foster the group's values. Clashes over censorship in schools often results from a confrontation between reference groups that subscribe to different values.

Proposition 7. *Most things that are outlawed in schools are banned for moral-value reasons. However, some things are banned for the sake of educational efficiency.*

The mission assigned to schools is that of teaching a body of subject matter, attitudes, and behaviors. To accomplish this mission, teachers are obliged to use school hours economically, ensuring that students stick at their learning tasks and not waste time. Thus, teachers may outlaw media that distract learners from their studies. Comic books and such tabloid weeklies as *Star*, *Globe*, and *Enquirer* may be banned as a waste of time. Computer games may be outlawed as time-wasters or models of destructive behavior. Likewise, students may not be allowed to bring Internet-capable cell phones to class so as to prevent them from interrupting their studies by talking with distant friends, exchanging e-mails and instant messages, joining chat groups, and viewing such social-network sites as MySpace, Facebook, and YouTube.

CONCLUSION

School personnel ban things that they believe (a) encourage students to adopt improper moral values or (b) waste time that should be spent pursuing the school's learning goals. Community groups—religious, political, fraternal, ethnic, and patriotic—often pressure schools to (a) ban media that feature values, ideas, and behaviors to which their group objects and (b) use media that promote values, ideas, and behaviors that their group favors. Controversies arise over what is prohibited whenever individuals or groups disagree about the kinds of events and values to which students should not be exposed.

The following chapters illustrate the censoring of things in schools by describing a wide variety of bans. Each chapter—2 through 15—addresses the same sequence of topics: (a) a particular ban's domain and, in some cases, its historical background, (b) representative cases of the ban's application, and (c) suggestions for school practice.

Books

The expressions *banned, censored, challenged,* or *forbidden* are commonly used in describing books, periodicals, and documents that are considered unsuitable for use in schools. Such censoring has been defined as "The removal, suppression, or restricted circulation of literary, artistic, or educational material—of images, ideas and information—on the grounds that these are morally or otherwise objectionable in light of standards applied by the censor" (Reichman in Mullally, 2007).

> People trying to ban books from libraries do not usually regard their efforts as censorship. A member of the community, school board member, or parent objects to, or "challenges," a book, requesting its removal or sequestration so that students may not have free access to it. Most frequently, books are challenged because they contain profanity or violence, sex or sex education, homosexuality, witchcraft and the occult, "secular humanism" or "new age" philosophies, portrayals of rebellious children, or "politically incorrect," racist, or sexist language. The American Library Association has documented more than 6,000 such challenges in the United States between 1990 and 2000. (Mullally, 2007)

Book banning is certainly nothing new. Since ancient times, there have always been people trying to prevent others from gaining access to reading matter that was considered dangerous. When Greek philosopher Anaxago-ras in 450 BCE wrote that he thought the sun was a "white hot stone and that the moon reflected the sun's rays," he was condemned for insulting the gods, his writings were burned, and he was expelled from Athens. His fellow philosopher, Plato, in 360 BCE approved of censorship in *The Republic*, where he planned to sanitize the reading matter available to people in his utopian society by proposing, "Our first business will be to supervise the making of fables and legends; rejecting all which are unsatisfactory."

In sixteenth-century England, William Tyndale, who partially completed translating the Bible into English, was captured, strangled, and burned at the stake (1536) by activists who opposed issuing bibles in the vernacular.

Books were not always banned outright. Instead, they could be published in expurgated editions that were trimmed of offensive contents. For instance, around 1830, publishers in the United States began issuing "family friendly" bibles from which "indelicate" passages had been deleted.

The best-organized effort at book censorship in the United States was launched in 1873 when Anthony Comstock created the New York Society for the Suppression of Vice. The main targets of Comstock's campaign were dime novels and "yellow dailies" that he dubbed "Feeders for brothels." In 1873, he convinced the U.S. Congress to pass the "Act of the Suppression of Trade in, and Circulation of, Obscene Literature and Articles of Immoral Use," a piece of legislation known as The Comstock Law that is still in effect today.

> For the next 42 years, until his death in 1915, Anthony . . . invaded publishers' pressrooms, pursued such people as Margaret Sanger, for her ideas on birth control, and Bernard Shaw for his "smutty" plays. Under Anthony's personal direction, more than 120 tons of literature was burned. Added to the more than 80 tons of literature by such authors as Dos Passos, Hemingway, and others burned after his death under the act that bears his name, Anthony weighs in at over 200 tons of burned books. The world's greatest tyrants have yet to match that figure. (Russell, 1998)

Controversies over censoring reading material have often led to court cases that set precedents affecting subsequent conflicts over bans. An especially influential judgment was the 1982 U.S. Supreme Court decision in *Board of Education, Island Trees Union Free School District v. Pico*. The trouble began in 1976 when the board of education in Levittown (New York) responded to the demand of a conservative community group—*Parents of New York United*—to remove eleven objectionable books from school libraries. The eleven were:

The Fixer by Bernard Malamud

Slaughterhouse Five by Kurt Vonnegut Jr.

The Naked Ape by Desmond Morris

Down These Mean Streets by Piri Thomas

Best Short Stories of Negro Writers, edited by Langston Hughes

Go Ask Alice, authorship anonymous

Laughing Boy by Oliver LaFarge

Black Boy by Richard Wright

A Hero Ain't Nothin' But a Sandwich by Alice Childress

Soul on Ice by Eldridge Cleaver

A Reader for Writers, edited by Jerome Archer

The board members yielded to the group's demand, ordered the eleven titles removed from library shelves, and defended their action by calling the controversial volumes "anti-American, anti-Christian, anti-Semitic, and just plain filthy" (Mullally, 2007). In response to the ban, a seventeen-year-old high-school student, Steven Pico, headed a group of fellow students who sued the school board in the U.S. District Court on a charge of violating the students' first-amendment free-speech rights. However, the court ruled that the school board could, indeed, remove the books, out of "respect for the traditional values of the community and deference to a school board's substantial control over educational content." The students reacted by taking the case to the U.S. Circuit Court of Appeals, where the district court's decision was reversed. The school board then appealed the reversal to the U.S. Supreme Court.

In June 1982, the Supreme Court—in a 5 to 4 decision—found in favor of the students. In writing the majority decision, Justice William Brennan interpreted the first-amendment's right to *express* ideas (freedom of speech and of the press) to mean an equal right to *receive* ideas. Even though school officials did have the authority to control the content of school curricula, that authority was not absolute, so "students may not be regarded as closed-circuit recipients of only that which the State chooses to communicate."

> While [school boards] might rightfully claim absolute discretion
> in matters of curriculum by reliance upon their duty to inculcate

community values in schools, [their] reliance upon that duty is misplaced where they attempt to extend their claim of absolute discretion beyond the compulsory environment of the classroom into the school library.... [School authorities] possess significant discretion to determine the content of their school libraries, but that discretion may not be exercised in a narrowly partisan or political manner. Whether [school officials'] removal of books from the libraries denied [students] their First Amendment rights depends upon the motivation behind the actions. Local school boards may not remove books from school libraries simply because they dislike the ideas contained in those books and seek by their removal to "prescribe what shall be orthodox in politics, nationalism, religion, or other matters of opinion." If such an intention was the decisive factor in [the Island Trees District] decision, then [board members] have exercised their discretion in violation of the Constitution. (Brennan, 1982)

Because the Pico decision recognized school officials' right to control the required curriculum, subsequent court cases have accepted the banning of classroom books that were judged to be vulgar.

In 1989, the 11th U.S. Circuit Court of Appeals upheld a Florida school board's removal of a previously approved classroom text because of its perceived vulgarity and sexual explicitness. Interestingly enough, the high school literature textbook was banned because it contained selections from Aristophanes' *Lysistrata* and Chaucer's *The Miller's Tale*, two authors whose works were among the thousands banned under the Comstock Law in the late nineteenth century. (Mullally, 2007)

In summary, censoring reading material has a long history that continues today in efforts to outlaw or restrict access to books in school classrooms and libraries. The multifaceted nature of this practice is reflected in the following cases.

ILLUSTRATIVE CASES

Challenges to reading materials in schools can usefully be analyzed from a variety of vantage points, such as (a) the extent to which people will go to outlaw books, (b) changes over time in reasons to ban books, and (c) types of "reality" to which students should be exposed.

The Harry Potter Saga

The twenty-first century's most-often-challenged school-library books have been the Harry Potter volumes, a series of seven titles created by British author J.K. Rowling. The first five books were made into highly successful movies.

Rowling's fantasy novels feature Harry Potter, a teenage boy enrolled in the Hogwarts School of Witchcraft and Wizardry, a training facility for young wizards. The novels' plots concern Harry Potter's fight against the evil wizard Lord Voldemort, who had killed Harry's parents as part of his plan to rule the wizardry world. By early 2007, the first six Potter books had sold more than 325 million copies and been translated into more than sixty-three languages. Critics of the Potter collection charged that the books damaged children by featuring wizardry, magic, and "Satanic influence."

A court case in the state of Georgia illustrates how persistent some critics of the Potter books have been in their attempts to rid the schools of Harry and his Hogwarts companions. Laura Mallory, a mother of two elementary-school children, attempted to have the Harry Potter volumes removed from the library of the school her children attended. Although she had not read any of the books, she charged that they fostered witchcraft and the occult, basing her complaints partly on testimonials by conservative Christian writers whose opinions she posted on her Internet Web site. She said, "Personally, I don't think it's a good idea to raise a whole generation of witches. I don't think it's good for our country" (Smith, 2007).

Mrs. Mallory's campaign began in 2005 at her children's school, J.C. Magill Elementary, whose principal refused to ban the Potter series. Thus, over the next two years, Mrs. Mallory carried her appeal to a sequence of increasingly influential authorities—the Gwinnett School Board and the Georgia State Board of Education. At each level, her request to ban Harry Potter was denied. The school board members said the books were good tools to encourage children to read and to stimulate their creativity and imagination.

The persistent mother then took her case to the Gwinnett Superior Court, where she argued that—for some people—witchcraft is a religion, so the Potter books should be banned because reading them in school violates the constitutional separation of church and state. When the judge denied her appeal, she vowed to continue her crusade, because "I have a dream that God will be welcomed back in our schools again. I think we need him" (Harry Potter, 2007).

In response to people who would ban Rowling's books from schools, defenders of Harry Potter have warned that outlawing the series would embolden censors to try cleansing the schools of other treasured fantasy tales—the Oz books, King Arthur legends, Greek and Roman myths, *Alice in Wonderland, Robin Hood, Winnie the Pooh, Aesop's Fables, Lord of the Rings,* and many more.

Reasons for Challenging Books

Objections to reading matter can vary by kind and amount, a point illustrated in (a) *And Tango Makes Three,* (b) *Bridge to Terabithia,* and (c) *I Know Why the Caged Bird Sings.*

And Tango Makes Three. This is a children's book about Roy and Silo, a pair of male penguins in New York City's Central Park Zoo. Over a six-year period, the two are inseparable—engaging in such ecstatic behavior as entwining their necks, vocalizing, and having sex. Zookeepers fail in their attempts to get the pair interested in female penguins. Then Roy and Silo display a parenting instinct by trying to hatch a stone. When sympathetic zookeepers replace the stone with an abandoned penguin egg, Roy and Silo hatch the egg and adopt the resulting female penguin as their child—Tango. The result is an unconventional family—a child with a pair of gay male parents.

When the book was published in 2005, it was lauded by some readers and condemned by others. It received several prestigious awards—a 2006 American Library Association Notable Children's Book citation and the Gustavus Myer Outstanding Book Award. It was a Nick Jr. Family Magazine Best Book of the Year and a Bank Street Best Book of the Year. At the same time, *And Tango Makes Three* was the most challenged book of 2006 for portraying homosexuality and a nontraditional family structure as acceptable life styles. The book was deemed particularly unsuitable for young children.

Bridge to Terabithia. Katherine Paterson's 1977 novel follows a pair of elementary-school friends as they create the vivid fantasy kingdom of Terabithia in woods near the rural Virginia community in which they live. The girl is Leslie, a very bright daughter of a pair of authors who left urban life to find their basic values in a small town. The boy is 10-year-old Jess, a hardworking son among four daughters in a family of modest means. Leslie and Jess yearn for the friendship of a companion who shares their capacity for imagination, sincerity, and emotional warmth. They find that companion in each other. However, after many adventures, tragedy strikes when Jess is away on a school excursion. Leslie drowns in a creek that the two friends always crossed on their way to their kingdom in the woods. The novel ends as Jess slowly recovers from the despair that followed Leslie's death, and he dedicates himself to helping others by offering them his friendship.

Bridge to Terabithia won the John Newbury Medal as the "most distinguished contribution to American literature for children" in 1978. Kent Bryson recommended the book as "an excellent novel for boys and girls ages nine to twelve because it deals with real life situations and problems that many children in the nine to twelve age group find difficult to cope with. Paterson is praised by many critics for creating a realistic boy-girl friendship, something 'so curiously unsung in literature' " (Bryson, 2007).

Other enthusiasts have applauded the book for its depiction of "friendship, individuality, honesty, and open-mindedness" and for "sensitively confronting issues such as death and prejudice" (Bertin, 2002).

However, Paterson's novel was the ninth most frequently challenged book of the 1990–2000 decade. Critics have banned *Bridge to Terabithia* for combining fantasy with reality, using profanity (*hell* and *damn*), and including children who fail to respect adults or religion. For instance, when Leslie attended church with Jess, she was interested in the story of Christ's crucifixion and resurrection but she considered it no more than a story that someone made up. She did not plan to become a Christian or to do what the Bible commanded. But, perhaps most objectionable was Leslie's death, a feature condemned by people who considered death an inappropriate subject for children. Paterson defended the inclusion of Leslie's death by explaining that

> Two of my children lost friends by the time they were eight years old. . . . [So] death was not appropriate for my children, but somehow, as their parents, we had to help them face death. . . . I feel that *Bridge* is kind of a rehearsal that you go through to mourn somebody's death that you care about. It's very *normal* to be angry when someone you love dies—even angry at the person who dies. . . . I'm always a little worried when somebody gives *Bridge* to somebody because someone has died, because I always think that it's too late. They should've read it before that. (Paterson in *Opinion*, 2007)

I Know Why the Caged Bird Sings. In this autobiography, Maya Angelou tells of her early life as an African-American child who is shunted from one home to another and on the way suffers neglect, insult, emotional abuse, rape, and self-doubt. These experiences contributed to her becoming an adult social activist honored by three American presidents—Ford, Carter, and Clinton—for her contributions to racial equality and justice.

Angelou's tale is a blunt recital of distressing life events, cast in the vocabulary of her childhood environment. Critics have objected to her candor, arguing that it soils the minds of teenage readers. As a consequence, *the Caged Bird Sings* was the third most frequently banned book of the 1990–2000 era.

There have been multiple charges against the autobiography—its rampant profanity, childhood sexual encounters, graphic portrayals of masturbation and rape, homosexuals, blatant child abuse, racial hatred, and disrespect for the law.

Typical complaints about *the Caged Bird Sings* are illustrated in passages cited on the Internet Web site of Citizens for Literary Standards in Schools:

> The [book's] crude language includes many references and comparisons to urine, pee, farting, and defecation, as well as general profanity and racial slurs such as Goddammit, shit, bitch, ass, titties, niggers, jigs, spooks, whore, hell, dykes, bulldaggers, pecker, peckerwood, and" "give me some trim." Sometimes the words are used as part of the actual conversation of the characters, but often, the words are used as Maya's personal choice of descriptive writing, "the plump brown face had been deflated and patted flat like a cow's ordurous dropping" or "the cotton truck spilled the pickers out and roared out of the yard with a sound like a giant's fart" or "I cried and hollered, passed gas and urine." Or "I decided I wouldn't pee on her if her heart was on fire." (Citizens, 2007)

In reacting to critics, proponents of *the Caged Bird Sings* praise such features of the book as its unblinking realism and its portrayal of black women of strong character.

> Though Maya struggles with insecurity and displacement throughout her childhood, she has a remarkable number of strong female role models in her family and community. Momma, Vivian, Grandmother Baxter, and Bertha Flowers have very different personalities and views on life, but they all chart their own paths and manage to maintain their dignity and self-respect. None of them ever capitulates to racist indignities. (I Know Why, 2007)

Summary. As shown by the above examples, different books can be censored for quite different reasons. *And Tango Makes Three* has been condemned for

depicting homosexuality and unconventional family structures as socially rep-
utable lifeways. *Bridge to Terabithia* has been faulted for mixing reality with
fantasy, confronting young readers with death, and lacking regard for Christianity. *I Know Why the Caged Bird Sings* has been challenged for its profanity,
child abuse, masturbation, rape, homosexuality, racism, and disrespect for
the law.

   Some schools have outlawed books for reasons somewhat rare.

   Laurence Yep's *Dragonwings* was challenged at the Apollo-Ridge schools in
Kittanning (Pennsylvania) in 1992 because it might encourage children to
"commit suicide because they think they can be reincarnated as something or
someone else."

   E.T. Suzuki's *Zen Buddhism: Selected Writings* was challenged at the
Plymouth-Canton (Michigan) school system in 1987 because "this book details
the teachings of the religion of Buddhism in such a way that the reader could
very likely embrace its teachings and choose this as his religion."

   Ellen Levine's *I Hate English* was challenged by a school board member in
the Queens (New York) school libraries in 1994 because "[t]he book says what
a burden it is they have to learn English. They should just learn English and
don't [sic] complain about it."

   Harry Allard's *The Stupids Die* was pulled from the shelves of the Howard
Miller Library in Zeeland (Michigan) in 1998 because a parent complained:
"Once you allow 'stupid' as a word to call people, who knows what they'll come
up with?" (New silly reasons, 1999).

The Incidence of Reasons

   The American Library Association's analysis of 6,364 challenges to books
over the 1990–2000 decade revealed that the eleven most frequent reasons
for condemning books were their:

   Sexually explicit material (25 percent)

   Offensive language (22 percent)

   Unsuitability for age group (20 percent)

   Occult theme or promoting the occult or Satanism (13 percent)

   Violence (12 percent)

   Homosexuality (8 percent)

   Promoting a religious viewpoint (6 percent)

Nudity (5 percent)

Racism (4 percent)

Sex education (4 percent)

Anti-family theme (3 percent)

The percentages total more than 100 percent because some books were challenged for more than one reason (American Library Association, 2007).

Shifts in Reasons for Banning Books

The reasons that self-appointed censors challenge books can change with the passing of time as a result of changes in the society within which the books are used. This point can be illustrated with Samuel L. Clemens' (Mark Twain's) first novel, *The Adventures of Tom Sawyer* (1876), and its sequel, *The Adventures of Huckleberry Finn* (1885).

When *Huckleberry Finn* was banned in 1885 from the Concord (Massachusetts) library as a book "more suited to the slums," Mark Twain explained that the "public library of Concord flung Huck out indignantly, partly because he was a liar, and partly because after deep meditation and careful deliberation he decided that if he'd got to betray [his Negro friend] Jim or go to hell, he would rather go to hell—which was profanity, and those Concord purists couldn't stand it" (New Mark Twain Letters, 1935).

In 1905, the young woman in charge of the children's room at the Brooklyn Public Library insisted on removing *Tom Sawyer* and *Huckleberry Finn* from the children's section because both boys' "coarseness, deceitfulness, and mischievous practices" set a "bad example for ingenuous youth" (New Mark Twain Letters, 1935). Professor Asa Don Dickinson, head librarian at Brooklyn College, was distressed about the young woman's decision and thus wrote to Mark Twain, informing him of what she had done. In response, Twain sent Dickinson the following letter:

Dear Sir:

I am greatly troubled by what you say. I wrote Tom Sawyer & Huck Finn for adults exclusively, & it always distresses me when I find that boys and girls have been allowed access to them. The mind that becomes soiled in youth can never again be washed clean. I know this by my own experience, & to this day I cherish an unappeased bitterness against the unfaithful guardians of my young life, who not only permitted but compelled me to read an unexpurgated Bible through before I was 15 years old. None can do that and ever draw a clean sweet breath again on this side of the grave. Ask that young lady—she will tell you so.

Most honestly do I wish I could say a softening word or two in defense of Huck's character, since you wish it, but really in my opinion it is no better than God's (in the Ahab & 97 others), & the rest of the sacred brotherhood.

If there is an Unexpurgated [Bible] in the Children's Department, won't you please help that young woman remove Tom & Huck from that questionable companionship?

Sincerely yours,

S. L. Clemens (New Mark Twain Letters, 1935)

Thus, in the late nineteenth and early twentieth centuries, the reason for preventing children from reading *Tom Sawyer* and *Huckleberry Finn* was to shield the young from the bad character traits and coarse language of the books' heroes. "Clemens' decision to include southern dialects and grammar may be one of the reasons Concord and *The New York Times* in 1885 attacked [*Huckleberry Finn*] and called it 'trashy' and 'vicious.'" The *Times* accused the author of lacking "a reliable sense of propriety" while the *New York Herald* dubbed the book "an unworthy production" (Railton, 1998).

But the twentieth century brought great social change to America. In particular, the black/white color barrier was officially broken down through antisegregation activists' efforts and legislation that accorded racial minorities deserved rights that they had never enjoyed before. African-Americans were no longer required to attend separate schools, to sit only in the back of buses, to enter buildings by separate doorways, and to be denied equal employment opportunities. Blacks rose to high political office and earned high status in sports, the entertainment world, academia, and business. Following such breakthroughs, the practice of labeling black Americans *niggers* fell increasingly into disrepute.

Thus, as a result of social progress, the main present-day reason for banning *Tom Sawyer* and *Huckleberry Finn* differs from the reasons of a century ago. Today, the chief objection to Twain's novels is their use of the word *nigger* for identifying people of African heritage—as in Huck's referring to his African-American companion as *Nigger Jim.* By the early twenty-first century many people had become so wary of saying *nigger* that they referred to the term as "the N word." A 2004 movie was *The N Word—Divided We Stand* and the 2007 book by Jabari Asim was titled *The N Word: Who Can Say It, Who*

Shouldn't, and Why. But avoiding the term *nigger* by substituting *N-word* proves to be an awkward solution to the problem of potentially denigrating African-Americans. The difficulty is that people can only understand the meaning of the expression *N-word* if they already have the word *nigger* in mind, and then they silently translate *N* into *nigger*. The potential error of using the initial letter of a term to represent the term itself was brought home to me by a first-grade teacher who said one of her pupils had rushed into the classroom during recess to report, "Michael said the F word." When the teacher inquired, "The F word?," the tattler answered, "Yeah, he said fart." So would it not make for more accurate communication to avoid the expression *N-word*—which could mean *Nordic* or *nobleman*, or *nincompoop* to the uninitiated—and to keep the word *nigger* in the vocabulary but to teach that it should not be used when it might be hurtful to people of African heritage?

Schools cope with the N-word problem in various ways. Some simply outlaw any book in which *nigger* appears. Others attempt to sensitize students to the historical background of racial issues by prefacing the reading of *Huckleberry Finn* or Harper Lee's *To Kill a Mockingbird* with lessons on insensitive words. For example, Montgomery County (Maryland) secondary-school students have prepared for Lee's book by first reading the essay *The Meaning of a Word* by the African-American writer Gloria Naylor, telling of the first time she heard a young classmate utter the N-word. Other teachers have used the poem *Incident* by Harlem Renaissance figure Countee Cullen to ready students for the *Mockingbird* tale. Parents of students in the Washington, DC, public schools can exempt their children from reading Lee's book, which has been taught after a preparatory lesson on Jim Crow, civil rights, and the justice system (de Vise, 2007).

So, in today's climate of social sensitivity and political correctness, schools puzzle over what to do about *Tom Sawyer, Huckleberry Finn*, and similar classics. Is outlawing the novels a good idea? Can studying those two books contribute positively to students understanding the history of America without appearing to endorse the pejorative use of such socially damaging slang as *nigger*?

When people attempt to answer such questions, they may choose to distinguish between (a) using *Huckleberry Finn* as a classroom textbook and (b) having the book available in the school library. The 1982 Supreme Court decision in *School Board v. Pico* drew such a distinction, allowing school authorities to fully control classroom textbooks but not have the right to remove books from a library without just cause. For example, consider a high-school class in

Cherry Hill (New Jersey) that included African-American students during the class's study of *Huckleberry Finn*. The teacher, before assigning the book, had not noted the more than 200 instances of the word *nigger* in the novel.

> As a result, according to one of the students, no one was pre-pared for the power of the word in class. White students would nervously "snicker" or "turn around and stare" at the handful of African-American students when the word was read aloud. The African-American students felt too ashamed to speak up or ask their teachers for help; instead, they simply stopped reading or attending class. (Controversy at Cherry Hill, 2007)

In such a situation, school officials might well outlaw *Huck Finn* as a required classroom text so as to protect the feelings of black students, yet still retain the book in the school library.

The question of what to do about *Huck Finn* is different for African Americans than for non-blacks, as implied in Mary Alward's essay "Should Huckleberry Finn Be Banned?"

> Since the 1950's, Huckleberry Finn has been the subject of much criticism. Twain's use of slang to describe people of color in the book has prompted efforts to have it banned time after time. . . . Though I don't agree with Twain's use of slang, I'm glad I had the opportunity to read Huckleberry Finn during my childhood. My father had taught us strict moral values. I loved being swept away to the shores of the Mississippi to join Huck on his adventures. It was a world of excitement, adventure, and wonder. It was a way of doing things in my imagination that were taboo in real life. I never would have thought of doing any of the things that Huck did. Though young, I knew that he faced many dangers. I had been brought up to know right from wrong. The things Huck done were wrong but that made the book more exciting. (Alward, 2001)

In a collection of high-school students' views of *The Adventures of Huckleberry Finn*, a white sophomore girl wrote:

> Huck Finn should not be banned from public schools. Although there are a lot of offensive racial remarks in it, it's important to remember that Mark Twain was not racist and wrote the book as a satirical criticism of the racist mindset many 19th century Americans had. It is crucial that students have access to it as a

historical document simply to prove how far we've come since then. (Yee, 2005)

Not only may non-African-Americans' attitudes toward *Huckleberry Finn* and *Tom Sawyer* change over time, but attitudes of blacks may change as well. For instance, in 1957 the National Association for the Advancement of Colored People (NAACP) charged that Huck Finn contained "racial slurs" and "belittling racial designations"—an accusation that resulted in the book being outlawed by a host of schools across the nation, including the Mark Twain Intermediate School in Fairfax (Virginia). But a more recent position adopted by the NAACP national headquarters contends that

> You don't ban Mark Twain; you explain Mark Twain! To study an idea is not necessarily to endorse the idea. Mark Twain's satirical novel, *Huckleberry Finn*, accurately portrays a time in history—the nineteenth century—and one of its evils, slavery. (Huck Finn— Teachers Guide, 2007)

Thus, the role of the teacher is crucial for determining whether *Huckleberry Finn* and *Tom Sawyer* should be used in classrooms. The way teachers guide students' interpretation of the books is a key factor determining the meaning learners assign to Mark Twain's tales.

Versions of Reality

Studying different people's lives helps us recognize that there are many versions of reality—with *reality* meaning individuals' experiences in the environments they inhabit. One of the values of novels and biographies is the opportunity they offer readers to understand realities other than their own.

Versions of reality can be either *actual* or *potential*. *The Autobiography of Benjamin Franklin* is an actual reality, if we accept that Franklin was telling the truth about his life. *The Adventures of Tom Sawyer* is also an actual reality, if Clemens was relating events from his boyhood days, including the sort of language used by the young in Hannibal (Missouri). In contrast, George Orwell's *1984* is a version of potential reality—what might happen by 1984 if socio-political trends were to continue on the trajectory that Orwell observed in 1949.

From the viewpoint of realities, book banning can be seen as the attempt to restrict the realities that students experience by eliminating books regarded as flawed models of human behavior that the young might imitate. Or the intent of a ban can be to shield students from realities that might frighten or depress still-innocent youths.

The contrast between acceptable and non-acceptable realities can be demonstrated by comparing books by Horatio Alger, Jr., with Robert Cormier's *The Chocolate War*.

Horatio Alger, Jr. Beginning at age thirty-five in 1867, Horatio Alger, Jr. (1832–1899) wrote more than 135 dime novels that sold over 200 million copies.

The stimulus for Alger's stories was his experience as a social worker in New York City at a time of massive immigration from Europe and the aftermath of the Civil War that resulted in 60,000 neglected or abandoned urchins running in the streets. Alger's novels envisioned how such waifs might raise themselves from lives of crime and despair to achieve middle-class respect and financial security by dint of hard work, courage, and concern for others' welfare. Luck might also play a role, but the transformation was mostly the product of grit, honesty, resourcefulness, and self-risk. All Alger stories end happily.

> Alger captured the essence, emotion, soul, and especially the spirit of an emerging America. His books all had the same message: no matter who they were, poor, orphaned or powerless, if they would persevere, if they would do their best, if they would always try to do the right thing, they would succeed. Through honesty, hard work, and strong determination, the American Dream was available to anyone willing to make the journey. (Bickford, 2002)

Although literary critics have scoffed at Alger's books as banal and unreasonably idealistic, there is ample evidence that the tales do, indeed, reflect the reality of some people's lives. Comedian Groucho Marx said, "Horatio Alger's books conveyed a powerful message to me and many of my young friends—that if you worked hard at your trade, the big chance would eventually come. As a child I didn't regard it as a myth, and as an old man I think of it as the story of my life." Since the Horatio Alger Association's creation in 1947, the organization has awarded citations to a wide range of Americans whose lives confirm the theme of Alger's stories. Award recipients have included Oprah Winfrey, Ray Kroc, Art Buchwald, Stan Musial, George Shearing, and Colin Powell (Kanfer, 2000).

Because Alger's books extol character traits that make for the good society—honesty, diligence, loyalty, courage, self-sacrifice—I can't imagine any of his works being banned from schools for the usual reasons that reading matter is outlawed or its access restricted.

The Chocolate War. During the 1990–2000 decade, Robert Cromier's 1974 novel *The Chocolate War* was the fourth most frequently banned book in the nation's schools. In 1995 the book was removed from school libraries in Grosse Pointe (Michigan) because it dealt with "gangs, peer pressure, and learning to make your own decisions." In 1998 and again in 2004, it was the year's most challenged book for its offensive language, violence, religious viewpoint, sexual content, and unsuitability for the junior-high-age group. In 2006, the book was dropped from the curriculum of an Idaho high school because a minister complained that it portrayed Christians in a negative fashion.

The Chocolate War is the story of a rather naive freshman football player, Jerry Renault, in a Catholic boys' school. Jerry's troubles begin when Archie Costello, the clever but sadistic leader of a school gang (The Vigils) commands Jerry to refuse to participate in the plan of the acting headmaster, Brother Leon, who intends to collect extra funds by selling 20,000 boxes of chocolates, with each boy assigned to pedal fifty boxes. Archie's assignment for Jerry is like a gang initiation rite, a form of hazing designed both to irritate Brother Leon and to demonstrate Archie's ability to dominate Jerry. Like Archie, Brother Leon is a sadist, getting pleasure from humiliating students. Brother Leon is also a spendthrift, running the school into debt during the real headmaster's absence. Archie's intent is to have Jerry refuse to sell chocolates for ten days, and then to cooperate with Brother Leon's campaign, with Archie taking credit for making Jerry capitulate.

But when the tenth day arrives, Jerry still refuses to sell chocolates, because he now considers the entire conduct of the school—The Vigils' oppressive antics and Brother Leon's exploitation of the students—to be a sham. Emboldened by a poster displayed inside his school locker ("Do I dare disturb the universe?"), Jerry decides to war against the system, using the chocolate sale as his weapon. He intends to follow his own judgment of what is right. But his continuing refusal to sell chocolates infuriates Archie and Brother Leon. The Vigils then take revenge. In chapter after chapter, they harass Jerry with phone calls throughout the night, damage the contents of his school locker, destroy his homework assignments, sabotage his efforts at football practice, accuse him of homosexuality, and finally stage a fight between Jerry and the school bully in the stadium, witnessed by the entire student body and Brother Leon. To the cheers of the crowd, Jerry is beaten so badly that he falls unconscious with a broken jaw and internal injuries. When he wakens and is about to be carried away in an ambulance, he tells his only friend not to disturb the universe—it isn't worth it.

As one analyst of *The Chocolate War* has observed,

> Cormier does not revisit Jerry in the last chapter, [thereby] leaving the reader with a dismal feeling about Jerry's future. We do not know the final prognosis of Jerry's injuries, nor do we know how this traumatic series of events will shape Jerry's future. The reader can hope that Jerry will prevail, but the tone at the end is bleak, suggesting that Jerry's recovery will be long coming, if ever. (Chocolate War, 2007)

So, how close to the truth is *The Chocolate War?* Reports of conditions in many American schools suggest that the events related in *The Chocolate War* do, indeed, represent many students' reality. And what about Jerry, the central character of the tale? He's not a bad person nor a bad role model for readers, for he exemplifies the same virtues as Horatio Alger's heroes—bravery, persistence, sensitivity to others' welfare, and intent to do the right thing. Why, then, has *The Chocolate War* been so widely banned in schools for more than three decades? Apparently it's because the book's reality is one that some people don't want students to witness. In the book, teenagers are not portrayed as noble, compassionate, and fair. As Archie says in Cormier's tale, "People are two things: greedy and cruel." And finally, quite unlike Horatio Alger's stories, virtue is not rewarded in *The Chocolate War.* There is no happy ending.

When Cormier was asked to defend his book, he said the language and controversial scenes simply reflected how kids talk and what they think about, so without those elements the book would lack credibility with young readers. "They're not looking for titillation, they're looking for validity. . . . [The book isn't] gratuitous. If it were, it wouldn't have been taught in hundreds of schools. . . . I feel like I must have done something right. There wouldn't be all these concerns about an ineffective book" (Chocolate War author, 2000).

Out of the Closet

Cultural changes that a society produces with the passing decades affect the kinds of books that are challenged during different eras. An example of this phenomenon is the issue of homosexuality. Among the top ten challenged books of the 1990–2000 decade, only one—Michael Willhoite's

Daddy's Roommate—blatantly addressed homosexuality in the guise of a non-traditional family. One other—Maya Angelou's autobiographical *I Know Why the Caged Bird Sings*—touched on lesbianism. But in 2006, four of the top ten censored books were condemned partly for their treatment of homosexuality:

> *And Tango Makes Three*, by Justin Richardson and Peter Parnell, was censored for its homosexuality, nontraditional family, and unsuitability for its age group.

> *Gossip Girl* series, by Cecily Von Ziegesar, was banned for the books' homosexuality, sexual content, alcohol, drugs, unsuitability for teenagers, and offensive language. The series—consisting of twelve books from 2002 through 2007—follows high-society teenagers in New York City's glamorous, sophisticated Upper East Side. The central characters are rich girls who shop, party, drink, and cope with issues of sex, drugs, and relationships. A blurb on the back jacket of the first in the series suggests the series central theme: "Welcome to New York City's Upper East Side, where my friends and I live, go to school, play, and sleep—sometimes with each other."

> *Athletic Shorts* by Chris Crutcher, was challenged for its homosexuality and racially offensive language. Crutcher's book of six short stories set in sports settings include one tale about a man dying of AIDS, thereby inviting complaints that the author was approving of homosexuality. In response to critics, Crutcher wrote,

>> [h]omosexuality is a reality in the world, and it always has been. Kids would much rather we found ways to discuss those tough issues than to pretend they don't exist. They say over and over that we don't understand. Why don't we see if we can prove them wrong? (Clutcher in Halls, 2005)

> *The Perks of Being a Wallflower* by Stephen Chbosky, was banned for homosexuality, explicit sexual scenes, offensive language, and unsuitability for its age group. The tale is cast as a sequence of letters written by Charlie, a shy, unpopular high-school freshman who recounts his experiences with such teenage concerns as sexuality, drug use, and introversion.

Several conditions have apparently contributed to the increase of challenges to books addressing homosexuality. One condition is the gay/lesbian social movement over the past two decades that drew widespread public attention to the vigorous public efforts of homosexuals to win opportunities and protec-tions denied to them in the past. As part of the movement, hosts of individuals, who previously had not been known as gay or lesbian, openly admitted their nontraditional sexual preference. With homosexuality becoming an increas-ingly open topic and more widely accepted, publishers were willing to issue more books with homosexual motifs. At the same time, more authors were disposed to write about such matters. And as public acceptance of homosex-uals grew, so also grew the threat to the moral values of people who accepted heterosexuality as the only normal, permissible sexual orientation. Under such a combination of conditions, it seems hardly surprising that the frequency of banning books with gay and lesbian characters would rise.

The Age Problem

Perhaps the most troublesome issue faced in the debate about banning books is reflected in the question, "At what age should children or youths be permitted to read a particular book?" Or, more precisely, "At what age can a particular book make a positive contribution to a person's life rather than cause damage." In effect, many of the controversies over censorship are not about whether the public should have access to certain books but, rather, at what age those books should be available. Hence, a typical complaint is the kind expressed by a mother whose fourteen-year-old son was obliged to read *The Chocolate War* in a middle-school English class—"We're not censoring anything. We don't want it banned. It has merit. But not for eighth-graders" (Chocolate War author, 2000).

There is little doubt that what children and youths read can affect their beliefs and behavior. That's the whole point of learning to read—to acquire new ideas, expand one's range of experience, understand other people's lives. But harm can result when readers model their behavior on examples of unsuitable beliefs and actions in books. And the younger the reader, the greater the danger that events portrayed in books will be misunderstood and mistakenly applied to the reader's own life. In particular, the young child cannot accurately predict the consequences of adopting beliefs and actions from stories. For these reasons people may approve of having certain books available to adults but not available to children below a given age—especially books featuring violence and sexual acts. The problem then becomes one of agreeing on what age that should be.

The difficulty of setting a reasonable age results primarily from the individ-ual differences among children—differences in their innate intellectual ability,

their parents' child-rearing practices, and their companions' attitudes and behavior. Some children's mental development is slower than that of others,
with the slow ones less adept at accurately predicting the consequences of
behavior, thus placing them at risk of harm from books that are beyond their
understanding. Some parents' child-raising methods establish constructive
values in children at an early age, thereby equipping the young to make wise
judgments about the desirability of copying ideas and actions in stories they
read. In contrast, other parents' abusive or neglectful child-raising habits—
along with harmful examples they offer by their own beliefs and actions—can
encourage their offspring to adopt objectionable behavior depicted in books.
And as children develop into adolescents, it's apparent that values held by
their companions can affect how students will react to scenes of violence, sex,
racism, illicit drugs, and religious views in books they read. Finally, whether a
book will harm the young rather than serve as a positive influence can depend
on the way a teacher guides students in interpreting the book's content.

One way to distinguish between *anti-ban* advocates (people who allow children to read controversial books at a younger age) and *pro-ban* advocates
(people who withhold such books from readers) is by identifying the principal
arguments offered in defense of the two groups' positions. Anti-ban proponents feature *preparation* and *expanded-experience* reasons. Pro-ban supporters
feature *confusion/fright* and *destructive-models* reasons.

The *preparation* argument contends that if children and youths meet a potentially distressing event (death, accident, rape, puberty changes, divorce,
premarital sex, drug addiction) in a book before they face it in their own lives,
they can be better prepared to respond to the event when it does appear in their
lives because they have already vicariously witnessed and thought about it. The
expanded-experience defense states that individuals can cope more adequately
with life if they understand other people's beliefs and behavior. Ergo, children
and youths at relatively early ages can profit from reading about many other
people's realities.

In contrast to such reasoning, pro-banners who withhold books from young
readers propose that stories rife with sex, violence, and alternative philosophical positions (religion, moral values) *confuse* and *frighten* readers who are too
immature to resolve such matters in their minds. In addition, immaturity can
lead to readers *modeling* themselves after a book's characters who behave in
antisocial and self-destructive ways (alcohol and drug addiction, irresponsible
sexual escapades, theft, fraud, exploitation).

Thus, in setting an acceptable age at which a controversial book should be
available to students, parents and school personnel are obliged to choose an

age that provides *preparation* and *expanded-experience* while avoiding *confusion/fright* and *bad models*. Because of the individual differences among children and youths, and because teachers differ in the way they help learners interpret stories, there is no age choice that will be proper for every reader or every classroom. The chosen age becomes a "best guess"—an age at which a book will perhaps do the most good with the least harm for the largest number of readers.

WHO CHALLENGES BOOKS?

There are various ways to categorize the people who ban books. Judith Saltman has divided censors along a political dimension ranging from conservatives on the right to liberals on the left.

> Conservatives object to frank language and profanity, images of nudity, references to sexuality, especially homosexuality, ideas that threaten their values, such as the undermining of authority and content believed too mature or inappropriate for children's understanding.
>
> The liberal side of the spectrum objects to perceived images of racism, sexism, ageism, elitism, materialism, and cultural appropriation, and judges children's books solely for positive images of women, ethnic minorities, senior citizens, and the disabled. Many adults judge children's books only on their perceived developmental or bibliotherapeutic values or commitment to social change. (Saltman, 1998)

> Heated battles over the matter of censoring books are often fought with emotionally charged language that reveals the religious and political positions of the adversaries. For instance, two residents of Cromwell (Connecticut) in 2002 petitioned the town's school board to withdraw *Bridge to Terabithia* from schools in order to "eliminate the study of materials containing information about witchcraft, magic, evil spells, or related material, now and forever. . . . We believe this material is satanic, a danger to our children, is being studied excessively, and has no place in our schools." (Grogan, 2002)

Then, from an opposing philosophical position, a book reviewer wrote,

> How could it be that a book as wonderful as *Bridge to Terabithia* is involved in a censorship controversy? Well, if you live in one

of the Conservative mid-Western or Southern states, you already
know why the book has been banned from school libraries there.
The right-wingers claim that there is a lot of profane language in
the book, but that is absurd. Oh, there are a few scattered uses of
the words *damn* and *hell*, but it's nothing that kids haven't heard on
"family friendly" TV shows. I think the real problem these right-
wingers have is with the book's attitudes toward religion and politics. Leslie Burke comes from a very liberal family; her father is a
political activist. The Burkes do not practice a religion. (Petersen,
2000)

Another way of classifying participants in book-banning debates is in terms
of groups that ban books versus groups that object to book censorship. For
example, the following organizations challenge reading matter in order to
promote their values by preventing readers from access to competing values
(Who is Doing, 2007).

Anti-Defamation League

Christian Voters League

Church of Scientology

Citizens for Literary Standards in Schools

Concerned Women of America

National Association for the Advancement of Colored People

National Association of Christian Educators

National Federation of Decency

New England Watch and Ward Society

Parents Against Bad Books in Schools

Roman Catholic Church's Index of Prohibited Books

Government departments at the national, state, and local levels may ban
books and periodicals, either to protect the organization's secrets or to prevent
readers from access to information that might harm the department's operations. Here are some U.S. government agencies that practice such censorship:

Bureau of Customs

Central Intelligence Agency

Federal Bureau of Investigation

Table 2.1. *Initiators of Book Challenges—2000–2005 (n = 3,050)*

Initiator	Number	Percentage
Parent	1,824	60.0
Patron	263	8.7
School administrator	207	6.9
School board member	72	2.4
Teacher	62	2.1
Government	57	1.9
Pressure group	51	1.7
Elected official	20	0.6
Religious organization	18	0.6
Clergy	10	0.3
Other groups	466	15.0

Source: Office of Intellectual Freedom, 2007.

Food and Drug Administration

Justice Department

National Security Agency

Treasury Department

The U.S. Postal Service has refused to deliver mail judged to be obscene, with the definition of obscenity varying somewhat from one era to another. Organizations that usually denounce book banning include:

American Booksellers Association

American Civil Liberties Union

American Library Association

Banned Books

Banned Books Online

First Amendment Center

People for the American Way

A final vantage point from which to view book banning focuses on the type of person or group that initiated the challenge to a book. For instance, consider the American Library Association's report of the percentages of different ban initiators in 3,050 challenges over the 2000–2005 period (see Table 2.1).

SUGGESTIONS FOR SCHOOL PRACTICE

For school personnel, deciding what should be done about challenges to books and periodicals is often not a simple task. It involves weighing the rights, the authority, the welfare, and the power of diverse participants—students, parents, teachers, the courts, and community groups. The following suggestions are offered as potential guidelines for coping with book-banning conflicts.

As a preparation for settling challenges to books and periodicals, school districts can prepare a statement of policies about reading materials used in classes and reading matter placed in libraries. The statement can include:

- A rationale explaining how a balance is sought between (a) freedom of speech and (b) harm students might suffer from unsuitable reading material. The rationale might refer to the legal principles behind the U.S. Supreme Court's decision in the Pico case described earlier in this chapter. To help ensure that the statement recognizes the concerns of those parties most intimately interested in book banning, the statement can be cooperatively developed by teachers, parents, administrators, and school-board members—perhaps after consultation with responsible high-school students—and with final formal approval by the school board.

- Criteria to be used in judging a book's suitability as a curriculum material (a book used in class assignments) or as a library holding.

- The procedure to be followed when a book is challenged—to whom the challenge should be sent, how evidence for and against a ban should be collected, who should participate in resolving the issue, and how a final decision will be reached.

Early in the semester, teachers can send parents a list of books to be used in their child's class, thereby avoiding the accusation that teachers surreptitiously assigned students reading matter that parents would consider unsuitable.

A reading list can be suggestive rather than obligatory, so students are able to avoid items on the list that they or their parents regard as damaging or distasteful.

For reading matter that some parents consider unsuitable but that others consider appropriate, parental permission can be required before a student is allowed access to the material.

Teachers or administrators can compile a file of material about a controversial book (reviews of the book from periodicals, court cases, authorities' opinions) as evidence to show parents, students, or community members who object to using the book for class assignments or as a library holding.

When a book is to serve as a text that all class members will study, any student can be exempted from the class sessions in which the book is used if the student's parents object to the book. However, this is usually an awkward solution to the problem, for it may stigmatize the exempted student in classmates' eyes.

Computers and the Internet

Whereas censoring books is the oldest form of education bans, censoring ways of using electronic computers is the newest form. Banning books—on papyrus, stone, or tree bark—began thousands of years ago. Banning ways of using computers began hardly two decades ago.

Before the 1980s, electronic computers were generally large machines used in research, business, and government to store and manipulate massive amounts of information that was often in a numerical form. The *personal computer* was introduced in the 1980s. It was small enough to rest on a desktop, simple enough that nonexperts could operate it successfully, and sufficiently affordable to be bought by a large portion of the population. Over the past two decades, the technology has developed so rapidly that computers have become by far the world's most popular communication, information-gathering, and data-storage devices. Computers assume a variety of forms, including desktop machines, "laptop" and "notebook" devices, cell phones, digital cameras, music players, hand-held calculating machines, or all sorts of functions combined in a single tiny instrument. Such devices are said to belong in the domain of *cybernetics*, a domain often defined as the science of communication and control in animals (including humans) and machines.

The world's computers are able to communicate with each other through *cyberspace* via the Internet, which is an enormous system of electronic networks. By means of the Internet, people send e-mail (electronic mail) instantly to nearly any place on earth, they chat with distant friends, and they access information posted on millions of sites of a World Wide Web.

The expansion of computers over the past two decades has been phenomenal. Analysts have estimated that by 2008 there were one billion personal computers in operation around the world, a quantity expected to double by 2015 (Chapman, 2007). In the United States during 2006, there were 14.2 million personal computers in schools, an average of one computer for every four students. All public schools had access to the Internet. By 2003, 83 percent of students, ages 3 to 17, had used a computer at school, and 43 percent had accessed the Internet. Seventy-five percent used the Internet for completing school assignments either at school, at home, or elsewhere. At home, pupils' second most common use of computers was to do school work, exceeded only by the time they spent playing computer games (U.S. Census Bureau, 2007).

So, in a very short period of time, personal computers and the Internet have become ubiquitous in American schools, bringing educational advantages as well as problems that have resulted in school personnel outlawing several ways that computers can be used. The purpose of this chapter is to analyze those ways and to suggest how schools might control misuse without stifling students' creativity or violating students' freedom of speech and access to information.

SCHOOLS' COMPUTER PROHIBITIONS

Schools typically ban the use of computers for (a) cheating on tests, (b) cheating on class assignments, (c) visiting forbidden Web sites, (d) storing forbidden information and images, (e) playing video games, and (f) hacking. A recent problem yet to be solved is that of students (g) using a video camera or camera-cell phone to place pictures of teachers on the Internet.

Cheating on Tests

Test cheating consists of a person's seeking the symbols of intellectual accomplishment without having acquired the knowledge and skill that the symbols are supposed to signify. Those symbols can be of various sorts—diplomas, certificates, degrees, high marks on school assignments, letters of recommendation, scholarships, job opportunities, public acclaim, and the phrase *magna cum laude* appended to a diploma.

Cheating on tests involves a student receiving illicit help in answering test questions when that person has failed to master the field of knowledge that the test has been designed to sample. Such help usually assumes one or both of the following two forms: (a) students study the test questions prior to the test session or (b) students receive unauthorized aid during the test session.

Traditional ways of getting unauthorized pretest assistance have included students

- Remembering items from a test and describing the items to schoolmates who will be taking the test later.

- Stealing test booklets during testing sessions, then passing the booklets on to friends who will be sitting for the tests at a later date.

- Breaking into a teacher's concealed collection of tests or test items, then selling or giving copies to classmates who will be taking the tests.

Traditional methods of cheating during the administration of a test include students

- Carrying unauthorized information into a test session in the form of notes slipped into one's sock or shirt pocket, symbols written on one's arm or palm, or cues taped under the classroom desktop the day before the test.

- Receiving notes from other test takers.

- Receiving signals from a classmate about which multiple-choice answers to mark.

- Peeking at classmates' test answers.

- Whispering answers to nearby test takers.

While students continue to use these time-honored styles of cheating, the popularity of such ruses has been dwarfed by schemes made possible with wireless communication devices known as *personal digital assistants* or PDAs, which include cell phones, pagers, and handheld computers. From inside or outside the classroom, students can communicate with each other during a test session by means of PDAs.

The high-stakes-testing movement that began in the 1980s and accelerated into the twenty-first century increased the pressure on students to score well on standardized achievement tests. That pressure reached a high point in 2002 with the introduction of the federal government's nationwide No-Child-Left-Behind program. An increasing number of states and school districts have since adopted graduation-test policies. Regardless of whether students passed all of their high-school classes, they are not awarded a high-school diploma unless they also pass graduation tests in such subject-matter fields as English, mathematics, and science. Thus, the temptation to cheat on standardized tests has increased dramatically in recent years. Moreover, with that increase, so has the temptation for students to use cybernetic devices for cheating.

The main method of pretest cybernetic cheating consists of students breaking into teachers' or schools' computers to copy test items, with the copies then given or sold to schoolmates.

Ways to cheat during tests sessions include students

- Bringing answers stored in a PDA.
- Receiving information by cell phone from a companion outside the classroom.
- Using a PDA as a calculator to carry out mathematical functions (find square roots, divide fractions, determine correlations) that students are expected to perform during the test session.
- Copying test items into a PDA for later use by classmates who will be taking the same test.

Because PDAs have been widely used for such purposes, it has become common practice for teachers to confiscate all such devices prior to administering tests. In some schools, cell phones are completely outlawed, not only to reduce test cheating but also to eliminate students' phoning friends during class sessions.

Cheating on Class Assignments

Plagiarism is the act of claiming to be the author of material that someone else actually wrote. Students may plagiarize book reports, term papers, essays, projects, and graduate-degree theses. Teachers—including college professors—may plagiarize journal articles, course materials, and textbooks. Researchers may plagiarize reports, articles, and book chapters.

Academic plagiarism is nothing new. However, what has been new since the latter years of the twentieth century is the ease with which writings on virtually any topic can be misappropriated with little risk of detection. The principal

instrument responsible for the recent rapid rise in academic plagiarism has
been the Internet, which John Barrie (a developer of software for detecting Web
plagiarism) calls "a 1.5 billion-page searchable, cut-and-pasteable encyclopedia"
(Barrie in Thomas, 2003).

Especially popular among assignment-cheaters are the online paper mills,
cheat sites, or essay banks, which are companies that give—or more often
sell—students essays, book reports, projects, or theses that can be submitted
in school under students' own names. By mid-2005, there were at least 780
paper mills worldwide, a 10 percent increase over 2004. Those on the World
Wide Web bear such names as *CheatHouse* (more than 70,000 essays on 190
subjects), *Term Paper Experts* (15,000 term papers), *Genius Papers, Research
Assistance, Cheat Factory Essay Warehouse, Superior Term Papers,* and *12,000 Pa-
pers.com.* In Germany, *Cheatwebsite* has advertised high-scoring essays, term
papers, stories, interpretations, book reports, and other types of school assignments. The site reported having between 3,000 and 5,000 high-school
and college users a day. The *School Sucks* paper mill not only offers 100,000
completed term papers but also customized papers written by "moonlighting
teachers," with custom papers priced at $50 per page for same-day service and
$25 per page for one-week delivery.

Paper mills that furnish essays at no cost include *4freeessays, Easy and free,
123 Free Student Essays,* and *All Free Essays.* Most free papers come from other
student users and are typically mediocre or less in quality so they are not always
easily recognized as plagiarized.

In an effort to avoid the cybercheating label, some sites claim they are
merely offering "sample essays" that serve as "models" for students to follow
in creating their own papers. Such Web pages also provide tips on how to cheat
on exams and how to order papers custom-made to suit specific topic and/or
length requirements.

The extent of cyber plagiarism was suggested in the results of a 2003 survey
of 11,000 high-school students by the Rutgers' University Center for Academic
Integrity in which 58 percent of respondents admitted copying unaccredited
material from the Internet for school assignments (Nearly 800, 2005).

In an effort to curtail the use of cheat sites, the world's most popular Internet
search engine, Google, in May 2007 began refusing paper-mill advertisements
(Andreatta, 2007).

Teachers' efforts to curtail plagiarism commonly assume the following three
forms: (a) instructing students in proper ways to acknowledge the sources of
quoted material, (b) watching for clues to plagiarized content in students'

assignments and (c) entering students' essays into Internet antiplagiarism sites.

Proper acknowledgement practices. Obviously, students do not naturally know acceptable ways to include content from other people's writings in their own essays. Thus, they must be taught about copyright laws, what constitutes "fair use" of copied material, how to acknowledge directly quoted passages, ways of paraphrasing an author's ideas, the use of footnotes and endnotes, bibliographic and reference styles, and the like. To aid with this task, teachers can assign class members to consult such Internet Web sites as the free Prentice-Hall tutorial on plagiarism which explains how to

- properly attribute sources you use in your papers
- properly quote material
- accurately summarize material
- carefully paraphrase material, and
- cite and attribute information retrieved from electronic or other unconventional sources (Understanding plagiarism, 2007).

Safeguards teachers can adopt at the outset of a writing assignment include (a) illustrating the difference between plagiarism and the honest identification of sources used in a paper, (b) giving assignments which specify the elements that the term paper or essay is to include, (c) requiring students to document the sources used throughout their entire paper, (d) insisting that students submit their paper in successive stages (intended topic, intended sources of data, outline of intended sections, first draft, corrected draft, final version), and (d) requiring students to incorporate material from their class in their writing, with the teacher discussing their paper's intended structure and sources ahead of time.

Clues to plagiarism. Teachers can often identify plagiarism by looking for suspicious signs in students' papers. Typical clues to cheating include these that Robert Harris described.

- *Lack of references or quotations.* Lengthy, well-written sections without documentation may have been taken from general knowledge sources, such as encyclopedias, popular magazines, or Web sites.
- *Unusual formatting.* Strange margins, skewed tables, lines broken in half, mixed subhead styles, and other formatting anomalies may indicate a hasty copy-and-paste job.

- *Off topic.* If the paper does not develop one of the assigned topics or even the topic it announces, it may have been borrowed at the last minute or downloaded. Similarly, if parts of the paper do develop the subject, but other parts seem oddly off, the product may be a cut and paste.

- *Signs of datedness.* If there are no references after some well-past date (e.g., 1985), or if a data table offers a company's sales from 1989 to 1994, either the student is using very old material or the paper itself is rather old.

- *Anachronisms.* If the paper refers to long-past events as current ("Only after the Gulf War is over will we see lower oil prices" or "Why isn't the Carter administration acting on this?"), you almost certainly have a recycled paper on your hands. (Harris, 2004)

Anti-plagiarism services. Not only has the Internet greatly expanded students' ability to plagiarize, but it has also enhanced teachers' ability to expose material lifted from Web sites. The most valuable tools for discovering cyber-plagiarism are Web checkers or verifiers. The typical Web checker is an Internet service that works the following way. A student's paper is entered into the checker's Web site. That Web site is programmed to compare the contents of the paper with the contents of billions of documents on the World Wide Web—books, journal articles, magazine stories, and students' essays. The Web verifier sends a report back to the teacher, showing how much of the student's paper is identical to, or highly similar to, documents on the World Wide Web; and the report identifies what those original documents were.

Plagiarism checkers usually charge for their services, either a flat annual fee or a stated amount for each paper processed. The most popular service is *Turnitin*, reported to be used by hundreds of educational institutions in eighty countries. *Turnitin* compares student papers (submitted via the Internet) to a database of over 4.5 billion World Wide Web pages, 10 million papers, and material from *ProQuest*, which provides access to 125 billion digital pages of the world's scholarship. *Turnitin* identifies each passage of eight consecutive words or more in a student paper that matches an identical passage in any document in the company's database. The Originality Report received by the teacher displays the student's suspected passages and the sources they match.

Another much-used checker has been *Essay Verification Engine* or *EVE2*, which sends teachers the result of a search in the form of the percent of the essay that has been plagiarized and an annotated copy of the essay showing all plagiarism highlighted in red.

In addition to using such services as *Turnitin* and *EVE2*, teachers can conduct a plagiarism hunt by employing a combination of the search engine Google and the University of Virginia's program WCopyFind.

Educators who have used Web-plagiarism checkers report that telling students that their papers will be Web-checked reduces the incidence of Internet plagiarism.

Visiting Forbidden Web Sites

Types of Internet Web pages that schools ban include ones containing pornography, information about how to conduct illegal activities, and students' personal identification. Computer software known as Web blockers or Web filters serve as the chief means by which schools and parents prevent students from visiting such sites. Those four topics—pornography, illegal activities, personal identification, and Web filters—are the focus of the following section.

Pornography. Illicit sexual material typically consists of pictures or descriptions of naked persons or of people engaged in sex acts. Individuals who exhibit such material to the young, or who have pornographic material available where children or youths might find it, are guilty of breaching child pornography regulations.

Child pornography—sometimes known as *kiddie porn*—is defined as

> visual depiction of minors (i.e. under 18) engaged in a sex act such as intercourse, oral sex, or masturbation as well as the lascivious depictions of the genitals. Various federal courts in the 1980s and 1990s concluded that "lewd" or "lascivious" depiction of the genitals does not require the genitals to be uncovered. Thus, for example, a video of underage teenage girls dancing erotically, with multiple close-up shots of their covered genitals, can be considered child porn. (Child Pornography, 2005)

The most common form of pornography violations in recent years has involved sexually explicit images on computers, particularly images from the Internet.

A forty-year-old woman substitute teacher at Kelly Middle School in Norwich (Connecticut) faced up to forty years in prison when convicted in court of exposing students to pornography on a school computer. During the trial, she claimed that the images just happened to appear on pop-up ads, but the prosecutor noted that the teacher had intentionally opened such blatantly pornographic Web sites as *meetlovers.com* and *femalesexual.com* (Substitute Teacher, 2007).

Not only may students or faculty members lift pornographic images from the Internet, but also they may create images by taking photographs of students in sexual poses. Or, as an alternative, a person may obtain nonpornographic photos of students, then alter the pictures by the use of computer software to render them sexually seductive.

A forty-eight-year-old fourth-grade teacher in Burnett County (Wisconsin) was arrested for obtaining photos of two high school girls, modifying the pictures to make them pornographic, storing them in his computer, and displaying them on the Internet. He was sentenced to six months in jail and ten years of probation for possession of child pornography (Belden, 2007).

With the advent of the Internet, seduction efforts have spread rapidly, often with members of a chat group displaying pornographic photos and inviting viewers to join in a personal relationship. A survey by the National Center for Missing and Exploited Children reported that 25 percent of children between ages ten and seventeen had been exposed to sexual material on the Internet (Karl & Associates, 2005). As the Internet has so efficiently promoted instant communication among individuals in different parts of the world, coalitions of sexual predators have mushroomed, resulting in greater threats to the safety of children and teenagers who search the World Wide Web.

The Internet allows pedophiles:

> Instant access to other predators worldwide;
>
> Open discussion of their sexual desires;
>
> Shared ideas about ways to lure victims;
>
> Mutual support of their adult–child sex philosophies;
>
> Instant access to potential child victims worldwide;
>
> Disguised identities for approaching children, even to the point of presenting themselves as members of teen groups;
>
> Ready access to "teen chat rooms" to find out how and who to target as potential victims;
>
> Means to identify and track down home contact information;

Ability to build a long-term Internet relationship with a potential victim, prior to attempting to engage the child in physical contact (Mahoney & Faulkner, 1997).

In the most extreme cases of parents' failure—or inability—to supervise youngsters' computer activities, disastrous consequences result.

A thirteen-year-old sixth-grade girl had come to Danbury (Connecticut) to live with her aunt, because the girl's parents had substance-abuse problems. In Danbury she attended a Catholic school where she earned good grades, was a cheerleader, and served as an altar girl at church. She became an avid computer user, continually visiting chat rooms where she assumed sexually provocative names for herself that attracted admirers with whom she set up sexual trysts. One of her sexual partners was a twenty-five-year-old married man, an undocumented immigrant from Brazil who worked in a local restaurant. During one of the girl's encounters with the man, he strangled her. When apprehended, he confessed the murder to the police and led them to the ravine in which he had dumped her body (Karl & Associates, 2005).

Illegal activities. The Internet is a worldwide communication channel that allows virtually anyone anywhere to put opinions, information, and images on Web sites available to nearly anyone anywhere. Although some governments forbid their people to visit certain sites, there really is no way to control what goes on the Internet. Consequently, information on the World Wide Web includes a variety of harmful activities, which, if seen by children and youths, may equip them to adopt behavior damaging to themselves and others. For example, consider the potential effects of the following:

> *Drugs.* When a researcher entered the term "no prescription codeine" into the computer search engine Google, fifty-three of the first 100 generated Web pages offered to sell opiate medication without a prescription. Thirty-five also sold barbiturates, benzodiazepines, hallucinogens, and other stimulates. Around half of the sources were registered outside the United States. One pledged to "reship your order for free in the event of confiscation." Another estimated that "there is less than a one-percent chance of your package being seized" because of the "high volume" of mail-order narcotics entering the United States (Internet boosts, 2007).

> *Bomb-making recipes.* Directions for constructing explosive devices are easily found on Web sites offering such terror manuals as *The*

Anarchist Cookbook IV and the *Terrorist's Handbook* that tell how to make plastic explosives, napalm, pipe bombs, ammonium nitrate, dynamite, TNT, Molotov cocktails, and phone bombs. The *Terrorist's Handbook* includes a "Checklist for Raids on Labs" that suggests "in the end, the serious terrorist would probably realize that if he/she wishes to make a truly useful explosive, he or she will have to steal the chemicals to make the explosive from a lab" (Bomb-making manuals, 2007).

Three high-school students in Ogden (Utah) admitted to police that they had learned from the *Anarchists Cookbook* Web site how to make the bomb they had set off at a Jehovah's Witnesses church. A pair of fifteen-year-old boys in Orem (Utah) were sent to a juvenile detention center for constructing a pipe bomb by following Web page instructions. And fourteen-year-olds in online discussions debated "which propellants are best to use, which Web sites have the best recipes, and whether tin or aluminum soda cans make better bomb casings" (Bomb-making manuals, 2007).

Weapons. Guns, swords, daggers, and knives are sold on the Internet, and juveniles may try to buy them with forged weapons licenses. For example, two juveniles in Montclair (New Jersey) were arrested after using a fraudulent gun license to order four weapons over the Internet from a gun dealer in Texas. The pair were caught when a package-delivery service reported them to the police after the driver delivered the guns to a residence, instead of to a gun store, and noticed that no adults were there to sign for the package (Clinton announces, 2000).

Internet auctions. Many Web sites are designed to auction off products, usually by connecting individual sellers or small businesses to individual buyers who bid for the advertised items. Ebay is perhaps the most popular auction site. However, some sellers are crooks, intent on bilking unwary buyers, so that purchasing items through auctions involves risk. Among the thousands of complaints about fraud that the U.S. Federal Trade Commission receives each year, a large proportion are about Internet auctions—failure to ship purchased items, products of poorer quality than advertised, and false online payment services. Teenagers can be either victims or perpetrators of fraudulent auction schemes, so school officials may try to prevent students from contacting auction sites from school computers.

Personal identity. The term *personal identity*, as used here, means material on a Web page telling about the life of the individual who posted the material. The information may include the person's name, e-mail address, home address, phone number, age, school attended, family's description, hobbies, activities, ambitions, friends' names, photographs, music, videos, and more. In effect, the posting is a type of *blog* (short for Web log)—an online journal of the writer's reflections and comments, sometimes embellished with links or hyperlinks (related Web sites).

A variety of Web sites—designed to display personal information and facilitate individuals communicating with each other—bear such names as *MySpace, Orkut, Friendster, iShoals, Yahoo! 360, Hi5, Bebo, Facebook,* and *Xanga.* One called *YouTube* specializes in members sharing videos.

Characteristics of personal-identity services can be illustrated with the most popular site—MySpace—one of the world's most frequently visited Web pages. It attracts 80 percent of the social-networking traffic. Individuals who are at least age fourteen can establish a *MySpace* account at no cost, then customize their profile with information about themselves and their friends.

In 2006, MySpace claimed to have well over 100 million accounts, with thousands of new customers registering each day. But, when one researcher studied how many members consistently used their accounts, he concluded that the number of active users was perhaps 43 million, which still is an enormous number (Barbarian, 2006).

However attractive Internet social-contact sites appear to be, they entail some potential harm. The danger risked by people who place their profiles in a social-network includes sexual abuse, property loss, and reputation damage.

Sexual abuse can occur when a visitor to a teenager's or young adult's place seduces the teenager into a tragic encounter—unrequited affection, disgusting sexual acts, rape, pregnancy. disease, or the like. For example, a thirty-four-year-old man created a MySpace site in which he described himself as a nineteen-year-old North Carolina State University student and, through searching MySpace profiles, persuaded two boys, ages fourteen and fifteen, to have sex with him, a ruse that landed him in prison. In December 2006, the operators of MySpace announced that new methods were being adopted to protect children from known sex offenders in the United States, but no details were given about what those methods would be. In February 2007, a U.S.

District Judge in Texas ruled that parents could not sue MySpace for negligence, fraud, and misrepresentation because their daughter had been sexually assaulted by a man she met through MySpace after she had misrepresented her age as 18 when she was 13. The judge reasoned that the parents, not MySpace, had the responsibility for protecting the girl. In May 2007, MySpace began screening their 177 million accounts worldwide for sex predators. Pressured by states' attorneys, the company released a list of 7,000 registered sex offenders who had MySpace profiles (North Carolina battling, 2007). During the same month, the North Carolina state senate passed a bill requiring youths below age 18 to have their parents' consent before they could sign up for a MySpace account (Weigl, 2007).

Property loss can result from someone stealing a space-holder's social-security number or credit-card number and using that information to extract funds or charge goods to the space-holder's account. Damage to a client's reputation occurs when a mean-spirited rival surreptitiously places damaging lies on the client's page.

Students can help protect their personal information by recognizing the danger of *phishing*, which consists of someone placing a bulletin on a student's MySpace through an advertisement that has a login screen. The screen is really a fake, so when the student logs in with his or her e-mail address and password, the creator of the bulletin can steal intimate information. Therefore, an intruder's purpose of phishing is to stealthily hook onto private data without the space holder's knowledge.

Educating teenagers about the risks of visiting potentially dangerous Web sites is one way to protect them from harm. But the way that gives parents and school personnel more secure control over what the young see on the Internet is to install Web filters on computers or computer systems.

Web filters—pro and con. Computer users gain access to the Internet via an ISP—Internet Service Provider. The ISP may be a commercial provider—such as America Online, MSN, ATT-Yahoo, or Earthlink—or it may be an institution, such as a university or school system. It is possible to install a device (a Web proxy server) between the ISP and the computers that students use at home or at school. A proxy server can be programmed to purge information from particular Web sites. Thus, parents and school personnel can prevent students from visiting Web sites that are considered harmful or perhaps a waste of time. Such proxy devices are known as Web filters or Web blockers.

A great variety of Web filters on the market are designed for use on home and/or school computers. Consider this sample of filters advertised on the

Internet: *WebBlocker, WiseChoice, Kid Safe, Net Nanny, CYBERsitter, CyberPatrol, Cyber Centinel, McAfee Parental Controls, Norton Parental Controls, MaxProtect, FilterPak, Safe Eyes, K9 Web Protection, Block Web Site Buddy, Netmop, WebWatcher, SpectorPro 6.0, SpyAgent, IamBigBrother, Content Protect, 8e6 Technologies, Websense, SurfControl, Symantec, N2H2, CyBlock, Untangle, Predator Guard,* and *Barracuda.*

Web blockers are distinguished from each other by such features as (a) the types of Web material they will screen out, (b) how easily they can be programmed, (c) cost, (d) reliability, and (e) flexibility (how different patterns of filtering can be suited to different types of users, such as young children versus teenagers).

In their advertising, Web filter companies emphasize qualities of their products that they consider particularly appealing to customers. *Smart Filter Bess*— designed for schools and libraries—not only allows administrators to block online plagiarism sites, but also displays on the computer screen the school's policy on plagiarism each time a student attempts to visit a cheatsite.

WebWatcher is touted as providing administrators with the ability to (a) block access to inappropriate Web sites, (b) see each Web site a user has visited, (c) read every e-mail sent or received, and (d) see both sides of the conversation of every Instant Message or Chat in which a user participated.

CyberPatrol is designed to block by (a) the particular individual using the computer, (b) groups of users (such as seventh graders), (c) the time of day that computers are used, (d) how long a user is online, (e) particular Web sites, and (d) specific kinds of banned material (pornography, racist, hate).

Sophos blocks computer games that lure students into wasting study time or that feature violence and sexual content regarded as harmful.

In one study that assessed the comparative advantages of twelve commercially available Web filters, the top three products were *Net Nanny, CYBERsitter,* and CyberPatrol. The systems were rated on such features as the sorts of Internet contents filtered, monitored, or blocked (chat groups, e-mail, pop-up ads, peer-to-peer connections, newsgroups), password controls, and how Internet users' profiles were displayed (Internet filter report, 2007).

Alorie Gilbert and Stefanie Olsen's (2006) evaluation of filter programs offers suggestions for parents and school personnel.

> Consider your Internet provider. Filtering comes free with [such servers as] AOL, EarthLink, or MSN. AOL and MSN both filtered effectively, but AOL blocked sites such as NewsMax, a conservative

political site, and Operation Truth, an advocacy site for Iraq War veterans. In both cases, a parent could override the block.

Weigh protection [of children] versus interference [with children's legitimate activities]. All filtering programs either overblock or underblock. For young children, look for maximum protection. For older children, look for filtering software that doesn't overly interfere [with what children should be allowed to do].

[Select which activities you need to control.] Older children are more likely to engage in activities such as e-mail, instant messaging, and gaming.

Decide how much customization you need. If your children aren't close in age, consider a program that can be customized by age. [Programs] that offer more filtering flexibility, make fine-tuning [by age] easier but may not offer [the most reliable protection]. (Gilbert & Olsen, 2006)

Some filter programs have come under attack by critics who accuse them of blocking Webpages that should be available to users. For example, operators of the Web site *Peacefire* are especially concerned about rights of free speech and open access to information.

The site has conducted long battles against the most commonly used filter programs, including, most famously, Net Nanny, Cyber-Patrol, and Bess. In particular, Peacefire has demonstrated that the filter programs suppress political speech and filter preferentially for corporate and conservative causes. In other cases, Peacefire has presented evidence that several filtering programs block some Web sites without having a human being review those sites first, despite the filtering companies' claims to the contrary. However, Peacefire is not usually active against filters that act in a more neutral way. (Peacefire, 2007)

In 1998, an Internet expert, Lawrence Lessig, warned that Web filters were poor devices for controlling people's access to harmful sites because "Filtering software is 'opaque' [and] necessarily relies on blunt, mechanistic key words and phrases to identify potentially troublesome material [so that] it censors far too much" (Heins, 2003). However, in 2000, Congress passed the Children's Internet Protection Act (CIPA) that was intended to shield minors from seeing sexually explicit material. The act required libraries and schools (those that received federal funds for Internet connections) to install filters on their computers whether the computers were used by minors or adults, including library staff members. When a lawsuit was filed in 2002 against the government by free-speech advocates, a three-judge federal court struck down the CIPA, citing problems of inaccuracy, overblocking, and secrecy that resulted in filters screening out "thousands of Web pages with no sexual content, on subjects ranging from religion to politics, careers to public health" (Heins, 2003). But, when the case was appealed to the U.S. Supreme Court in 2003, the justices, in a 6 to 3 decision, reversed the lower court's ruling, thereby reinstating the CIPA.

So it is that the debate continues about which Internet sources to block, with the debate accompanied by computer buffs figuring out new ways to bypass filters and companies that sell filters inventing new ways to foil the bypassers.

Storing Forbidden Information and Images

Schools' rapid adoption of computers over the past two decades has confronted teachers and administrators with problems of protecting students from illicit images and information stored on school computers.

The most prominent kind of forbidden display is pornography that exposes school children to seductive images of naked people, adult sexual activities, or minor children performing sex acts in photos or videos. For example, at Castlemont Elementary School in San Jose (California), a third-grade boy saw pictures of a partially robed girl on his teacher's computer screen. When the boy reported this to his mother, she informed the police, who seized computers from the forty-four-year-old teacher's home, his classroom, and a relative's home. The police found additional pictures of children in sexual poses on the computers as well as a folder in the classroom containing explicitly sexual photos of children. Authorities arrested the teacher on a charge of possessing child pornography (Buchanan, 2004).

There are various sources of computer-stored pornography, including images from Web sites, digital photos or videos taken by students or teachers, and pictures from magazines scanned onto a computer's had drive.

Other kinds of objectionable stored content are pictures of violent acts, descriptions of how to create homemade bombs, sources of harmful drugs, methods of using such substances as cannabis and cocaine, recipes for manufacturing methamphetamine, and the like.

Playing Computer Games

As the number of computer-game programs has burgeoned in the twenty-first century, school personnel and parents have faced the need to identify which games are appropriate for children and youths. In 1994, as a response to public pressure and threats of congressional legislation, game producers formed an Entertainment Software Rating Board (ESRB) that labels games for their suitability at different age levels.

EC (Early Childhood). Ages 3 and older; no material parents would find objectionable.

E (Everyone). Ages 6 and older; minimal cartoon, fantasy, or mild violence

E 10+ (Everyone over age 9). More cartoon, fantasy, or mild violence; minimal sexually suggestive themes.

T (Teens). Age 13 and older. Violence, suggestive themes, crude humor, minimal blood, simulated gambling, infrequent use of strong language.

M (Mature). Age 17 and older; intense violence, blood and gore, sexual content, strong language.

AO (Adults only). Age 18 and older; prolonged scenes of intense violence and/or graphic sexual content and nudity (ESRB, 2007).

Hacking/Cracking

In popular publications, such as newspapers and magazines, the term *hacking* has referred the act of secretly, illegally breaking into a computer system to steal information or to alter the operation of computers. In such cases, a computer's legitimate operator has not given permission to alter the computer, and the operator usually is unaware of the break-in. However, experts in the computer world object to such a deprecating application of the words hacking and hacker. Hence, they reserve the term hacker for identifying "a person who enjoys exploring the details of programmable systems and how to stretch their capabilities, as opposed to most users, who prefer to learn only the minimum necessary" (Definition of hacking, 2007).

> Hackers are computer-programming experts. They are the people who invented the Internet and run it today. They are creative

and brilliant, always inventing new computer technologies and solutions. They are also the people creating computer software and computer games. Without them there would be no computers and no Internet. Hackers are the Internet equivalent of engineers who can build cars, take cars apart and make them run better, or even customize cars into amazing styles. Most of us who use the Internet are like the drivers of cars. Sure, we can drive, but could we actually BUILD a car? (Hatcher, 2001)

So the computer world's "true hackers" use the term *cracker* to identify "a malicious meddler who tries to discover sensitive information by poking around" (Definition of hacking, 2007).

Crackers are also hackers, and also computer programming experts, but they use their hacking skills to do harm to other people's computer networks. Crackers are the people who break into government Web sites and leave rude messages. Crackers are the people who break into other people's computers and steal or destroy valuable data. Crackers are people who crack security codes on software in order to deal in pirate software, which is an illegal activity. (Hatcher, 2001)

A cracker is someone who breaks into someone else's computer system, often on a network; bypasses passwords or licenses in computer programs; or in other ways intentionally breaches computer security. A cracker can be doing this for profit, maliciously, for some altruistic purpose or cause, or because the challenge is there. Some breaking-and-entering has been done ostensibly to point out weaknesses in a site's security system. The term "cracker" is not to be confused with "hacker." Hackers generally deplore cracking. (Sjohon, 2007)

Thus, crackers are the kind of hackers that concern us in this chapter.

Modern-day schools typically store sensitive records in computers that cannot be entered without a secret password or special set of operations. Sensitive records include test items, students' grades and personal data, teachers and administrator's private information, budget expenditures, and more. Passwords are reserved for authorized personnel. Other people—students, parents, members of the community, and some members of a school's staff—are banned from entering secured files.

However, sophisticated computer buffs can sometimes crack into secure systems, usually with the aid of software programs known as *spyware* that are surreptitiously installed in a computer without the user's informed consent. Such software can be added secretly when someone else is using the computer, when the computer is being repaired, or when the user is intentionally downloading other information from the Internet. Spyware is one form of a broader class of invasive, unwanted programs known as *malware* or *badware* that includes such irritating and destructive computer intruders *viruses*, *worms*, *trojan horses*, and dishonest *adware*. Spyware can intercept information sent to the computer, take partial control over how a person uses the computer, monitor the user's behavior (such as keeping track of the sequence of keys that are tapped when an e-mail is composed), and collect the computer's stored data.

Although teachers still keep grade books in which they record the scores students earn on tests, essays, and projects, schools today store semester-end grades in master computer files whose access is available only to authorized personnel. However, students with a sophisticated knowledge of computer programming are sometimes able to crack into such files by circumventing the system's security walls. Crackers can then change students' grades in the files—raise an F to a respectable C or elevate a B to an A.

A typical case of grade changing was the successful effort of a pair of students at Western High School in Davie (Florida) to crack the school's supposedly secure central computer system. The intent of the two was to change various schoolmates' grades for tests and quizzes. The scam was exposed when a teacher noted that a zero she had awarded a student on a test had been changed to 100 percent. A check of other grade-records showed similar tampering. When the two crackers were caught, they were suspended from school. An official said he did not know how many grades had been changed, but one of the culprits admitted altering twenty grades or attendance records for $5 each occasion (Farrell, 2002).

The aim of crackers may not be to change students' records but, rather, to collect classified information. For instance, Cedarburg (Wisconsin) High School students used a school computer to find confidential information on the school district's computer network about former and current employees' names, addresses, Social Security numbers, and bank account information. School officials discovered the breach after a student told a teacher that some schoolmates had broken into the district's ostensibly secure network (Students use Cedarburg, 2007).

To prevent crackers from entering secured files, schools can adopt antispyware programs that prevent the installation of spyware and/or cleanse systems of spyware already in a computer. Examples of antispyware programs are *Windows Defender, Spy Sweeper, Spyware Doctor,* and *CounterSpy V2.*

Administrators sometimes invite a hacker to try breaking into protected files so as to determine how cracker-proof a school's computer-security system is. For instance, the principal of Anzar High School in San Juan Bautista (California) asked a fifteen-year-old computer buff to try penetrating the secured files. Within less than one second, the youth, aided by three spyware programs, discovered the system's password—*Silvia* (the school secretary's name). He then left evidence in the files to prove that he had been the surreptitious visitor. Because he was already a straight-A student with a 4.0 grade-point average, he could not raise his GPA, so he lowered his average to 1.9—D+. As a result, school officials began plugging the holes in the security system. The student explained, "I'm helping them with it. I basically came up with three pages to improve the security of the network in general. [And] I made sure it was really easy for them to change [my grade average] back to 4.0" (Legon, 2002).

However, school authorities did not appreciate a seventeen-year-old hacker's exposing weaknesses in a computer security system at Turlock High School (California). The officials had him arrested for breaking into the system without school officials' knowledge or permission.

Posting Classroom Scenes on the Internet

Since the advent of camera cell phones and such social-network sites as MySpace and YouTube, students have increasingly been taking video or still photos of their teachers during class sessions, then posting the results on the Internet. The postings often portray teachers in embarrassing poses, with the pictures accompanied by students' rude comments. A representative of the American Federation of Teachers warned that such practices could damage the educational process by causing teachers to change their spontaneous ways of interacting with students for fear of being photographed.

The task of curbing such antics has been difficult, particularly because judges in two court cases (*Evans v. L.A. Unified School District* and *Roberts v. Houston Independent School District*) declared that teachers have no privacy rights in their classrooms, which means that they can legally be photographed during class sessions. It is true, however, that students can be cited for misconduct if their picture taking has seriously disrupted the learning program. Some schools have coped with the problem by outlawing cell phones, at least in classrooms, thereby reducing students' opportunities to photograph teachers in unbecoming poses (Honawar, 2007).

SUGGESTIONS FOR SCHOOL PRACTICE

Schools can profitably (a) offer students guidance in using the Internet, (b) distribute a computer-policy statement to students and their parents, and (c) install Web-filtering software on their computer networks.

Guiding Students' Computer Use

To protect pupils from predators who surf the Internet to find candidates for sexual exploitation, the U.S. Federal Bureau of Investigation has recommended that, when children have access to the computer Internet, their teachers and parents should warn them to:

Never arrange a face-to-face meeting with someone they met on-line.

Never display pictures of themselves on the Internet to people they do not personally know.

Never give out identifying information such as their name, home address, school name, or telephone number.

Never download pictures from an unknown source, as there is a good chance there could be sexually explicit images.

Never respond to messages or bulletin board postings that are suggestive, obscene, belligerent, or harassing. (Freeh, 2005)

In addition, children need to learn that whatever they are told over the Internet may or may not be true.

Most children that fall victim to computer sex-offenders spend large amounts of time on-line, particularly in chat rooms. They may go on-line after dinner and on the weekends. . . . They go on-line to chat with friends, make new friends, pass time, and sometimes look for sexually explicit information. Children on-line are at the greatest risk during the evening hours. . . . [because most sex] offenders work during the day and spend their evenings on-line trying to locate and lure children or seeking pornography. (Freeh, 2005)

To help prevent students from committing plagiarism, teachers should explain to students

- The meaning of plagiarism and the nature of copyright laws,
- Proper ways to cite sources of information that students use in writing essays and term papers,
- Ways that teachers can discover plagiarism in students' written work—ways that include the use of Web-plagiarism checkers, and
- The consequences of being caught plagiarizing.

Teachers should also describe (a) the school's rules about the sorts of material that students are not allowed to store on school computers and (b) the consequences to be expected by persons who break those rules.

Distributing a Statement of Computer-Use Policy

To help ensure that concerned members of the community understand the permissible use of school computers, school officials can distribute a formal policy statement to students and their parents. The statement can address issues of

- Plagiarism,
- Internet filters and access to Web sites,
- Restrictions on personal digital assistants (cell phones, pagers, cameras),
- Rules governing social-network sites (MySpace, Friendster, YouTube, and the like),
- Playing games on school computers, and
- Procedures to follow for resolving conflicts over computer use.

Installing Web Filters

To control the Web sites that students are permitted to visit on school computers, school officials can install filter software. Because many filter products are on the market, officials can profitably collect information about a variety of different types so as to choose a system best suited to the particular school's needs. The search can be guided by such questions as the following. Sales representatives for each company's filter software can be asked to provide written answers to the questions so the school has a record of each company's claims about its product.

- What kinds of material can the filter eliminate—pornography, online games, social-network sites, chat groups, cheatsites, and the like?

- How can the school customize the kinds of material that are blocked so as to fit (a) different groups of users (by age, by grade level) (b) individual computer users, (c) time of day, and (d) subject-matter fields?

- What is the total cost of the filter system?

- What provisions are made for correcting problems with the system?

- How readily can hackers bypass the system, and by what means does the system foil efforts to bypass it?

Movies, Television, and Photographs

For untold centuries, people have banned pictures they regarded as offensive. Before the invention of photography in the 1830s, all banned pictures were the products of an artist's pencil, pen, paintbrush, print-blocks, or etching tools. Although by the twenty-first century there continued to be hand-drawn pictures that were censored, by far the greatest number of condemned images were photographic—both moving pictures and still pictures.

Over the past 170 years, photographic technology has expanded at an accelerating pace in types of cameras, ease of operating cameras, quality of pictures, printing processes, and the numbers of people taking pictures. As a result, most Americans today can afford to buy cameras that produce high-quality photos (either still or moving) and to purchase devices for viewing them— cell phones, i-pods, computers, and printers. Thus, members of the general public—including students—find it easier than ever before to take and distribute pictures that critics may deem offensive enough to be banned from schools. At the same time, there has been a marked expansion of commercially produced movies and photographs that can also be judged unsuitable for schools.

In parallel with the development of photographic technology, changes have evolved in American culture. Hence, some kinds of pictures considered censorable in the past are no longer judged so at present, and vice versa. World War II—and particularly the 1960s—represented a shift in attitudes about sexual behavior so that (a) unmarried couples living together became increasingly acceptable, (b) premarital sex among teenagers and young adults became more common, and (c) portrayals of sexual behavior in movies and on television grew more explicit.

> The landmark *Miracle* Supreme Court decision of the early 1950s declared that films were protected as "free speech" by the first amendment to the Constitution, and most censorship was ruled unconstitutional. In a remarkable 9-0 decision, the Supreme Court decided that the New York Board of Regents could not ban Roberto Rossellini's short film *The Miracle* (1952) under regulations barring "sacrilegious" films....
>
> [In the twenty-first century] sexy and erotic images in film scenes can be displayed in many kinds of films. Sexual scenes may appear in art-house films, horror/slasher films, erotic dramas, foreign-language films, and mainstream films. They may be "old-fashioned," risque, blatant, mature, PG-13, excessive, suggestive, cheap, exploitative, outrageous, innovative, infantile, soft hued and soft focused, campy, voyeuristic, trashy, sensual, highly-charged, symbolic or visually metaphoric, carnal, highly-choreographed and artsy, prurient or soft-core NC-17. Erotic films, unlike pornography, do not have as their sole purpose the explicit and graphic display of sex and nudity. Erotica sometimes is explicit, but can often be teasing, intriguing, s[t]ylized, unique and imaginative. However, trends in recent art-house films (that are unrated) suggest that simulated sex is becoming more explicit, unsimulated sex—bordering on pornographic! Although most theatrical releases are often edited to obtain an R-rating, the DVD releases include the "director's cut," with unrated, explicit extra material. (Dirk, 2007)

In a similar trend, the amount of violence in films has also increased.

> In a content analysis of movie violence, we randomly selected twelve top-grossing American war films from four decades (1970 to 2002). We coded for implements of violence, length of violence, gore, and violence directed at noncombatants. We hypothesized that recently released war movies would be more violent than those released earlier. We found that films released since 1990 did contain more violence compared to others. Further, the intensity of gore increased in recently released movies. (Monk-Turner, et al., 2004)

These changes in "standards of decency" have led to increasing controversies over what sorts of photographic matter are appropriate for schools and for students of different age levels—controversies that array proponents of conserving traditional standards against advocates of free access to photographs and films of all kinds.

The purpose of this chapter is to analyze the controversies in terms of (a) typical conflicts over forbidding pictorial material in schools and (b) suggestions for the position school personnel might adopt toward such issues.

TYPICAL CONTROVERSIES

The movies, television programs, and photographs banned in schools are ones that (a) glamorize and encourage violence, (b) foster unacceptable sexual behavior, (c) denigrate ethnic or religious groups, or (d) are politically contentious.

Glamorizing and Encouraging Violence

Teachers obtain instructional motion pictures from several sources: (a) movies on DVDs (digital video discs) or on magnetic tape, available from the school district's instructional-materials department or from a rental store, (b) television programs that a class watches during school hours, (c) television or theater motion pictures that students are assigned to watch during nonschool hours, and (d) television shows that teachers or students copy onto magnetic tape or discs so the programs can be watched at convenient times during the school day. TV channels particularly useful as sources of educational programs include *History, Discovery, Biography, Classic Movies, National Geographic, Travel,* and *Public Broadcasting Service.*

When a teacher contemplates using a movie to depict a historical event, a famous person's life, or a social problem, there is a chance that the movie will cast the event in a violent form that could do more damage than good for the students. The fact that portrayals of raw violence have grown dramatically over the past century is reflected in this reminiscence—

> The first violent film that "moved" an audience was the *Great Train Robbery* in 1903. Ticket holders reportedly ran from the theaters in terror when the villain pointed his phony prop gun directly into

the camera. In 1931, when James Cagney starred in *Public Enemy*, a New York Times film critic berated the picture as "sensational and incoherent ending in general slaughter." In fact, there were a total of eight deaths, each one taking place off screen. Compare that with the 1990 Bruce Willis film *Die Hard 2* with 264 brutal killings, all in front of the camera. Another disturbing trend has been showing up over the past few years. Humor is being introduced in violent movies to inoculate the audience from the horror of violence. Films like *Natural Born Killers* and *Pulp Fiction* exemplified that tend. The comedic elements in *Pulp Fiction* worked so well that the audience lost touch with the seriousness of the crimes. Many even empathized with the criminals. A majority of audience members interviewed in exit polls felt the villains were "somewhat justified" in their murderous acts. (Rolfe, 1997)

The extent of brutality on television during the mid-1990s was reported in a National Television Violence Study that covered more than 6,000 hours of television programming on 23 channels over a three-year period (1994–1997). Sixty percent of the programs contained violent scenes. In one-third of the programs the villains were never punished, and 70 percent of those who committed violence showed no remorse about their deeds. In 40 percent of the cases, the hero was the perpetrator of violence. Fewer than 5 percent of the brutal programs included antiviolence messages (*National Television Violence Study*, 1997).

The question of whether violent movies and television programs damage children and youths has been a highly controversial issue. However, the preponderance of evidence suggests that damage can, indeed, result. The harm includes—

- Increased antisocial behavior and aggression
- Violence desensitization and lower levels of empathy toward others
- Increased levels of fear due to perceiving the world as violent
- Acceptance of violence as a way of settling conflict
- Higher tolerance and threshold of violence leading to a desire to experience more violence in both video games and real life (Violence, 2007).

In response to public clamor about brutality in entertainment media, the movie and television industries responded with rating systems designed to warn parents and school personnel about who might suffer harm from particular motion pictures and TV programs. Both industries' rating methods are based on the assumption that younger viewers are more susceptible than older ones to violent, sexual, and profane content. In short, both systems are age graded.

The Motion Picture Association of America introduced its scheme in 1968 and has made periodic adjustments to it ever since. The most recent code letters and their meanings are as follows:

G: General Audiences—All ages admitted.

PG: Parental guidance suggested—Some material may not be suitable for children.

PG-13: Parents strongly cautioned—Some material may be inappropriate for children under age 13.

R: Restricted—Viewers under age 17 must be accompanied by a parent or adult guardian.

NC-17: No one age 17 and under admitted.

NR: Film is not rated.

Following the passage of the federal government's Telecommunications Act of 1996, a rating system was created by the television industry in collaboration with child advocacy organizations. It was a voluntary-participation system with no legal force, but it was adopted by most broadcast and cable networks. The system was designed to utilize the V-chip, a device built into all television sets that allowed parents and school officials to block certain categories of programs. Television networks often display the rating of a program by a symbol in the corner of the television screen. The symbols bear the following meanings.

TV-Y—Appropriate for all children

TV-Y7—Directed to older children; may not be suitable for children under age 7.

TV-Y7-FV—May not be suitable for children under 7; contains fantasy violence.

TV-G—General audience; for viewers of all ages.

TV-PG—Unsuitable for young children without the guidance of a parent.

TV-14—Parents strongly cautioned that content may be offensive.

TV-MA—For mature adult viewers only.

Several codes may be added to the TV-PG, TV-14, and TV-MA ratings—V = intense violence; S = intense sexual situations; L = strong, coarse language; and D = intensely suggestive dialogue.

Schools have frequently used the movie- and television-rating schemes as guides to what sorts of films and TV programs will be permitted at different grade levels. However, both rating schemes have been criticized for inconsistency and a measure of secrecy in how their standards are applied. Furthermore, teachers have complained that strictly applying a rating system without allowing exceptions can result in denying students valuable learning experiences. As noted in Chapter 1, the Newburgh (New York) school system prevented teachers from using any R-rated films, so two highly regarded movies, *Schindler's List* and *Saving Private Ryan*, could not be shown in high-school classes because of the films' scenes of violence.

Fostering Unacceptable Sexual Behavior

Banning views of erotic portions of the human body and of erotic acts has been of even greater concern to the public than has banning violence, as shown by the movie and television rating standards. And over the past century, public standards of sexual morality have undergone marked changes. Consider, for example, the greater flesh exposure accepted in female swim attire over the nine decades between 1918's full-body garments with knee-length bloomers and 2008's skimpy string-thongs. Schools are caught in this transition, obliged to set standards of dress that encourage students to concentrate on their studies without being distracted by classmates' erotic displays of body contours that copy styles from films, television, and advertising photos.

In a similar trend, the kinds of sexually suggestive acts permitted in public have also changed over the past century, with increasingly permissive behavior reflected in the movie and TV fare to which students are exposed. Schools are thus confronted with the task of monitoring teens' actions and speech so that students' sexually tinged behavior neither offends others—classmates, parents, school personnel—nor diverts learners from their studies.

Problems that educators often face with pictorial portrayals of sex are illustrated by the following cases.

Sexual behavior in school. The entertainment media have been blamed—at least partly—for portraying sexual behavior that teenagers then copy at school, thus allegedly helping produce such events as these in the state of Virginia during 2005:

- Two girls and three boys at Osbourn High School in Manassas were suspended from school for engaging in oral sex in the darkened school auditorium.
- Two students were apprehended having sex in an Anne Arundel County high school gym.
- Four students at Colonel Zadok Magruder High in Rockville were arrested after performing sex acts in the school parking lot.
- A boy and a girl at Springbrook High in Silver Spring were caught "touching inappropriately" in a school bathroom.
- Three teenage boys at Mount Hebron High in Howard County were arrested after a girl accused them of sexually assaulting her in a school restroom, but charges were dropped after the boys said the sex was consensual and the girl recanted.
- A graduate of Dunbar Senior High reported that during his years there, "Students would have intercourse on the stairwells, locked classrooms, in the locker rooms." (Bahrampour & Shapira, 2005).

Pornography. Schools have always been forced to cope with students or staff members' collecting and sharing sexually explicit drawings, cartoons, and photos. However, until the arrival of the Internet and its World Wide Web, individuals were never in such a favorable position to collect and distribute erotica in the form of "dirty pictures" (both moving and still) as they are today. Some students or teachers pursue the compelling pastime of finding sexually stimulating pictures on the Internet and storing them in a computer— either a school computer or a laptop, or hand-held device brought from home.

For example, a sixty-nine-year-old middle-school art teacher in Westport (Connecticut) was sentenced to ten years in federal prison and assessed a $30,00 fine for amassing more than three million illicit images—including many of very young children—and for watching "snuff films" depicting the rape and murder of children. The accused teacher had also taken photographs from "underneath school desks of unsuspecting female adolescents who were wearing skirts and dresses" (Breslow, 2007).

In another case, a sixty-eight-year-old Kansas City elementary-school teacher was arrested for using four boys, ages twelve and fourteen, to make erotic videos with a motion-detector camera at his home. Police found 150 photos and forty movie files of child pornography on the teacher's computer (Former KC teacher, 2007).

Denigrating Ethnic or Religious Groups

Schools are apt to forbid teachers to assign students to view films that appear to advocate hatred of an ethnic or religious community.

The early progenitor of modern-day hate-provoking movies was D. W. Griffith's 1915 *Birth of a Nation*, which glorified the Ku Klux Klan and disparaged Negroes in its depiction of events prior to and following the American Civil War. Griffith's film set off riots in several cities and was banned from theaters in Chicago, Denver, Pittsburgh, St. Louis, Kansas City, and Minneapolis.

A controversial modern-day motion picture that public schools are likely to prohibit is *The Passion of the Christ*, a 2004 portrayal of the trial and crucifixion of Jesus. Critics have deemed the film unsuitable for school use on several counts—(a) its implication that Jews were responsible for Jesus' death, (b) its violence, and (c) its exalting Christianity and thus appearing to be aimed at attracting believers to the faith in violation of the Constitution's first-amendment separation of church and state. The Anti-Defamation League charged that *The Passion of the Christ* represented

> one of the most troublesome texts, relative to anti-Semitic potential, that any of us had seen in twenty-five years. It must be emphasized that the main storyline presented Jesus as having been relentlessly pursued by an evil cabal of Jews, headed by the high priest Caiaphas, who finally blackmailed a weak-kneed Pilate into putting Jesus to death. This is precisely the storyline that fueled centuries of anti-Semitism within Christian societies. (Passion of the Christ, 2007)

The banning of *The Passion of the Christ* in schools was publicized when officials at Florida's Indian River Community College in 2004 denied the Christian Student Fellowship permission to show the film on campus on the grounds that school rules prohibited all R-rated movies. The Foundation for Individual Rights in Education (FIRE) came to the Fellowship's aid, pointing out that the college had permitted other R-rated movies and dramas. FIRE representatives suggested that Indian River officials

> seem to understand that adult students have a legitimate educational interest in watching an R-rated film in some cases, but rejects the idea that the same students should be able to watch a movie about their faith in a private student group meeting. These distinctions are juvenile and demonstrate precisely why the state should not be regulating the speech of adults. (Ban on The Passion, 2005)

Indian River administrators reversed their decision in early 2005 and allowed the student-organized screening of the movie.

Promoting a Controversial Political Cause

Members of a community—and particularly parents—are apt to complain to school authorities if a film shown in school presents material that conflicts with their political views.

A case in point is the documentary *An Inconvenient Truth*, produced by Al Gore, who had been vice president of the United States during the Clinton administration. In 2007, the film earned Gore a motion-picture award (*Oscar*), a television award (*Emmy*), and the Nobel Peace Prize. The movie warned that the earth's atmosphere was heating up at a dangerous pace that was significantly hastened by such human activities as burning fossil fuels in automobiles and factories. Whereas some schools accepted Gore's offer to show the film to their students, others turned down the offer when critics charged that the movie was not an objective scientific revelation but, instead, was a political statement supporting a Democratic Party agenda.

An example of the stir *An Inconvenient Truth* could cause in a community appeared in the 22,500-student Federal Way (Washington) School District, where a forty-three-year-old father of seven children—who identified himself as a computer consultant and evangelical Christian—e-mailed the school board: "No, you will not teach or show that propagandist Al Gore video to my child, blaming our nation—the greatest nation ever to exist on this planet—for global warming." The father said he believed that a warming planet is "one of the signs" of Jesus Christ's imminent return to Earth for Judgment Day. The school board responded to the complaint by ordering the middle-school principal to send a disciplinary letter to the teacher who had planned to show the film to seventh graders. The letter berated the teacher for failing to abide by board rules that required written permission to present "controversial" materials in class. Board members reported that they were then bombarded with thousands of e-mails and phone calls, "many of them hurtful and obscene, accusing them of scientific ignorance." In the board's final judgment, the members decided that *An Inconvenient Truth* could be shown, but only with the written permission of a principal and only when it was balanced by alternative views that were approved by both a principal and the superintendent of schools (Harden, 2007).

Another motion picture widely banned in schools for its political character was *Fahrenheit 9/11*. The 2004 documentary criticized the George W. Bush administration's responding to terrorism by launching the Iraq war, and it faulted the nation's news media for their early representation of the war. The movie won the grand prize for documentaries at the Cannes Film Festival and set a record for box office receipts for a generally released documentary. Among the limited number of places that allowed the showing of *Fahrenheit 9/11* was Henry M. Jackson High School in Mill Creek (Washington), where a teacher received permission from the principal and students' parents to use the movie in her government class as part of a lesson on government and politics (Tryon, 2004).

SUGGESTIONS FOR SCHOOL PRACTICE

Schools have found it useful to (a) cast policies governing films, television, and photos in detailed, printed form and (b) distribute the descriptions to students and parents. Such policy statements can profitably—

- Define *pornography*, list the forms of pornography that will not be permitted (printed photos, Internet sites, computer-stored photos), and describe the sanctions to be imposed for violating the ban.
- Specify the standards used for determining the acceptability of films, television programs, and photos for classroom use or to be viewed outside of class. The movie and television rating systems described earlier in this chapter are convenient criteria for schools to adopt. However, it is well to provide for exceptions to those standards by permitting teachers to explain why an otherwise prohibited film or

TV program is of sufficient educational value to warrant its use with
the kinds of students who would see it.

- Inform parents of the intended future use of a particular film, television program, or set of photos that some people might find offensive. Students who objected to a film or program—or whose parents
objected—would be free to absent themselves without penalty from
the class sessions in which the film or program was shown and discussed.

Garb

Throughout this chapter, the word *garb* refers to clothing, decorative accoutrements (jewelry, insignia), markings on the body or face (tattoos, lip gloss, sketched eyebrows), and items that students habitually carry.

All schools—past, present, and future—have rules about permissible garb. A collection of rules in written form is typically called a *dress code*. There also are unwritten rules, ones widely recognized throughout the society and referred to as *commonsense* or *customary* expectations. An obvious example of a customary rule is "Don't come to school naked." Thus, students are obliged to abide by both dress codes and customs, and school personnel are expected to enforce garb policies.

SIGNIFICANT SOCIETAL CONDITIONS

Two societal conditions that cause problems for schools in defining and applying garb rules are *subgroup differences* and *cultural change*.

Subgroup Differences

When the expression *group* is used to mean a collection of everyone in a given society (such as everyone in the United States), then *subgroup* can mean smaller collectivities within that *group* whose members have a cluster of characteristics in common—beliefs, habits, and even garb. Subgroups whose members might share similar beliefs about suitable garb can be religious (Amish, Catholic, Islamic, Jewish, Pentecostal, Unitarian), ethnic (Arabic, Afro-American, Latino), or generational (teenagers, young adults, the elderly). In schools, such subgroups' opinions about garb often lead to controversies with which teachers and school administrators must cope.

It is also the case that schools—especially junior and senior high schools—include social subgroups or cliques within their student populations. The subgroups are distinguished from each other by their members' reputed interests, abilities, character traits, and general worthiness. In addition, membership in a school subgroup is often signified by the members' distinctive garb. Consequently, a student's clothing, ornaments, and body markings can be interpreted by schoolmates as indicators of the wearer's beliefs, behavior, and position in the school's social-prestige hierarchy.

For convenience of analysis, it is useful to recognize two ways of grouping students in schools—the administrative and the voluntary-spontaneous. Administrative groups are those formed by school officials to facilitate the learning program. Students are assigned to grade levels, to classes, and sometimes to "tracks" in a way intended to foster efficient learning. In contrast, voluntary-spontaneous groups are ones formed by students themselves through informal social dynamics that produce a social-interaction structure that is unimportant for understanding administrative groups (grades, classes) but very important for understanding the significance of subgroup garbs. This point can be illustrated with an example of the student-determined social structure of one high school in a medium-sized, seaside California city (Cortenbach, 2007). Table 5.1 sketches the school's social structure as described in interviews with two students—a girl and a boy—who attended the school. The two students (both would likely qualify as "preps") agreed on the kinds of groups, their appropriate titles, and the sorts of garb typically associated with each group's members. The table identifies (a) group titles, (b) estimated percent of the school's student population that belong in each group, (c) significant group features, and (d) garb typical of group members.

In describing the social structure in Table 5.1, the pair of interviewees recognized two other racial/ethnic groups—Asians and blacks—with each group represented by hardly more than a handful of students. The Asians

Table 5.1. One High School's Spontaneous Social Structure

Mexicans (50%)

Significant features—Families recently from Central or South America and speak
Spanish at home. Kids not well assimilated into the dominant U.S. culture.

Typical garb—Boys wear baggy pants and "really clean clothes" (very white shirts,
fresh-looking shoes). Girls are referred to as *cholas* who draw their eyebrows on
with a black marking pen. They wear high-waisted jeans, tight tank tops, and clean
tennis shoes.

Preps/Cool Kids (20%)

Significant features—Mostly ethnic whites or offspring of prestigious, long-established
Latino families. Leaders in school activities. Successful in academics and sports.
Have financially successful, socially active parents. (The boy interviewee divided this
group between "rich kids" and "goody-two-shoes who always do the right thing.")

Typical garb—Wear tight pants, such as name-brand jeans (such brands as Frankee
B's, True Religion, Sevens, Hudsons) and name-brand shirts like Volcom or from
surf companies or skate companies. Preps usually wear hats. As footwear, girls
prefer Uggs, flats, or sandals, "but NEVER tennis shoes." They also like
"cute-loose" tank tops, short skirts, and little cashmere sweaters.

Gangsters (15%)

Significant features—These are tough guys and tough gals, known as troublemakers,
an ethnic mixture of whites, Latinos, and blacks.

Typical garb—Usually the same as the Mexicans wear.

Losers (12%)

Significant features—Students who, in the opinion of their schoolmates, are
undesirably different from the majority in physical or mental attributes and social
skills.

Typical garb—"Tend to wear the stuff nobody ever wears anymore, like overalls,
running shoes, high-water pants (not form-fitting, high on the waist, leg length
above the shoes), baggy shirts, and clothes that don't fit properly."

Skaters/Surfers (10%)

Significant features—They ride skateboards or surf at a nearby beach.

Typical garb—Carry skateboards or have in-line skates. Wear what the preps
wear—skinny jeans and skater shirts.

Nerds/Geeks (7%)

Significant features—Most are ethnic whites with bookish interests and are
"non-athletic."

Typical garb—Eye glasses, high-water jeans, random shirt styles, and running shoes.
Girls wear their hair ponytail style.

Emos/Gothics (5%)

Significant features—Usually show no emotion and "appear not to care about
anything."

Typical garb—Wear all black clothing, with very skinny jeans. Usually have multiple
body piercings—nose, tongue, eyebrow, or lip, such as the Marilyn-Manson
upper-lip stud. "Sometimes guys stretch their ear holes to the the size of quarters."

---

and blacks were distributed among the other groups and did not form by themselves a significant component of the social-interaction structure. The boy who was interviewed added one further group that the girl had not mentioned—Rockers, who spent their time listening to loud music on portable audiotape players.

It is apparent that one school's social structure can differ from another's because of the differences between schools in the socioeconomic, ethnic, cultural, and religious composition of the student population. Thus, understanding the relationship between any school's social categories and garb requires the analysis of that particular school's social system. And school personnel (board members, administrators, teachers) are more prone to advocate banning the garb of some student groups—such as Goths and gangsters—than of other groups—preps and nerds.

Cultural Change

For the intent of this chapter, the term *culture* is defined to mean beliefs shared by members of a group, including beliefs about what constitutes proper behavior and proper garb. Such beliefs within a group are not static but, rather, are subject to change that can be either slow or rapid. Prior to World War II, the change was gradual, but it suddenly accelerated during 1960s and continued in a manner that bore consequences for school-garb standards as America moved into the twenty-first century. Table 5.2 displays several trends across the past five decades. Although such changes have not been adopted by all students, an ever-growing number appear to subscribe to the twenty-first-century standards and have thereby startled school personnel into devising garb regulations at an accelerating rate.

Such cultural change in attitudes about garb has produced a generational conflict. Youths of the 2000s often disagree with people who were students in the 1950s over which standards of personal appearance should prevail in today's schools. The adults often believe that the rules about dress from their years in school were proper and should be retained. Today's teenagers frequently argue that greater latitude is needed in garb rules if young people are to express their personalities and keep pace with their peers' styles.

In summary, differences between groups and differences across generations in people's preferences for modes of dress and adornment can cause heated controversies about what garb is proper in schools.

Table 5.2. Trends in Students' Garb, 1955–2005

Girls' skirt length	
Knee-length or lower	Mini-skirts barely below the buttocks

Boys' pants	
Extend down from waist to instep	Oversized, sagging down from below the buttocks to drag on the ground

Body piercing	
Girls wear a set of earrings	Girls wear multiple sets of earrings. Boys wear earrings. Girls wear rings in nose, lips, or chin; studs in the tongue; gems in the side of the nose

Facial and body paint	
Girls wear red lipstick, blackened eyelashes, drawn eyebrows, cheek rouge, eye shadow	Girls and boys wear tattoos. Girls wear different colors of lipgloss, eyelashes, eyebrows, eye shadow

Hair styles	
Boys and girls wear their natural-color hair or dye their hair blond or brunette	Boys and girls dye hair such unusual shades as pink, blue, purple, or green

Insignia	
Sweaters (school teams, clubs), religious pendants (Christian cross, Jewish star), club clothing and badges (Scouts, Campfire Girls)	Jackets (school teams, clubs), professional sports teams' jerseys and hats, religious pendants (Christian cross, Jewish star, Satanist pentagram), street-gang colors and logos, Muslim girls' headscarves

FEATURES OF THE GARB DEBATE

One useful way to view the conflict over what students should wear in schools is in terms of (a) who participates in the debate and what are their rationales and (b) efforts to settle the controversy.

The Debate's Participants

A simple way to categorize people who engage in garb controversies is to divide them between *conservatives* and *liberals*.

Conservatives include (a) parents and adult members of the community who subscribe to the dominant dress standards applied when they themselves were school, (b) current students who agree with their conservative parents, and (c) most school personnel (schoolboard members, administrators, teachers). In support of their position, conservatives propose that rules limiting the kinds of garb permitted in schools help:

- Students concentrate on their studies rather than being distracted by classmates' garb.
- Parents and students to resist peer pressure to buy expensive garb.
- School officials identify intruders who enter schools.
- Prevent street-gang members from wearing gang colors and insignia at school.
- Reduce theft and violence among students over designer clothing and shoes.

Liberals include (a) students attracted by fads in garb that have been popularized by current movie and television stars, sports figures, hip-hop personalities, and street gangs, (b) parents and community members who were in—or who admired—the "flower children" counter-culture movement of the 1960s and 1970s. To bolster their position, liberals contend that curtailing students' choice of garb:

- Stifles creativity in personal appearance that is important for forming children's and adolescents' self-concepts.
- Violates students' right to freedom of expression as implied in the portion of the first amendment of the U.S. Constitution that states: "Congress shall make no law . . . abridging the freedom of speech." Freedom of expression is also implied in the fourteenth amendment, which reads: "No state shall make or enforce any law which shall abridge the privileges or immunities of citizens of the United States; nor shall any state . . . deny to any person within its jurisdiction the equal protection of the laws."
- Does not improve students' school performance, as advocates of school uniforms have proposed.

Efforts to Settle the Garb Controversy

Two increasingly popular attempts to solve conflicts over what students wear at school are those of adopting school uniforms and establishing dress codes.

Uniforms. The Long Beach (California) Unified School District has been credited as the first public school system in modern times to oblige elementary and junior-high pupils to don uniforms. To avoid imposing uniforms on families without the families' approval, district officials (a) specified that at least two-thirds of the district's parents would need to agree with the plan and (b) allowed parents to opt out of the plan if they so desired. In 1995, after the program had been in effect for a year, the district superintendent announced that "suspensions [of pupils from school] had decreased by 32%, school crime by 36%, fighting by 51%, and vandalism by 18%" (Isaacson, 1998).

Advocates of uniforms say uniforms make schools safer, reduce gang influence, and help identify trespassers. Furthermore, parents are relieved of the pressure of children insisting they need the latest fashions, so parents spend less on children's clothing. Uniforms are also said to eliminate obvious cultural and economic differences among pupils, enhance school pride, improve attendance, and increase students' self-concepts, classroom behavior, and academic performance.

Opponents charge that uniforms stifle students' creativity and take away the liberty students deserve to express their individual identities. In support of these claims, opponents cite the first and fourteenth amendments to the U.S. Constitution that address people's rights of expression and control over their personal appearance.

During the latter 1990s and into the twenty-first century, the number of school districts adopting uniforms continued to grow. By 2005, thirty-seven states and the District of Columbia had some sort of school-uniform policy, usually in the form of giving local districts the authority to require students to wear uniforms (Cox, 2005).

Dress codes. A dress code describes the types of garb that are acceptable and the types that are not acceptable in school. A policy regarding uniforms is sometimes part of a dress code. The contents of codes vary markedly from one school district to another. Some codes are brief and rather general. Others are long and very specific. The example in Table 5.3 of a lengthy, detailed code is the student dress policy introduced in 2005 in the Stafford (Virginia) County

Table 5.3. Student Dress Code—Stafford, Virginia

Students in all grades will be prohibited from wearing:

- Clothing and accessories that promote alcohol, tobacco, or drug usage or which display weapons or violence and which cause or are likely to cause a disruption within the school environment.
- Clothing and accessories that contain vulgar, derogatory or suggestive diagrams, pictures, slogans, or words that may be interpreted as racially, religiously, ethnically, or sexually offensive and which cause or are likely to cause a disruption within the school environment.
- Clothing symbolic of gangs or disruptive groups associated with threatening behavior, harassment, or discrimination and which cause or are likely to cause a disruption within the school environment.
- Clothing, accessories and/or any words, pictures, diagrams, etc., thereon which are lewd, vulgar, indecent, plainly offensive, or which cause or are likely to cause a material disruption.
- Head coverings of any kind in the building (except for religious or medical reasons). Bandanas may not be worn anywhere on one's person.
- Curlers, picks, combs, or hair rakes in the hair.
- Sunglasses or permanently tinted glasses.
- Dog collars, chains, wallet chains, safety pins, spike jewelry, or fishhooks worn as jewelry, accessories or ornamentation.
- Tank tops, tube tops, mesh tops, sheer tops, sleeveless tops, halters, or bare midriff tops. Shirts cannot have necklines that are lower than the straight line from top of underarm across to opposite underarm. Shirts must cover shoulders, must have sleeves, and must extend past the top of the pants. Display of cleavage is not permitted. Tops may not expose the midriff, and clothing must cover undergarments at all times. Note that at the elementary level, sleeveless tops and dresses are permitted providing they do not violate any other part of the dress code.
- Gloves in the building.
- Pajamas, loungewear, and dorm pants.
- Leggings or tight fitting spandex[-]type pants, pants with side slits or holes above the knees, see-through pants, tights, or leotards worn as outer garments.
- Sagging pants, pants worn low on the hip so as to reveal underwear or skin. Pants must be worn with both legs down (not one leg rolled up), and pants legs may not extend past the sole of the shoe. Clothing must cover undergarments at all times.
- Dresses, skirts, shorts, culottes, and sk[i]rts that are shorter than the extended tip of the longest finger with arms hanging naturally at the sides.
- Bedroom slippers, roller sneakers, or heels higher than 3 inches. Shoes must be worn at all times. Athletic shoes or closed shoes with a rubber sole should be worn for physical education and recess. At the elementary level, high heels, loose fitting sandals, and flip-flops are discouraged for safety reasons.
- Fringed garments in CTE areas or in Drama and Art areas which contain machinery.
- Items of clothing that would impair the health and safety of the student during normal school activities.

Source: Student Dress Code, 2005.

public schools. Note that the Stafford policy is limited to prohibited styles of attire. Other schools' codes, such as the one from Redwood Middle School, later in this chapter, identify both appropriate and inappropriate styles.

By 2000, an estimated 11 million public school students in the United States participated in school-dress-code programs, representing 22 percent of the public school population.

ILLUSTRATIVE CASES

Typical controversies and attempts to resolve them are illustrated in the following three cases. The first two cases—the Tigger affair and the forbidden jeans—demonstrate how court decisions in school-garb disputes are (a) usually argued in terms of the first and fourth amendments to the U.S. Constitution and (b) may be decided on somewhat disputable technical points. The third case—a sagging-pants controversy—shows how both a garb style's origins and the style's conformity with traditional community values may influence how the style is treated in dress codes.

The Tigger Affair

As described in Chapter 1, a fourteen-year-old honor student at Redwood Middle School in Napa Valley (California) was placed in a detention program called Students With Attitude Problems because she had worn socks embroidered with a figure of Tigger from the Winnie-the-Pooh stories. The punishment was for violating the school's dress code that permitted only solid-color clothing without pictures or logos. In response to the detention, the girl's parents filed a lawsuit against the school on behalf of their daughter and five other students, charging that the school's "unconstitutionally vague, over-broad, and restrictive uniform dress code policy" flouted state law, violated freedom of expression, and wasted teachers' and students' time (Bulwa & Egelko, 2007).

In a Napa superior-court ruling in early July 2007, Judge Raymond A. Guadagni noted that, under the school's attire policy, the student plaintiffs had been disciplined "for wearing, inter alia, blue jeans, socks with the image of Winnie-the-Pooh's Tigger character, an American Cancer Society pink ribbon for breast-cancer awareness, a Vintage High School sweatshirt, a backpack with the band name 'Jansport' written in red, a heart sticker on Valentine's

Day, a t-shirt with the words 'D.A.R.E. to resist drugs and violence,' and a
t-shirt reading 'Jesus Freak'" (Guadagni, 2007).

The judge ruled that Napa school officials failed to offer "facts which might
reasonably have led school authorities to forecast substantial disruption of or
material interference with school activities," which was a principle established
in a 1969 U.S. Supreme Court case (*Tinker v. DesMoines*). He also stated
that the attire policy violated the following portion of the California Education
Code.

> Students of the public schools shall have the right to exercise free-
> dom of speech and of the press including, but not limited to bulletin
> boards, the distribution of printed materials or petitions, the wear-
> ing of buttons, badges, and other insignia . . . except that expression
> shall be prohibited which is obscene, libelous, or slanderous. Also
> prohibited shall be material, which so incites students as to create
> a clear and present danger of the commission of unlawful acts on
> school premises or the violation of lawful school regulations, or
> the substantial disruption of the orderly operation of the school.
> (California Education Code, 2007)

Judge Guadagni concluded that the Napa attire policy, as currently written,
was too broad in restricting students' rights of expression (free speech), as
in the message implied by the cancer campaign's pink ribbon, the Valentine
heart, and the D.A.R.E. drug-warning. Consequently, the court granted the
plaintiffs a preliminary injunction that would prevent the school from enforcing the dress code as currently written (see Table 5.4). A noteworthy feature
of the dress policy was its extensive list of prohibited elements that school
officials associated with street gangs, such as the color *red*; the initials *S, N,
BP*; and the numbers *13, 14, XIV, XIII*.

In December 2007, the final settlement of the case required the school
district to pay at least $95,000 in lawyers' fees that had accumulated for the
five families that had filed the suit.

The Forbidden Blue Jeans

In 2001, the Highlands Middle School in Fort Thomas (Kentucky) adopted
a dress code whose announced purpose was "to provide an appropriate educational environment while allowing students to dress comfortably within limits
to facilitate learning" (Farris, 2005). In its details, the code was similar to the

Table 5.4. Student Dress Code—Napa Valley (California)

APPROPRIATE ATTIRE POLICY 2006–2007

This policy was developed to insure the safety and protect the instructional time of *all* students and is part of a larger "positive and safe school climate" program which includes discipline, facilities, school day and curriculum. Nothing which promotes drugs, alcohol, violence, gangs, racist, immoral ideas, profane or inappropriate ideas may be worn at any time.

- All clothes will be plain (no pictures, patterns, stripes or logos of any size or kind) and must fit appropriately.
- Colors—Solid Colors Only—Acceptable colors are blue, white, green, yellow, khaki, gray, brown, and black for all apparel including jackets (students are encouraged to also not dress in the same color i.e. all black or all blue). School colors apply to all items of clothing or accessories including shoes, shoelaces, socks, belts, scarves, mufflers, hair ties, etc.
- Fabrics—No jeans, denim, denim-looking, sweat pants, sports-nylon or fleece material may be worn. All pants, shorts, skirts or dresses must be cotton twill, chino or corduroy.
- Shirts—Must have sleeves that cover a student's shoulder and the mid part of an upper arm, be long enough to be tucked in and remain tucked in with normal movement and not display any cleavage. Shirts must not be oversized. Shirts must be worn right side out and cannot be turned inside out to hide a graphic.
- Pants/Shorts/Skirts—Must fit appropriately in the waist and the length (i.e., appropriate size for the students' height and weight) be fitted at the waist and/or hips and must not sag or drag and must be hemmed. Shorts and skirts must be no higher than mid thigh.
- Shoes—All shoes and shoelaces must follow the school colors. The heels of shoes must NOT be higher than 2 inches, as measured by the back of the heel, and must have a back or strap. Shoes may not have any red/pink/burgundy, gang symbols, or numbers on them. Sandals or flip[-]flops are not considered shoes.
- Sweaters/Sweatshirts/Vests—Must follow all dress[-]code rules regarding colors and logos. Sweatshirts and sweaters may not be worn inside out.
- Jackets—All jackets must follow the school colors and fabrics outlined above. Jackets may have a college or "small" brand logo. They must not contain ANY red or burgundy inside or out. Jackets and sweatshirts may not hide non-dress acceptable items or be worn inside out. A jacket is classified as any material other than cotton/polyester that has a full zipper or set of buttons and is usually waist long. Cotton/polyester sweatshirts or sweaters with a zipper are NOT considered a jacket. Jean jackets are not allowed.
- Backpacks—All backpacks must follow the school colors outlined above and must be solid colors (i.e. blue, white, green, yellow, gray, khaki, brown, and black).
- Any Redwood School, Redwood team logo or RMS club activity clothing is acceptable.

(Continued)

Table 5.4 (*Continued*)

- Restricted Items—Professional Sports teams and any *gang symbols* such as, but not limited to, bandanas or rags, belt buckles with the initials S, N, West Side, or BP, clothing with old English-style writing, low riders, drama masks, laugh now-cry later, prison insignia, tears, the numbers 13, 14, XIV, XIII, and the brand names or clothing tags with the words Homey, No Fear, Eight Ball, BK, CK, *Ben Davis* and *Dickey* are not permitted.

- Other Restricted Items—Black trench coats, nonauthorized hats, or head coverings, any unusual/unnatural (nontraditional) hair color or hair style that is distractive to the learning environment or takes away from the educational process, hair nets, excessive piercing such as nose, eyebrow, lip, tongue and chin, shaved eyebrows, spiked jewelry, hanging belts or chains, graffiti, patches or writing on backpacks, buttons or jewelry with pictures, colors, sayings, or writing, which cause or threaten to cause a disruption of the educational process or school activities are prohibited.

Source: Appropriate Attire Policy, 2006.

attire policy in Stafford (Virginia) that was described earlier in this chapter (see Table 5.3).

When a sixth-grade girl, Amanda Blau, was told she had violated the Highlands code by wearing blue jeans to school, her father—Robert Blau, a lawyer—filed a lawsuit in a district court, charging that the dress code violated the first and fourteenth amendments to the U.S. Constitution. The district court responded by ruling that the dress code did not violate Amanda's first-amendment right to freedom of speech because Amanda admitted that her blue jeans were not intended to represent "any particular message that she wished to convey through her clothing" (Farris, 2005). Instead, her reason for opposing the dress code was merely that she liked to wear clothes that "looked nice on her," that she "felt good in," and that expressed her individuality. The court also rejected the Blaus' claim that, under the fourteenth amendment, Amanda had a fundamental right to wear clothes to school that were entirely of her own choosing. In addition, the judge dismissed Attorney Blau's contention that a parent's right under the fourteenth amendment to control the education of his or her child extended to determining how Amanda would be dressed at school. The court likened the dress code to the school's curriculum, asserting that parents were neither entitled under the fourteenth amendment to dictate the contents of the curriculum nor to override a "reasonable" dress policy.

When the Blaus appealed the ruling to the sixth circuit court in 2005, the court's three-judge panel concurred with the district court's decision, so the Blaus lost the appeal.

A Sagging-Pants Controversy

From the 1980s through the early 2000s, an increasing number of teenage boys wore oversize pants with the beltline just below their buttocks so their underwear or bare skin was exposed between the bottom of the shirt and top of the pants. The origin of the style has been traced to prisons where inmates were given baggy uniform pants but not given belts that might be used for hangings and beatings. By the late 1980s, sagging pants had made their way into "gangsta" rap videos, most of them created by Afro-American hip-hop enthusiasts. The drooping-trouser fad then spread to skateboarders in the suburbs and high-school hallways, engaging youths of all ethnic backgrounds.

Because baggy pants have been associated with a segment of hip-hop culture that denigrates women, glamorizes violence, and appears to violate traditional clothing standards, sagging pants have been outlawed in many school-garb policies, including those of Stafford, Napa, and Fort Thomas schools. The condemnation of sagging trousers has extended well beyond the schools, with an increasing number of communities including baggy pants in their indecency ordinances. In 2007, youths caught wearing baggy trousers in Delcambre (Louisiana) were subject to a fine of up to $500 or a six months jail sentence. In Shreveport (Louisiana), the fine was $150 or up to fifteen days in jail. Similar legislation was planned in Trenton (New Jersey) and Atlanta (Georgia) (Evans, 2007; Koppel, 2007).

SUGGESTIONS FOR SCHOOL PRACTICE

When school-district officials face the question of establishing a garb policy, they can usefully consider options ranging from the least to the most restrictive:

- No dress code.
- A general policy, with each school's principal authorized to set specific rules adjusted to that school's student population, problems of disruptive behavior, and parents' attitudes.
- A detailed policy specifying rules to be applied throughout the district.
- Rules that define forbidden kinds of garb and provide for student to voluntarily wear school uniforms.

- Mandatory school uniforms, with a provision for parents to opt out of the uniform program.
- Mandatory school uniforms; no opt-out provision.

At the first stage of formulating a garb policy, a school can publicly announce the intention to issue a formal dress code and can thereby invite the opinions of interested parties (administrators, teachers, parents, students, community members) who submit their ideas during an open meeting or by correspondence (phone calls, letters, e-mails).

Next, a small working committee can be appointed with its membership including administrators, teachers, parents, and students. The committee's task is to use ideas collected during the first stage for drafting a dress code in its tentative form. Questions that may be considered as the draft is prepared can include

- Are all of the rules necessary for maintaining a school environment that promotes the learning program, or do some rules merely express preferences in dress style not necessary for maintaining order?
- Are all of the rules legal? That is, in a court challenge, could any of the rules be declared invalid by their violating the U.S. Constitution's free-expression provision under the first amendment or by breaching the right to direct one's own life under the fourteenth amendment?
- Do any rules impose an undue financial burden on families, such as by a mandate to purchase uniforms?
- Can all of the rules be effectively enforced?
- Will any of the rules damage an amicable relationship between students and teachers?

Once a draft of the policy has been produced, it can be distributed to administrators, teachers, students, and parents for their reactions. Their responses can be used to refine the code before it is officially adopted.

Food and Drink

The first decade of the twenty-first century witnessed a heated debate over whether schools have the right to outlaw or curtail foods and drinks on school premises. And if schools do have that right, which things should be banned and why?

Chapter 6 addresses those issues in a sequence of three topics: (a) the adversaries, (b) illustrative cases, and (c) suggestions for school practice.

THE ADVERSARIES

The controversy over banning foods and drinks has pitted two groups of adversaries against each other—nutrition advocates and proponents of snacks and fast foods.

Nutrition Advocates

People who favor outlawing certain foods and drinks in schools assert that banning is necessary in order to protect and enhance students' health. They say that allowing students to choose just what they want from an unlimited array of edibles just doesn't work. Left to their own tastes, most young people choose harmful items, so their choices should be limited to a selection of healthful foods and beverages.

The drive for controlling foods in schools began during the twentieth century when nutrition experts at an increasing pace urged schools to offer health-promoting foods in lunch programs, and students were taught lessons that emphasized the importance of a well-balanced diet. During World War II and thereafter, the nature of such a diet was widely advertised through posters distributed by the U.S. Department of Agriculture displaying *basic-7 food groups.* Americans were advised to maximize their health by including items from each group in their day's meals.

1. Green and yellow vegetables

2. Oranges, tomatoes, and grapefruit

3. Potatoes and other vegetables and fruits

4. Milk and milk products

5. Meat, poultry, fish, or eggs

6. Bread, flour, and cereals

7. Butter and fortified margarine

As the science of nutrition advanced into the twenty-first century, the more refined variations of a balanced diet that replaced the basic seven were often cast as a pyramid, with the foods that should comprise the largest portion of meals at the pyramid's base and those forming the smallest portion at the peak (see Figure 6.1).

Subsequently, for the purpose of analyzing students' diets, nutritionists divided foods at schools into three categories: (a) government-financed lunches and breakfasts, (b) *competitive foods* available for students to purchase, and (c) lunches and snacks students bring from home. Although the government-supported foods are required to meet federal nutrition standards, suppliers of competitive foods have not traditionally been obliged to comply with any nutrition standards, nor have the foods students bring to school. However, in recent years competitive foods have come under attack as the numbers of overweight children and teenagers have risen at an alarming rate. Surveys of weight among American children and youths have revealed that between the mid-1970s and 2004 the incidence of overweight children aged 2–5 rose from 5.0 to 13.9 percent, among children aged 6–11 it rose from 6.5 to 18.8 percent, and among adolescents aged 12–19 it increased from 5.0 to 17.4 percent. One

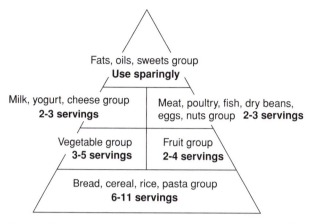

Figure 6.1. Food Pyramid (Adapted from ProHealth, 2007)

of every three American children was now in danger of becoming overweight, and one in six was obese (Overweight and obesity, 2007).

Analysts have suggested that, while the causes for the dramatic rise in obesity are complex, unhealthy diets are likely a highly potent cause, especially when linked to young people's increasingly sedentary lifestyles that find them spending long hours viewing television and playing video games rather than getting physical exercise. Children and teenagers who watch television four hours a day are more likely to be overweight than ones who watch two hours or less (Gavin, 2005).

In their attacks on dangerous diets, health-food advocates have made soft drinks and fat-laden foods their principal targets.

> Sweetened drinks (fruitades, fruit drinks, soft drinks, etc.) con-
> stitute the primary source of added sugar in the daily diet of chil-
> dren. High-fructose corn syrup, the principal nutrient in sweetened
> drinks, is not a problem food when consumed in smaller amounts,
> but each 12-ounce serving of a carbonated, sweetened soft drink con-
> tains the equivalent of 10 teaspoons of sugar. Soft drink consump-
> tion increased by 300% in 20 years, and serving sizes have in-
> creased from 6.5 ounces in the 1950s to 12 ounces in the 1960s and
> 20 ounces by the late 1990s. Between 56% and 85% of children in
> school consume at least 1 soft drink daily, with the highest amounts
> ingested by adolescent males. Of this group, 20% consume 4 or
> more servings daily. (American Academy of Pediatrics, 2004)

Nutritionists have assailed fast-food restaurants for the high levels of fat in their most popular products, including hamburgers, french-fried potatoes, fried chicken, sausages, sauces, and salad dressings. Analyses of foods' fat content have revealed that 55 percent of the calories in a traditional Big Mac hamburger came from fat, along with 83 mg (milligrams) of cholesterol. A cheeseburger's fat content is 45 percent (41 mg of cholesterol). A McDonald's sausage patty is 92 percent fat, a Domino's pizza (thin crust) 59 percent, a Kentucky Fried Chicken thigh 64 percent, Taco Bell guacamole 73 percent, and Wendy's caesar dressing 100 percent fat. In comparison, beans are only 4 percent fat, rice is 1–5 percent (depending on the variety of rice), and a baked potato less than 1 percent (Barnard, 1993; Fat calories, 2007).

As people consume more drinks, fast foods, and candy, they fill up on high-caloric fats and sugars that put on weight but lack a proper balance of nutrients.

To reverse the obesity trend, nutritionists, medical doctors, parents' organizations, and school personnel have mounted campaigns to improve the quality of competitive foods at schools and to encourage students to adopt healthful diets. An example of the kinds of school food recommended by nutrition experts is the set of standards issued in 2007 by the U.S. Institute of Medicine.

- At least one serving of fruit, vegetable, whole grain, nonfat or low-fat dairy food.
- Sugar should form no more than 35 percent of total calories.
- No snack should have more than 200 calories per portion.
- No more than 200 mg of sodium (salt) per snack portion or 480 mg per a-la-carte entrée item.
- Fat should form no more than 35 percent of the total calorie value of a food item.
- Total ban on items containing trans fats.
- Juice drinks limited to 4-ounce servings in elementary and middle, 8-ounce serving in high schools.
- Water should be freely available, tap or bottled. (U.S. school food, 2007)

The Institute's voluntary standards favor such items as "apples, dried fruit, baby carrots, low-sugar cereals, low-fat with low-sugar yogurt, turkey sandwich, water, skimmed milk, soya drinks, and 100 percent fruit and vegetable juices (in restricted quantities because of their high calorie value)." Students are discouraged from drinking caffeinated beverages because of "the potential for negative effects, including headaches, moodiness, and other results that could disrupt students' abilities to concentrate and learn" (U.S. school food, 2007).

In addition to recommending proper meals, health-food campaigners warn that diets which lead to overweight place children at risk for developing a variety of medical disorders, including:

High blood pressure

Heart disease

Stroke

Diabetes

Bone and joint problems (osteoarthritis)

Dyslipidemia (high cholesterol, high levels of triglycerides)

Liver and gallbladder disease

Sleep apnea (breathing problems that disturb sleep)

Certain cancers (breast, colon, prostate)

Shortness of breath (makes exercising difficult, may lead to asthma)

Depression

In summary, health-food advocates urge the elimination of unhealthy foods and drinks from schools.

Anti-Ban Forces

Prominent groups arrayed against the food-ban activists have included (a) the fast-foods-and-snacks industry, (b) students addicted to sugary drinks and fat foods, (c) school administrators who profit from soft-drink and snack sales, and (d) people who object to a government or institution (school) curtailing their freedom of choice.

It seems highly unlikely that the snack-food industry would willingly abandon the sale of "junk food" in schools in view of the fact that $165 billion a year is spent by children and adolescents on food and beverages. Nor are school administrators prone to oust sugary-and-fat snacks from schools and thereby lose the money that purveyors of edibles (Coca-Cola, Pepsi Cola, Cadbury Schweppes, American Beverage Association) have paid them for the right to sell products to students through vending machines, school stores, sporting events, and fund drives. That is, in exchange for the exclusive right to peddle its drinks and snacks on school property, a company pays a school district a portion of the profit from sales. By 2003, such *exclusive-pouring-rights* contracts had funneled over $200 million of unrestricted revenue into school-districts' coffers (American Academy of Pediatrics, 2004).

In parallel with soft-drink and snack companies' efforts to exploit students' enthusiasm for sugary drinks and candy, fast-food restaurants have taken advantage of youths' taste for fat-laden lunches by locating eateries near schools. Researchers who studied 1,292 schools and 613 fast-food restaurants in Chicago estimated that three to four times as many restaurants were clustered near schools than in areas without schools. The research team charged that such facilities were "deliberately built within walking distance of schools. Thirty-five percent of the schools were within a five-minute walk of a fast-food place; 80 percent had at least one restaurant within a ten-minute walk" (Childhood obesity, 2007).

As obesity among children and adolescents has become an increasingly worrisome problem, health-food activists' accusations are met with several sorts of response from soft-drink companies and restaurants. The responses include (a) denying that their products were significant causes of young people's overweight and (b) blaming students, their parents, and schools' health-education programs for failing to ensure that children and youths consumed heavy-caloric foods in moderation.

Typical of the denials that soft drinks contribute to childhood obesity was the retort of a spokesman for the American Soft Drinks Association when San Francisco's board of education eliminated sugary drinks from school lunches in 2003.

> We are in agreement that obesity among children is a problem, but we feel very strongly that banning soft drinks will have no impact on that problem. If [board members] want to be constructive in addressing obesity, they should focus on more nutrition education and daily physical education classes. (Delgado, 2003)

However, growing public pressure has forced fast-food suppliers to improve the quality of their offerings by adding more healthful alternatives to the array of drinks and foods traditionally available in school stores and vending machines. For example, in January 2007, the company *Bravo! Brands* began selling a 150-calorie, 8-ounce bottle of flavored milk in school vending machines as part of Coca Cola Enterprise's effort to supply nutritious drinks to schools that already bought its sodas. Bravo's low-fat milks contained a calorie-free sweetener, were fortified with vitamins and minerals, and met schools' nutritional guidelines.

Fast-food restaurants also began including salads on their menus and providing more grilled and fewer fat-fried items. However, health-food advocates note that making a informed choice about which foods to select still requires an understanding of different items' dietary value. For example, after the McDonald's chain added salads to their offerings, nutritional analysis revealed that the restaurants' *Caesar Salad with Chicken Premiere* contained 18.4 grams of fat (20 percent of a man's and 26 percent of a woman's recommended daily amount), while the standard cheeseburger had only 11.5 grams of fat. The salad dressing, in particular, had piled on extra calories (McDonald's salad, 2004). Hence, nutritionists have sought to equip customers to select wisely among the innovations by offering such advice as "Ordering a burger without the cheese and mayo could save you 8 grams of fat and 100 calories, and you might choose grilled chicken over breaded chicken when you find out what a big caloric difference it makes" (Fast food nutrition links, 2007).

Even as the evidence about children's unhealthy diets has mounted, school-board members and school administrators often fail to eliminate sugary drinks, candy, and fat-linked snacks from campuses because the dollars school districts receive from vending-machine contracts trump appeals about students' health. District officials argue that the extra funds enable them to provide school services that otherwise would not be possible, so students as well as taxpayers profit from the contracts.

However, as concern about obesity has gained momentum, public pressure on politicians and school administrators has accelerated the banning of sugary drinks, candy, and fatty foods from schools.

ILLUSTRATIVE CASES

As shown by the following examples, recent bans on food and drink in schools are only partial victories for health-food advocates, since policy makers commonly accept compromises urged on them by proponents of free enterprise who want market forces rather than regulations to determine the products available to children and youths.

In 2006, the Connecticut state legislature passed a bill heralded by its Democratic-senator sponsor as "the best and strongest bill in terms of standards for nutritious beverages in the country." While the legislation restricted vending-machine sales of sodas and sugary drinks in schools, it allowed the sale of chips and candy and permitted sodas at school-sponsored events on weekends or after school. The new law was a watered-down version of an earlier bill that Republican Governor M. Jodi Rell had vetoed—a proposal that sought to limit the sale of some snack foods, required at least twenty minutes a day of vigorous exercise in elementary schools, and ordered schools to meet nutritional guidelines set by the state's department of education (Stowe, 2006).

In June 2007, Oregon Governor Ted Kulongoski signed into law a bill that (a) limited the amount of fat and calories as well as the serving sizes for snacks sold in Oregon public schools and (b) restricted the types of beverages sold to students. In elementary and middle schools, only water, milk, or fruit or vegetable juice would be allowed; but high-school students could also buy sugar-free sodas and sports-performance drinks. The law would not apply to after-school and sporting events attended by the public. Two years earlier, a similar bill was defeated by legislators who said decisions about foods and drinks should be left up to individual schools. However, observers noted that those legislators had received campaign contributions from the Oregon Soft Drink Association, which gave a total of $91,000 to lawmakers before the 2004 election (Cain, 2005; Jacks, 2007).

Several Oregon cities had already introduced school wellness policies a year before the statewide law was enacted. In 2006, the school board in Eugene required schools to eliminate on-campus sources of soda pop, candy popcorn, and candy (except chocolate). The policy also strongly discouraged the use of candy as rewards for good behavior or academic performance. At the same time, the local Pepsi-Cola bottling company in Eugene—responding to "community wishes"—voluntarily removed soda from high-school vending machines and substituted sports drinks, fruit drinks, fruit juice, and water (Williams, 2006). The Portland 2006 wellness policy banned soda in vending machines at all grade levels and limited servings of cookies and French fries in high schools. Salad bars with fresh fruits and vegetables were added in all school cafeterias along with veggie burgers, tofu, pita, and hummus platters (J. Anderson, 2006).

New York State's Governor Eliot Spitzer introduced legislation in 2007 titled *The Healthy Schools Act* that would allow students to purchase only fruits, vegetables, whole grains, and low-fat or nonfat dairy items during the school day. After hours, high-school students could buy additional snack items that met limits for fat, sugar, and sodium. Beverages sold in schools would be limited to water, 100 percent fruit or vegetable juice, and low-fat or nonfat regular or flavored milk. The plan favored granola bars, yogurt, fat-free puddings, and baked (rather than fried) chips in smaller packages. In addition, high schools could serve hot chocolate and decaffeinated coffee and tea during breakfast hours and could sell sugar-free, noncarbonated beverages after school. No sodas would be allowed, but sports drinks would be available to students who engaged in afterschool sports. The New York plan linked diet and exercise by requiring that students in eighth grade and under have a recess period involving physical activity of up to thirty consecutive minutes on each day that students did not attend a physical-education class. Furthermore, school districts' policymakers were obligated to develop a wellness plan and to consider adding nutrition-education to the curriculum (Spitzer, 2007).

After Arizona's state legislators refused in 2007 to curtail the sale of junk foods in public high schools, the state's superintendent of education, Tom Horne, launched a voluntary healthy-food campaign that encouraged school districts to create their own wellness plans that would eliminate such staples as potato chips, candy, and sodas from campus vending machines. Horne's campaign was in response to the legislators having acceded to fast-food-industry lobbyists' requests that no restrictions be placed on the availability of sugary drinks and greasy chips in high schools. The standards that Horne recommended would allow no more than 35 percent of a food item's calories from fat, with a 10 percent limit on saturated fats and trans-fatty acids combined. The total sugar could not exceed 35 percent of the weight of the item, and the item would need to contain at least 1 gram of fiber (Fischer, 2007).

In summary, as the foregoing cases show, the struggles between health-food advocates and school-food libertarians have resulted in a variety of compromises that differ in their details from one school district or state to another. Yet the trend has been toward the increased banning of junk foods from campuses. A September 2007 report from the beverage industry noted that significant progress had been made in removing nondiet sodas from schools, as the proportion of sugary drinks sold in schools had declined from 47 percent in 2004 to 32 percent in 2007. The report predicted even more rapid replacement of nondiet drinks in the years ahead (Report, 2007). Thus, it appears that, as students' obesity increases and their fitness deteriorates, health-food proponents will gain further ground in eliminating sugar- and fat-laden foods and drinks in schools.

However, serious questions remain about how effective improved food offerings in schools will be in reversing the obesity trend among students. A 2007 Associated Press review of fifty-seven healthy-school-food programs concluded that only four showed significant progress in changing children's eating habits. Much of the blame for such meager success was placed on advertising aimed at children. Although the federal government spent $1 billion in 2007 on nutrition education ("lively lessons about how great you will feel if you eat well"), a Kaiser Family Foundation study reported that "Children age 8 to 12 see an average of 21 television ads each day for candy, snacks, cereal, and fast food—more than 7,600 a year. . . . Not one of the 8,854 ads reviewed promoted fruits or vegetables"(Mendoza, 2007). Furthermore,

> Experts agree that parents have the greatest influence—even a biological influence—over what their children will eat. "If the mother is eating Cheetos and white bread, the fetus will be born with those taste buds. If the mother is eating carrots and oatmeal, the child will be born with those taste buds," according to Dr. Robert Trevino of the Social and Health Research Center in San Antonio. (Mendoza, 2007)

Consequently, improved foods in schools cannot be expected to significantly alter the obesity trend without the support of other forces in the society.

SUGGESTIONS FOR SCHOOL PRACTICE

A 2006 addition to the federal government's National School Lunch and School Breakfast programs required all schools that receive federal funds to issue a wellness policy that conforms to government nutritional guidelines. The resulting policies have varied markedly in quality. Some are in great detail, specifying recommended portion sizes for foods and drinks. Others consist of only general goals. By early 2007, an estimated 54 percent of schools nationwide had met all of the minimum federal requirements.

A typical process through which schools can fulfill their wellness-policy obligation consists of four phases.

1. A planning committee is appointed, with members representing several concerned groups—nutritionists, the school board, school administrators, teachers, students, and parents. The committee is

assigned to consult other school districts' wellness policies and the federal government's nutrition standards in order to prepare a tentative wellness policy.

2. The committee's draft of the policy is distributed to the school board, a broad range of school personnel (administrators, teachers, cafeteria workers), students, parents, and such interested groups as the schools' food suppliers (including the beverage industry) and the public press. Those recipients are asked to submit written comments about the policy to the planning committee.

3. On the basis of responses to the initial draft, the planning committee revises the wellness policy into its final form and announces the date when the policy will take effect. In setting that date, the committee considers such matters as (a) the costs the plan will incur, (b) current contracts with food suppliers (such as venders' *exclusive-pouring rights*), and (c) when sources of new foods will be available. The committee also devises a system for monitoring effects of the policy. The monitoring system provides a record of (a) the popularity among students of different cafeteria and vending-machine foods and drinks and (b) alternative sources of edibles that students use in preference to the school cafeteria and vending machines (bag lunches, nearby restaurants, convenience stores).

4. The wellness policy is implemented along with its monitoring system.

Speech

Probably at no time in American history have freedom-of-speech issues been more contentious than during the past half century, and particularly issues relating to schools.

The basic guides to the kinds of speech permitted in schools and in the general society are found in the opening section of the first amendment to the U.S. Constitution that was mentioned in earlier chapters.

> Congress shall make no law respecting an establishment of religion, or prohibiting the free exercise thereof; or abridging the freedom of speech; or of the press. . . .

The first portion of this section is known as the *religion-establishment* clause. The second portion is the *religious-freedom* clause. The third is the *free-speech* clause. The fourth is the *free-press* clause. How those principles apply in specific cases has been decided over the years in state and federal courts, with the ultimate, definitive rulings issued by the U.S. Supreme Court. And those rulings have made clear that the freedom for Americans to express opinions in public is not without limits. For instance, courts have permitted the banning of speech that is obscene, defamatory (libelous, slanderous, hateful), likely to incite imminent lawless action, or designed to recruit believers into a religious faith. Furthermore, the limits on speech have been stricter for elementary and secondary schools than for either higher education institutions or the general society.

This chapter's discussion of speech bans is offered under six topics—(a) the evolution of speech policies, (b) the influence of personal values, (c) word-meaning problems, (d) political considerations, (e) schools' speech codes, and (f) suggestions for school practice.

THE EVOLUTION OF SPEECH POLICIES

Until the mid-twentieth century, two features of American public schools that were inherited from the nation's colonial past were:

- Christian (chiefly Protestant) content in school programs (prayers, Bible reading, the recitation of Christian maxims), and

- School officials' complete control over the sorts of opinions students and teachers were allowed to express.

Prior to the 1960s, there was little or no effective opposition to these traditions. However, a spirit of rebellion among youths in the 1960s, along with the growing multiculturalism of American society, would ignite a movement that produced intense controversy that continues today regarding what students and teachers are allowed to say without being punished. One part of the movement has been aimed at changing the religious content of schooling and the other part at reducing the control school officials wield over students' and teachers' expressions of opinion.

The pattern in which the movement developed over the past five decades is reflected in the following parade of litigation and legislation that established the legal borderlines for the sorts of speech permitted in public schools. The principles behind all of those decisions were drawn from the Constitution's First Amendment.

First, the 1962 U.S. Supreme Court case of *Engel versus Vitale* banned the prayer that the New York State Board of Regents during the 1950s had required students and teachers to repeat each morning in all of the state's public schools: "Almighty God, we acknowledge our dependence upon Thee, and we beg Thy blessings upon us, our parents, our teachers, and our country." The prayer was seen as a violation of the religious-establishment clause that prohibited government agencies from promoting religion.

Next, in the 1963 case of *Abington Township School District versus Schempp*, the Court forbade the Bible reading and recitation of scripture passages that had long formed a daily routine in America's public schools. Again, the practice was ruled to be an offence to the establishment clause.

The 1965 *Tinker versus Des Moines School District* case struck a blow at school officials' complete control over student expression by ruling that neither students nor teachers "shed their constitutional rights to freedom of speech or expression at the schoolhouse gate" (Fortas, 1969). Thus, Des Moines school administrators had erred in punishing five secondary-school students for wearing black armbands in protest to the Vietnam War.

The conditions under which schools could accommodate speech that advocated a particular religion were further defined in 1984 when the U.S. Congress passed the Equal Access Act (EAA) that would permit the establishment of Bible-study, fellowship, and prayer clubs in public high schools. The act specified conditions under which religious clubs could be formed. First, a qualifying school must (a) be a public secondary school, (b) receive federal financial assistance, and (c) have designated certain facilities as a limited open forum. The phrase *limited open forum* refers to a school's allowing noncurriculum (outside the normal course of study) student groups to meet on school premises during noninstructional time. That time could be either after school or during a free-activity period within the school day. A school is providing a limited open forum if it permits such noncurriculum clubs as ones focusing on chess, skiing, stamp collection, folk dancing, scuba diving, environment protection, and the like. If those sorts of groups are accepted, then religious clubs must be accepted as well. As a result of the act, the number of Christian Bible clubs rose from around 100 in 1980 to an estimated 15,000 by 1995 (Robinson, 2003).

Whether students should be allowed to include obscenities in their public discourse in school was the issue at stake in the 1986 case of *Bethel School District No. 403 versus Fraser*. A high-school student had alluded to sexual intercourse in an assembly speech in which he spoke in favor of a candidate for a student-government office. After school authorities disciplined the youthful campaigner, he claimed that his free-speech right had been violated and he filed a lawsuit. When the suit reached the U.S. Supreme Court, the justices—in a 7-2 decision—upheld the school-district's right to punish the lad on the grounds that obscene public speech is not protected under the First Amendment.

The operating definition of *obscene* used in *Bethel versus Fraser* had been described a decade earlier during the U.S. Supreme Court 1973 ruling in

Miller versus California. Three questions must be answered in determining if speech—oral or written—should be classified as obscene:

- whether the average person, applying contemporary community standards, would find that the work, taken as a whole, appeals to the prurient interest;
- whether the work depicts or describes, in a patently offensive way, sexual conduct; and
- whether the work, taken as a whole, lacks serious literary, artistic, political, or scientific value.

If the answer to each question is yes, then the utterance enjoys no free-speech protection (Burger, 1973).

As noted earlier, the Constitution's First Amendment not only addresses religion and free speech, but also guarantees freedom of the press—books, newspapers, radio, television, and the like. A combination of speech and press freedom was at issue in the 1988 case of *Hazelwood School District versus Kuhlmeier.* The student editors of a school newspaper wanted to publish two controversial articles, one about pregnancy among students (who were identified by name) and the other about students of divorced parents. When the school principal censored both articles, the student editors sued. The Supreme Court, in a 5-3 judgment, supported the school district by reasoning that when an activity is school sponsored, school officials may censor speech as long as such censorship is reasonably related to legitimate educational concerns. In effect, officials could ban material that was "ungrammatical, poorly written, inadequately researched, biased or prejudiced, vulgar or profane, unsuitable for immature audiences, or inconsistent with shared values of a civilized social order" (White, 1988). To bolster their decision, the justices cited a principle introduced in the 1986 *Bethel School District No. 403 versus Fraser* case: students' rights "are not automatically coextensive with the rights of adults in other settings."

The Supreme Court returned again to the religion-establishment clause when it outlawed public prayer at schools' graduation exercises in the 1992 case of *Lee versus Weisman.* The 2000 ruling in *Santa Fe Independent School District versus Doe* extended the ban to prayer at school-sponsored sporting events, such as football games.

The 1990s brought to fruition an *anti-hate-speech* campaign that had been developing since World War II. The National Congress of American Indians was founded in 1944 to take action against U.S. Government policies that violated Indians' rights. By 2007, the Congress—with a membership of 250 tribes—included in its agenda the protection of Indian cultural resources and religious-freedom rights, including the right to be free of insulting stereotypes of Indians from the past. In the mid-1950s, African-Americans' civil rights took center stage in the nation's social discourse after the Supreme Court's 1954 decision in *Brown versus Board of Education,* which ruled that separate educational facilities for whites and blacks were inherently unequal. Thereafter, a broadscale, continuing effort was launched to accord blacks equal rights in all aspects of life, including freedom from derogatory epithets. Two years later the Mattachine Society emerged as a national organization promoting homosexuality as a socially acceptable lifestyle that offered equal rights and respect for homosexual men (gays), women (lesbians), bisexuals, and transgender people. In the late 1960s, activists of Latino origin established branches of La Raza in several western states. The branches worked for the equal treatment and social progress of people of Latin-American heritage. La Raza Unida's first national convention in 1972 melded together the groups from the states.

Over the following years other minority groups founded associations to further their members' welfare. A key aim of such bodies was to eliminate— or at least reduce—speech in public settings that could be interpreted as denigrating the members. By the 1990s, such speech was widely being referred to as *hate speech* or *harassment,* or *politically incorrect speech.*

> *Hate speech* is a controversial term for speech intended to degrade, intimidate, or incite violence or prejudicial action against a person or group of people based on their race, gender, age, ethnicity, nationality, religion, sexual orientation, gender identity, disability, language ability, moral or political views, socioeconomic class, occupation or appearance (such as height, weight, and hair color), mental capacity and any other distinction-liability. The term covers written as well as oral communication and some forms of behaviors in a public setting. (Hate speech, 2007)

Harassment in its broadest sense consists of uninvited, unwelcome behavior that demeans, threatens, or offends the victim and results in a hostile environment for the victim. Harassing acts may include epithets, derogatory comments, lewd propositions, physical assault, blocking movements, offensive touching, and visual insults, such as disparaging posters or cartoons. (The present chapter's discussion of harassment is limited to spoken insults.

Physically aggressive versions of harassment and lewd advances are treated in Chapter 8: Bullying and Sexual Annoyances.)

Social pressure generated by the expanding array of equal-rights groups forced employers, social organizations, and schools to establish and enforce formal statements of policy—*speech codes*—regarding what sorts of public expression would be allowed and what sanctions would be applied to people who violated the policies. Consequently, during the opening decade of the twenty-first century, schools were faced with a host of speech problems that pitted two sorts of freedom against each other (a) freedom to express one's opinions, however distasteful others might find those opinions, and (b) freedom from individuals feeling insulted by hurtful comments. In short, the issue became: Is it against the law to say anything that could hurt someone's feelings?

Although hate-speech and harassment controversies provided a large portion of the banned-speech troubles for school personnel in recent times, the traditional religious-speech issues did not disappear. In June 2007, Texas Governor Rick Perry signed into law a bill that (a) protected students' expression of religious viewpoints, (b) furnished guidelines for student speakers at graduation ceremonies and other events, (c) protected religious expression in class assignments, and (d) allowed students to organize religious groups and activities. Observers waited for someone to file a lawsuit objecting to the legislation so that the ultimate fate of the law might be settled in the courts (Rendon, 2007).

In summary, the past six decades have witnessed a decrease in the traditional role of religious speech in public schools and in the degree of control school administrators wield over what students and teachers are legally permitted to say. The amount of free speech allowed in general public discourse and in higher education institutions has been greater than in elementary and secondary schools. Over the same era, legal and social restrictions on people's public comments about members of minority groups have increased, so that saying hurtful things can invite punitive sanctions.

THE INFLUENCE OF PERSONAL VALUES

Theoretically, court decisions about acceptable speech are objective judgments based on the moral values asserted in the U.S. Constitution's First Amendment. However, the amendment's principles are cast in such broad terms that they leave a great deal of room for people—such as federal judges, school administrators, teachers, parents, and students—to apply their own values when interpreting how the principles should apply in daily-life situations. Because of people's differences in personal values, U.S. Supreme Court cases bearing on school speech have rarely resulted in unanimous decisions, and judgments of lower courts have frequently been overturned when appealed to higher courts. Ways that such values can affect freedom-of-speech decisions are illustrated in the following two cases. The first example demonstrates two opposing lines of reasoning in the 1969 *Tinker versus Des Moines* litigation that set the tone for so many subsequent cases of school speech. The second example features conflicting values held by judges in the 2007 case of *Harper versus Poway* that concerned speech regarded as unacceptable in the current political climate.

Tinker Versus Des Moines Independent School District

In December 1965, five secondary-school students in Des Moines (Iowa) planned to wear black armbands to school as a protest to the Vietnam War, a war that they and their parents thought was unwise and unjust. When Des Moines school principals learned of the plan, they "adopted a policy that any student wearing an armband to school would be asked to remove it, and if he refused he would be suspended until he returned without the armband" (Fortas, 1969). The students did, indeed, wear armbands and were suspended from school. In response, they filed a lawsuit against the school district, claiming that the no-armband regulation violated their constitutional First Amendment right to free speech as well as their Fourteenth Amendment due-process right (the right to a fair hearing).

When the case was argued in a district court, the judges ruled in favor of the school district, contending that school officials had the authority to decide what opinions students could express in school. When the students contested that decision in an appeals court, the appeals jurists also supported the school district. However, when the appeals decision advanced to the U.S. Supreme Court, the judgment was reversed. Seven of the nine justices found in favor of the students, thereby setting a precedent that would affect all schools free-speech cases thereafter. As proposed by Justice Abe Fortas, who wrote the majority opinion, a key principle underlying the decision was that neither students nor teachers "shed their constitutional rights to freedom of speech or expression at the schoolhouse gate" (Fortas, 1969). Speaking for the majority, Fortas declared that

The school officials banned and sought to punish petitioners for a silent, passive expression of opinion, unaccompanied by any disorder or disturbance on the part of petitioners. There is here no evidence whatever of petitioners' interference, actual or nascent, with the schools' work or of collision with the rights of other students to be secure and to be let alone. Accordingly, this case does not concern speech or action that intrudes upon the work of the schools or the rights of other students. . . .

In order for the State in the person of school officials to justify prohibition of a particular expression of opinion, it must be able to show that its action was caused by something more than a mere desire to avoid the discomfort and unpleasantness that always accompany an unpopular viewpoint. Certainly where there is no finding and no showing that engaging in the forbidden conduct would "materially and substantially interfere with the requirements of appropriate discipline in the operation of the school," the prohibition cannot be sustained. (Fortas, 1969)

However, Justice Hugo Black—one of the two judges who opposed the majority—denied that pupils enjoyed the same rights as adults, because immature children were sent to school to learn, not to engage in political action. He warned that permitting pupils to use the school for expounding political views could lead to unbridled rebellion against an orderly society.

I deny that it has been the "unmistakable holding of this Court for almost 50 years" that "students" and "teachers" take with them into the "schoolhouse gate" constitutional rights to "freedom of speech or expression". . . . The original idea of schools . . . was that children had not yet reached the point of experience and wisdom which enabled them to teach their elders. . . . Here a very small number of students have crisply and summarily refused to obey a school order designed to give pupils who want to learn the opportunity to do so. One does not need to be a prophet . . . to know that, after the Court's holding today, some students will be ready, able, and willing to defy their teachers on practically all orders. This is the more unfortunate for the schools since groups of students all over the land are already running loose, conducting break-ins, sit-ins, lie-ins, and smash-ins. Many of these student groups . . . have already engaged in rioting, property seizures, and destruction. (Black, 1969)

Thus, the case revealed a difference in values between seven justices and two of their colleagues. The majority valued students' right to express their opinions, so long as they did not disrupt the peaceful conduct of schooling nor affront their schoolmates or teachers. In contrast, the minority valued adult control over immature youths who, if allowed to express their opinions unchecked, could destroy the social order.

Harper versus Poway

On April 21, 2004, officials at Poway High School in California permitted members of the Gay-Straight Alliance to hold a *Day of Silence* at the school. An assistant principal explained that the purpose of the event was to "teach tolerance of others, particularly those of a different sexual orientation" (Reinhardt, 2006). For that occasion,

> participating students wore duct tape over their mouths to symbolize the silencing effect of intolerance upon gays and lesbians; these students would not speak in class except through a designated representative. Some students wore black T-shirts that said "National Day of Silence" and contained a purple square with a yellow equal sign in the middle. The Gay-Straight Alliance, with the permission of the School, also put up several posters promoting awareness of harassment on the basis of sexual orientation. (Reinhardt, 2006)

In objection to the event, a sophomore boy, Tyler Chase Harper, the following day wore a T-shirt with the message "I will not accept what God has condemned" written on the front and "Homosexuality is shameful—'Romans 1:27'" on the back. He was ordered by school personnel to remove the T-shirt or be punished. He refused and was ordered to spend the rest of the day alone in a conference room. He and his parents then filed a lawsuit against the school, claiming that the authorities had violated his freedom-of-speech and freedom-of-religion rights. The lawsuit alleged that the school's "true purpose" of the *Day of Silence* was "to endorse, promote, and encourage homosexual activity" (Reinhardt, 2006). A district court judge rejected Harper's claims and supported the school's right to penalize the student for his actions. When the Harper family appealed the case to the Ninth District Court of Appeals, two of the three jurists—Reinhardt and Thomas—endorsed the lower court's decision. The third judge, Alex Kozinski, dissented, thereby revealing how the three jurists' personal values affected their decisions in the case.

First, consider the majority position. Judges Reinhardt and Thomas supported the district court's denial that Poway school officials had violated Tyler Harper's free-speech rights (as defined in the earlier *Tinker* and *Bethel* cases) or had violated viewpoint-discrimination laws.

> The school is permitted to prohibit Harper's conduct if it can demonstrate that the restriction was necessary to prevent either the violation of the rights of other students or substantial disruption of school activities.... Injurious speech that may be so limited is not immune from regulation simply because it reflects the speaker's religious views.... [In the majority opinion, Reinhardt quoted from *Tinker vs. Des Moines:*] "The First Amendment rights of students in public schools are not automatically coextensive with the rights of adults in other settings, and must be applied in light of the special characteristics of the school environment." Thus, while Harper's shirt embodies the very sort of political speech that would be afforded First Amendment protection outside of the public school setting, his rights in the case before us must be determined "in light of [those] special characteristics." (Reinhardt, 2006)

Next, consider Judge Kozinski's minority opinion in which he (a) contested the notion that Harper's T-shirt message would substantially disrupt schooling and (b) contended that school officials were prejudicially censoring Tyler Harper's political and religious views while tacitly endorsing the views of the Gay-Straight Alliance.

> The school authorities have shown precious little to support an inference that Harper's T-shirt would "materially disrupt classwork." [One teacher testified that] several students were "off-task" talking about [the T-shirt].... Surely, however, it is not unusual in a high school classroom for students to be "off-task." [And there is] no indication that the distracted students refused to get on task once they were admonished, or that the T-shirt caused a commotion or otherwise materially interfered with class activities. As this is the only evidence that Harper's T-shirt interfered with classroom learning, I find it ludicrously weak support for banning Harper's T-shirt on the ground that it would materially disrupt classwork.
>
> Harper's T-shirt was not an out-of-the-blue affront to fellow students who were minding their own business. Rather, Harper wore

his T-shirt in response to the Day of Silence, a political activity
that was sponsored or at the very least tolerated by school authorities. . . . (Kozinski, 2006)

To support his rejection of his two colleagues' ruling, Kozinski quoted
Judge Gerald Rosen who, in *Hansen versus Ann Arbor Public Schools—2003*,
had written,

> [The proposal that] "defendants can say with apparent sincerity that
> they were advancing the goal of promoting 'acceptance and toler-
> ance for minority points of view' by their demonstrated intolerance
> for a viewpoint that was not consistent with their own is hardly
> worthy of serious comment." [The government has no] "authority
> to license one side of a debate to fight freestyle, while requiring the
> other to follow Marquis of Queensberry rules." (Kozinski, 2006)

To summarize, Reinhardt and Thomas particularly valued (a) school authorities' right to prevent potential disturbance to school routines and (b) the
Gay-Straight Alliance's right to publicly urge greater tolerance of nontraditional sexual orientations. In contrast, Kozinski more highly valued students'
right to free speech (a) that did not substantially disrupt school routines and
(b) that was provoked by other students who publicly demonstrated speech
that conflicted with their own beliefs.

After the Harper family's suit was rejected by the appeals court, it arrived at
the U.S. Supreme Court where—on March 5, 2007—the justices in an 8-to-1
ruling, declared that the Ninth Circuit Court's ruling had been poorly reasoned
so that the issues at stake remained *moot*—unresolved. A lawyer for the
Harper family welcomed the Supreme Court's rejection of the Ninth Court's
ruling because "The Ninth Circuit decision armed school officials with a wide-
ranging, politically-correct justification to censor any student viewpoints it did
not want expressed in the school" (Mauro, 2007). The case thus reverted to the
original district court where further litigation was expected that might result
in a clarification of the basic legal principles underlying *Harper versus Poway*.

WORD-MEANING PROBLEMS

The fact that not everyone assigns the same meanings to certain words can
cause problems for determining if a speech ban has been violated. This point
is illustrated in a pair of 2007 court cases.

Rice Versus Gans-Rugebregt

When Rebekah Rice, a freshman at Maria Carillo High School in Santa Rosa (California), was teased by classmates in 2003 about her Mormon heritage ("Do you have 10 moms?"), she answered back, "That's so gay." A teacher, Claudine Gans-Rugebregt, reacted to Rebekah's retort by sending her to the principal's office, where she was warned not to use such expressions, and a report of the incident was placed in her disciplinary record. Rebekah's parents filed a lawsuit on her behalf, charging that the teacher and two administrators had violated their daughter's free-speech rights by punishing her for uttering a phrase which, according to the suit, "enjoys widespread currency in youth culture" to mean anything that was *absurd* or *inane* (Pearlman, 2007).

When the case was tried before a superior court judge in 2007, the teacher and the administrators defended their action by claiming that the phrase "that's so gay" made homosexuals feel uncomfortable or hurt. But Rebekah said she had used the expression simply to mean, "That's so stupid, that's so silly, that's so dumb" after classmates taunted her about being a Mormon. Thus, a pivotal issue at the trial concerned the meaning that people assigned to Rebekah's expression. If she had not been referring to homosexuals, punishment would hardly have been warranted.

In adjudicating the case, Judge Elaine Rushing ruled in favor of the school by concluding that the Rices had failed to prove that school personnel had violated any state laws or had singled the girl out for punishment. Judge Rushing brushed off Rebekah's hurt feelings at being teased about being a Mormon. The jurist wrote,

> All of us have probably felt at some time that we were unfairly punished by a callous teacher, or picked on and teased by boorish and uncaring bullies. Unfortunately, this is part of what teenagers endure in becoming adults. The law, with all its majesty and might, is simply too crude and imprecise an instrument to satisfactorily soothe deeply hurt feelings. (Teen punished, 2007)

The judge also rejected the lawsuit's claim that the school had used a double standard by protecting homosexuals from hurtful speech but failing to protect Rebekah from students making denigrating comments about her religion. Judge Rushing not only ignored the Rices' complaint but also admonished Rebekah's parents for creating a miserable situation for their daughter by advertising their dissatisfaction with the school's handling of the incident. Rushing wrote,

> If the Rice family had not told everyone that Rebekah had been given a referral for saying "That's so gay," then no one else would have known it either, and she would not have been referred to [by other students] as the "That's so gay girl." (Teen punished, 2007)

Morse Versus Frederick

On the day in 2002 that a runner carrying the Olympic torch followed a route past Juneau-Douglas High School in Alaska, the school's classes were dismissed so students could witness the event. As television cameras focused on the scene, one student—Joseph Frederick—unfurled a 14-foot-long banner that read "Bong Hits 4 Jesus." The school principal, Deborah Morse, snatched the banner from Frederick and suspended him for ten days. "The school board upheld the suspension, agreeing with Morse that Frederick's message insinuated approval of smoking marijuana and that it was counter to the school's mission of discouraging illegal drug use" (Barnes, 2007). Frederick then filed a lawsuit, claiming that Morse had violated his free-speech rights.

A key issue in the case involved the meaning that Frederick intended by his banner's message as compared to the meaning observers might attribute to the message. The principal and school board apparently recognized that, among users of illicit drugs, a *bong* is a pipe for smoking marijuana and *hits* is the act of inhaling bong smoke. But when Frederick was questioned in court, he said the message was a joke, merely intended to amuse the television audience that watched the Olympic torch parade.

When the suit was tried in a district court, the judge ruled that principal Morse and the Juneau school board had not infringed on Frederick's speech rights. Thus, Frederick lost the suit, so he challenged the decision in the Ninth Circuit Court of Appeals, where the district court's ruling was reversed. The Ninth Circuit justices decided that, even though the banner expressed a positive sentiment about marijuana use, the school officials had violated Frederick's free-speech rights because they had punished him without demonstrating that his speech "materially or substantially disrupted the work and discipline of the school" (Roberts, 2007).

The school district next took the case to the U.S. Supreme Court, where the majority (five justices) reversed the Ninth Circuit Court's decision by agreeing with principal Morse that the 14-foot banner could be read as either encouraging viewers to smoke marijuana or celebrating drug use. Moreover, as the ruling noted, school officials did have the responsibility to punish behavior that promoted illegal activity.

However, three justices disagreed. Their dissent was founded on their doubt that Frederick's banner was urging people to smoke marijuana. Justice John Paul Stevens, author of the minority opinion, wrote that the Constitution's freedom-of-speech provision should not be restricted by a "nonsense banner's . . . oblique reference to drugs" (Roberts, 2007).

> [I]t is one thing to restrict speech that advocates drug use. It is another thing entirely to prohibit an obscure message with a drug theme that a third party subjectively—and not very reasonably— thinks is tantamount to expressing advocacy. . . . [I]t is a gross non sequitur to draw . . . the remarkable conclusion that the school may suppress student speech that was never meant to persuade anyone to do anything. In my judgment, the First Amendment protects student speech if the message itself neither violates a permissible rule nor expressly advocates conduct that is illegal and harmful to students. This nonsense banner does neither, and the Court does serious violence to the First Amendment in upholding—indeed, lauding—a school's decision to punish Frederick for expressing a view with which it disagreed. (Roberts, 2007)

So it was that the various judges' disagreement over the case of *Morse versus Frederick* was heavily influenced by what the justices assumed the phrase *Bong hits 4 Jesus* (a) was intended to mean by the creator of the banner and (b) was interpreted to mean by "third-parties" who saw the banner.

To summarize, individuals' conflicting interpretations of word meanings are significant factors in controversies over the banning of speech in schools. Hence, an important question is: Should students' speech be judged by the intent behind their words or, instead, by the interpretation that listeners or readers place on those words?

POLITICAL CONSIDERATIONS

The role that politics may play in schools' speech bans was illustrated in the U.S. Supreme Court's 2007 decision in the case of *Mayer v. Monroe County Community School Corporation*. In 2003, a Monroe County (Indiana) primary-school teacher had led a class discussion of an article in an edition of *TIME for Kids* about peace marchers in the nation's capital who protested the Iraq war. When pupils asked the teacher if she would ever participate in such a demonstration, she said that she once had honked her car's horn as she drove past marchers who held signs urging drivers to "Honk for Peace." The teacher later explained, "I went on to say that I thought it was important for people to seek out peaceful solutions to problems before going to war, and that we train kids to be mediators on the playground so they can seek out peaceful solutions to their own problems" (Walsh, 2007).

After several parents complained about the teacher's class discussion, the school principal forbid the teacher from mentioning "peace" in her classroom and canceled the schools' traditional "peace month." The principal also announced, "We absolutely do not, as a school, promote any particular view on foreign policy related to the situation with Iraq. That is not our business" (Walsh, 2007). When the teacher's contract was not renewed for the coming year, she filed a lawsuit, charging that she had been dismissed over the "peace affair." School officials denied the charge, declaring that she had been fired for incompetence.

When the lawsuit went to trial, both the U.S. District Court and a Court of Appeals rejected the teacher's claim and, instead, found in favor of the school district. The appeals-court ruling stated,

> The First Amendment does not entitle primary and secondary teachers, when conducting the education of captive audiences, to cover topics, or advocate viewpoints, that depart from the curriculum adopted by the school system. (Walsh, 2007)

The teacher's attorneys then appealed the ruling to the U.S. Supreme Court, seeking clarification of the issue of free speech in the classroom because "Teachers need to know if their in-class speech is ever entitled to First Amendment protection and, if so, when" (Walsh, 2007). The Supreme Court justices declined to accept the case, thereby letting the appeals-court's judgment stand. A journalist who had followed the lawsuit concluded that

> The case was notable because it led to a fairly broad ruling by a federal appeals court that teachers have virtually no First Amendment protection for statements made in the classroom, even on a topic of such public importance as the war. (Walsh, 2007)

Other observers speculated that the political-party composition of the courts may have influenced the judgment in *Mayer v. Monroe County*, because eight of the nine Supreme Court justices were appointees of Republican presidents, and the current Republican administration had launched the Iraq war. Would a teacher who had spoken in favor of the war have been censored by the school principal, and if so, would the courts have defended the teacher's actions as constitutionally acceptable freedom of speech?

SCHOOLS' SPEECH CODES

Prior to the black-armband ruling in *Tinker versus Des Moines* in 1965, the notion that elementary- and secondary-school students had freedom of speech was not a serious issue. Students were expected, without question, to abide by school authorities' best judgment regarding what students should not say. Rarely was such "best judgment" cast in written form. Rather, the authorities' reasons were simply *common sense* or *custom*. But the social climate changed when the 1960s brought students' free-speech rights to the fore during students' clashes with "the establishment" over the Vietnam War. From that time on, public confrontations between students and officials over what could be said and written in schools mounted at an accelerating pace. Although the most vitriolic and widely publicized conflicts broke out in colleges and universities, disagreements increased in secondary schools as well.

By the 1980s, and at an increased rate in the 1990s, educational administrators were trying to cope with free-speech challenges by issuing formal *speech codes*—regulations prohibiting speech or other conduct that could be interpreted as abusive, threatening, or demeaning toward women, ethnic minorities, religious groups, and such. Codes typically forbid students from calling other people degrading names or telling jokes and making pejorative references about others' national origin, religion, sexual preference, appearance, traditions, or customs.

The task faced by administrators in fashioning workable speech codes has involved their (a) describing prohibited behaviors in terms that make clear to students and staff members precisely what students may and may not do, and yet (b) keeping definitions general so as to accommodate potential improper behavior that cannot be foreseen, and still not (c) infringing on speech freedoms that students rightfully deserve. Frequently, university and school authorities have failed to perform this balancing act satisfactorily. As a result, courts have struck down a host of codes whose prohibitions were unduly vague, all-encompassing, or blatant violations of the free-speech provision of the U.S. Constitution. Consider, for example, restrictive provisions in some questionable higher education codes.

- Bowdoin College banned jokes and stories "experienced by others as harassing."
- Brown University banned "verbal behavior" that produces "feelings of impotence, anger, or disenfranchisement," whether "intentional or unintentional."
- Colby College outlawed speech that causes "a vague sense of danger" or a loss of "self-esteem."
- The University of Connecticut outlawed "inconsiderate jokes," "stereotyping" and even "inappropriately directed laughter."
- The University of Buffalo Law School stated that students' free speech is limited by "the responsibility to promote equality and justice."
- Syracuse University outlawed "offensive remarks... sexually suggestive staring... [and] sexual, sexist, or heterosexist remarks or jokes."
- West Virginia University instructed incoming students and faculty that they must "use language that is not gender specific.... Instead of referring to anyone's romantic partner as 'girlfriend' or 'boyfriend,' use positive generic terms such as 'friend,' 'lover,' or 'partner.'"
- The University of North Dakota defined as harassment anything that intentionally produces "psychological discomfort, embarrassment, or ridicule" (a category of no small scope. About speech codes, 2007).

Difficulties resulting from authorities expressing speech prohibitions in all-embracing language were illustrated in the proposal by the University of Alabama's faculty senate that would deny university funds for "any behavior which demeans or reduces an individual based on group affiliation or personal characteristics, or which promotes hate or discrimination, in any approved university program or activity." So critics asked, "Would this all-inclusive language apply to fans who heckle Auburn players or students at football games? It is hard to see why it would not" (Beito, Luker, & Johnson, 2005).

Virtually all colleges and universities today have published speech codes. And while all elementary and secondary schools also limit the kinds of speech

students may use, those restrictions are rarely called *codes*. Instead, speech limitations appear in student handbooks under such titles as *harassment, freedom
of expression, disparaging remarks*, and *obscenity*. Here are three such statements.

> **Harassment.** [The school is] committed to maintaining an envi-
> ronment that is free of harassment based on race, color, religion,
> national origin, gender, sexual orientation, age or disability. Ha-
> rassment includes physical or verbal conduct that is derogatory;
> this may include jokes, gestures, unsolicited remarks, or other be-
> havior that creates an intimidating or offensive working or learning
> environment. (Acton-Boxborough Regional High School, 2007)
>
> **Freedom of Expression.** Students will be allowed to express their
> viewpoints and opinions as long as the expression is responsible.
> The expression shall not, in the judgment of the administration,
> encourage the breaking of laws, cause defamation of persons, be
> obscene or indecent, or cause a material and substantial disrup-
> tion to the educational program. The administration, when making
> this judgment, shall consider whether the activity in which the
> expression was made is school-sponsored and whether review or
> prohibition of the students' speech furthers an educational pur-
> pose. The expression must be done in a reasonable time, place, and
> manner that is not disruptive to the orderly and efficient operation
> of the school district.
>
> Any expressions made by students, including student expres-
> sion in official school publications, is not an expression of official
> school policy. The school district, the board, and the employees or
> officials are not liable in any civil or criminal action for any student
> expression made or published by students.
>
> Official school publications [such as a student newspaper] are free
> from prior restraint by employees or officials except as provided by
> law. A faculty advisory shall supervise student writers to maintain
> professional standards of English and journalism and to comply
> with the law including, but not limited to, the restrictions against
> unlawful speech. (East Central High School, 2007)
>
> **Obscenity, Profanity, Vulgarity, Disparaging Remarks.** Students
> may not engage in obscene acts or engage in habitual profanity or
> vulgarity, which includes: writing, speaking, gesturing, or acting in
> contempt of sacred or holy things, or using irreverent, or coarse lan-
> guage. Inappropriate language, put-downs, disparaging remarks,

and racial slurs will not be tolerated. (Mount Miguel High School, 2004)

Speech codes continue to be highly controversial. Proponents of codes cite their ability to promote a civil climate of discourse in schools and to protect individuals from hurtful comments. Nevertheless, critics charge that strict codes poison the educational environment by inhibiting the free exchange of ideas that is the essence of a truly great education. The Foundation for Individual Rights in Education (FIRE) has warned,

> If universities applied these [speech codes] to the letter, major voices of public criticism, satire, and commentary would be silenced on American campuses, and some of our greatest authors, artists, and filmmakers would be banned. These codes also lead students to believe they have an absolute right to be free from offense, embarrassment, or discomfort. As a result, other students begin the compromise of self-censorship. These attitudes stay with students long after graduation. If students on our nation's campuses learn that jokes, remarks, and visual displays that "offend" someone may rightly be banned, they will not find it odd or dangerous when the government itself seeks to censor and to demand moral conformity in the expression of its citizens. A nation that does not educate in freedom will not survive in freedom, and will not even know when it has lost it. (About speech codes, 2007)

SUGGESTIONS FOR SCHOOL PRACTICE

As school personnel (board members, administrators, teachers, support staff) face the question of what kinds of speech can legally be banned, they may be aided by such summaries as one offered by Ken Petress.

> Various court rulings [have] struck a common chord. Utterances are protected as long as they do not: (a) directly impede government operations (such as treason or perjury); (b) incite a clear and present danger (like a riot or a lynching); (c) perpetrate fraud; (d) defame another (such as libel or slander); (e) violate legal confidences; or (f) commit face-to-face verbal assault. Hurtful speech, while painful, intrusive, and inconvenient, is nonetheless protected. The recourse to abusive speech, said the courts, is to speak back, rebut others'

speech, or ignore hateful speech, giving it less standing in the public's eye. (Petress, 2007)

It seems clear that many university speech codes—and probably many elementary and secondary schools' speech rules—unduly restrict students' rights as provided by the U.S. Constitution. However, until someone contests a school's code in court, the code can remain in force. The more often issues of students speech rights end up in court—and particularly in the U.S. Supreme Court—the greater the legal guidance schools receive about what sorts of student expressions can be banned and what sorts cannot. The 2007 ruling in *Bong Hits 4 Jesus* is an example of a case that shed additional light on students' speech rights.

Finally, students and their parents obviously find it helpful if a school's speech standards are in printed form and clearly specify both the types of banned speech and the consequences to be suffered by those who violate the rules.

Bullying and Sexual Annoyances

This chapter is an extension of Chapter 7, carrying bans beyond spoken and written words to include additional acts that qualify as bullying, hazing, or sexual harassment.

BULLYING

Bullying is the act of tormenting a person in ways the person detests. Until recent years, bullying was not considered a noteworthy problem in schools. Taunting, ridiculing, goading, shoving, and punching were regarded as normal incidents of childhood and adolescence—experiences that did no serious or lasting damage. But over the past two decades, bullying has increasingly been considered quite harmful to victims. Not only does bullying make students' lives miserable during the years they are being attacked, but the residue of badgering may have undesirable long-term consequences. Thus, schools have adopted antibullying policies, and legislators have passed laws designed to punish both bullies and school personnel who fail to protect students from attacks.

Measures to curtail bullying have been adopted not only in the United States, but in other nations as well. In 2007, the Ontario legislature in Canada amended the provincial *Safe Schools Act* to provide for expelling or suspending students who bullied others directly or via the Internet (Bullying officially illegal, 2007). Also in 2007, an Australian court awarded a youth US$187,000 in a lawsuit charging that the boy had been so consistently brutalized by an older pupil when he was in a public school's primary grades that his mother had to remove him from school. Despite repeated pleas from the mother, school authorities had done nothing to prevent the attacks. The judge who awarded the monetary settlement said that the youth's "adolescence has been all but destroyed; his adulthood will not be any better. He will never know the satisfaction of employment. He will suffer anxiety and depression, almost certainly, for the rest of his life" (Lamont, 2007).

The seriousness of bullying in schools is reflected in research, which shows that

- About 10 to 15 percent of children in the United States say they are regularly bullied. Half of all students are bullied at some time during their school career. In one survey, almost one million students (4 percent), aged twelve through eighteen years, reported fearing an attack in the school vicinity during the previous six months.

- Bullying occurs most often where there is little or no adult supervision—on the playground, in the hallways and cafeteria, and in the classroom before lessons begin.

- Bullying begins in elementary school, peaks in middle school, and decreases in high school.

- Boys bully both boys and girls. Girls tend to bully girls. Boys are more often the perpetrators and victims of verbal and physical bullying. Girls tend to bully in more indirect ways—manipulating friendships, ostracizing classmates, and spreading malicious rumors.

- Victims are usually loners who appear to be friendless or different in appearance from others (mental or physical handicaps). Boys who are chronically victimized tend to be more passive and physically weaker than their tormentors. In middle school, girls who mature early are commonly victims of harassment.

- Both bullies and onlookers tend to blame the victims for the treatment they receive.

- A study of thirty-seven recent shootings in schools revealed that in two-thirds of the cases, the shooters had felt "persecuted, bullied, threatened, attacked, or injured by others," and that revenge was an underlying motive for the shooters' attacks. (Lyznicki, Mc-Caffree, & Robinowitz, 2004; Facts about bullying, 2007; Noll, 2001)

Forms of Bullying

Bullying can assume many guises—direct verbal taunts, physical abuse, property damage, theft, written messages, rumor spreading, activity exclusion, and cyber attacks.

Direct verbal taunts and threats. Perhaps the most common form of bullying is that of oral assaults—threats, derogatory name-calling, and insulting remarks about a person's appearance, mental ability, race, religion, habits, family background, mode of speech, lifestyle, friends, sexual orientation, and more.

"My name is Dennis. Kids used to call me Menace when I was young, and I didn't like it at all."

A high-school girl reported that after having an argument with a schoolmate, she thought their differences had been resolved. But the next day the schoolmate arrived with friends who said "they were going to get me after school. They didn't get me, but I was scared for two weeks."

After an 11-year-old girl was told by her family physician that she was overweight, she reported that "Someone found out I'd been to the doctor about my weight and then they started picking on me. They do it when the teachers aren't around—calling me 'earthquake' and 'whale.' Sometimes it makes me cry. I used to play sports but now I don't do that any more because people laugh at me" (Real life, 2005).

Physical abuse. Physical torment can include pushing, kicking, hitting, biting, pinching, twisting, hair pulling, and the like. Although students of either sex may engage in physical bullying, boys inflict physical damage more often than girls.

A news reporter interviewed a Duquesne (Pennsylvania) fifth-grade girl who was hospitalized for a concussion suffered when the girl had been assaulted by schoolmates, despite the presence of security guards (Welles, 2005).

> Interviewer: "How many girls were there and what were they doing?"
>
> Student: "There was five girls kicking me in my head."
>
> Interviewer: "So, you're down on the floor?"

Student: "Yeah and everybody's on top of me. The security guard's on top of me. Children are on top of the security guard. That's how it was that I couldn't breathe, couldn't move. I passed out like twice."

A teacher calls two students to the front of the class to complete a math problem on the blackboard. As one of the students walks to the front, a boy sticks out his foot and trips him. The student falls clumsily to the floor as the rest of the class laughs (Bullying, 2005).

Property damage and theft. Bullies often damage, destroy, or steal their victims' belongings. There are various ways of despoiling property. For instance, a second-grade boy was distressed by a classmate's spitting on his lunch. The locker in which a high-school band member kept his drumsticks was raided, and the sticks were broken in two before they were returned to the locker. Middle-school bullies stole epilepsy medicine from the book bag of a thirteen-year-old epileptic schoolmate. When a high-school girl put her lunch tray on a table near a group of other girls, one of them picked up the new arrival's milk carton and poured milk over the victim's enchilada. After a middle-school girl hung her jacket on a clothing rack outside the classroom, another girl searched through the jacket pockets and removed a comb, loose change, and a package of gum.

Written messages. Written threats and insults can be issued in several forms—notes passed around a classroom or left in a victim's notebook, graffiti on walls, letters sent through the mail, and e-mails sent from a computer.

A fifteen-year-old girl, whose younger brother suffered from a severe illness, was sent a note saying, "I hope your brother dies." The girl also received threats to beat her up, and she once came home with footprints on her stomach where she had been kicked. Her parents felt school personnel had failed to confront the bullies. The girl was removed from school by her doctor to protect her from future assaults (Woolf, 2004).

Rumor spreading. Rather than say insulting things directly to a fellow student, bullies often create hurtful rumors about the student and spread the tales through the school's hearsay network. Rumors are apparently the most frequent of the various forms of bullying, especially among teenage girls. Making up vicious gossip is a popular means of tormenting schoolmates because (a) it does not require that bullies confront their victims face-to-face and (b) it extends its damaging effect well beyond the creator of the rumor by influencing other people's impression of the rumor's target.

Four girls attending a boarding school in Virginia disliked a recently arrived sixteen-year-old classmate and sought to "get her good" by telling people that the sixteen-year-old had been "busted for smoking pot." School authorities, under their no-tolerance drug policy, locked the accused student out of her dormitory room, pending a complete search of the room, and ordered her to sleep on a couch outside a guard's office over the weekend. A drug test showed that the accusations had been false, so the girl was reinstated, but nothing was done to punish the rumormongers (Is there a potential, 2007).

Activity exclusion. Bullying is not limited to direct assaults or spreading rumors, but can also take the form of preventing a student from joining a group or engaging in attractive activities. That kind of bullying is especially common among girls. Thus, a bully may reject a girl in the lunchroom or on a school outing, encourage basketball teammates to never pass the ball to her, never invite her to a party, or never choose her to be on a committee.

Cyberbullying. Over the past two decades, students' ability to bully at a distance and to remain anonymous has been greatly enhanced by the advent of the desktop computer and its associated gadgets—cell phones, digital cameras, pagers, hand-held computers, or all of these components in one small instrument. Such devices are the tools of cyberbullying, which consists of humiliating, intimidating, or threatening others via the Internet. The Internet services that can be used for cyberbullying include e-mail, chat groups, Web pages, blogs, opinion polls, and instant messaging that enables users to engage in multiple written conversations simultaneously.

As explained in Chapter 3, blogs are sites on the World Wide Web in the form of personal-opinion journals or logs containing entries on any subject of the writer's choice. The opinions are e-mailed to selected recipients or shared with others through links on the Internet. Some blogging sites require users to register personal identifying information and to conform to the site's rules. In addition, such polling or voting Web sites as www.freevote.com offer users the chance to create online voting booths that enable cyberbullies to encourage Internet users to vote for whichever schoolmates they regard as the ugliest, fattest, dumbest, or the like.

Popular forms of cyberbullying by teenagers include

Sending cruel, vicious, and sometimes threatening messages.

Creating Web sites that have stories, cartoons, pictures, and jokes ridiculing others.

Breaking into an e-mail account and sending vicious or embarrassing material to others.

Engaging someone in instant messaging, tricking that person into revealing sensitive personal information, and forwarding that information to others.

Posting pictures of classmates online and asking students to rate them on such derogatory features as boring, repulsive, bad smelling, and disgusting.

Using a digital phone camera to take a photo of a person undressed in the locker room and sending that picture to others. (Center for safe, 2005)

The extent of cyberbullying among youths has been suggested in a survey of 1,400 adolescents. The researchers reported that over one-third of respondents said they had been victims of cyberbullying. Most victims (56 percent) had been bullied in a chat room or via computer text messaging (49 percent). Forty-one percent did not tell anyone about the bullying incident (Patchin & Hinduja, 2005).

Some typical ways that cyberbullying operates are illustrated in the following cases.

One of the most widely publicized examples of cyberbullying is the Web site created by Eric Harris—one of the two killers in the 1999 massacre at Colorado's Columbine High School—where he discussed his plan to murder fellow students.

As a prank, two eleven-year-old Duxbury (Massachusetts) pupils used the name of a thirteen-year-old neighbor girl when they entered an Internet chat room where they gave an older man the neighbor girl's personal contact information. When the man's Internet request to meet the thirteen-year-old arrived in her home computer, her parents phoned the police. The girl said, "I didn't know who this guy was. He said he wanted to meet me. It was scary" (Crane, 2005).

A high-school boy, enraged because his girlfriend had rejected him, used a photo-editing program on his computer to paste her face on a pornographic photo, which he sent to his entire e-mail list. The girl was emotionally devastated. When the school principal learned of the event, he removed the boy's Web site. The girl had to seek counseling and was transferred to a different school (Paulson, 2003).

During a school trip to Costa Rica for Milton (Massachusetts) High School students, two girls logged onto the Internet's LiveJournal.com Web site where users shared journal entries with friends. On the Web site, the two girls posted a fictitious entry under the name of one of their sixteen-year-old classmates. Included in their fake entry was the admission of a sexual liaison that their sixteen-year-old classmate supposedly had with a Costa Rican. The impersonators had written:

> "I was in the elevator going to my room last night and it stopped all of a sudden. The only other person in there was this older man named Juan. His hands were so gentle and loving. I thought I could be there all night just stuck in the elevator."

When the sixteen-year-old victim of the hoax later discovered the false material on the Web site, she said she fell apart emotionally.

> "I keep asking myself why they would do such a thing—because there was nothing I had ever done to make them hate me. Anyone in the world could read this stuff. Anyone in the school could say, 'Wow, look at what kind of person she is.' They could judge me by what other people wrote about me."

School authorities responded by reprimanding the two impersonators and eliminating access to the LiveJournal.com Web site from school computers. However, when the victim's mother reported the incident to the police, they told her that there was nothing they could do about it, because there were no laws preventing such behavior (Welles, 2005).

As a reaction to the threat of cyberbullying, some officials have completely banned the use of cell phones, messaging, and computer instant messaging at school. Others have published rules, backed by strict penalties, to prevent cyberbullying via school computers that students use.

HAZING

Hazing is a subtype of bullying that involves someone being forced to submit to humiliating treatment in order to earn membership in the group that is responsible for the hazing. For schools, a typical definition of hazing is this description in the handbook for students at Edina Senior High School (Minnesota).

"Hazing" means committing an act against an individual, or coercing an individual into committing an act that creates substantial risk of harm to a person. This includes a student initiated into or having an affiliation with a student organization. The term *hazing* includes, but is not limited to:

1. Any type of physical brutality, such as hitting, taping, whipping, beating, striking, branding, electronic shocking, or placing a substance on the body.

2. Any type of physical activity such as sleep deprivation, exposure to the weather, and confinement in a restricted area, or other activity that subjects the individual to an unreasonable risk of harm or that adversely affects the mental or physical health or safety of the individual.

3. Any activity involving the consumption of any alcoholic beverage, drug, tobacco product or other food, liquid, or substance that subjects the individual to an unreasonable risk of harm or that adversely affects the mental or physical health or safety of the individual.

4. Any activity that intimidates or threatens the individual with ostracism, that subjects the individual to mental stress, embarrassment, or shame or humiliation, that adversely affects the mental health or dignity of the individual or discourages the student from remaining in school.

5. Any activity that causes or requires the individual to perform a task that involves violation of state or federal law or district policies or regulations.

6. Any situation that causes an individual to be subjected to a hostile and/or intimidating environment or causes a disruption to the school learning environment. (Definitions of hazing, 2007)

The extent of hazing in schools has been suggested in a survey of more than 1,500 high-school students from various sections of the United States.

Forty-eight percent of students who belong to groups reported being subjected to hazing activities.

Forty-three percent reported being subjected to humiliating activities.

Thirty percent reported performing potentially illegal acts as part of their initiation.

Both female and male students report high levels of hazing, although male students are at highest risk, especially for dangerous hazing.

Even groups usually considered safe haze new members—24 percent of students involved in church groups were subjected to hazing activities.

Seventy-one percent of the students subjected to hazing reported negative consequences, such as getting into fights, being injured, fighting with parents, doing poorly in school, hurting other people, having difficulty eating, sleeping, or concentrating, or feeling angry, confused, embarrassed, or guilty (Hoover & Pollard, 2000).

In the past, people not only tolerated hazing as an initiation rite, but some thought hazing was a desirable test of individuals' mettle, toughening them to cope with difficult times they would face later in life. However, in recent times, schools have increasingly recognized hazing as a harmful practice that calls for such measures as those described in the student handbook of a New Jersey secondary school.

Under no circumstances will hazing in any form be tolerated within the scope of the programs (including extra-curricular and co-curricular) sponsored by Washington Township Public Schools. Students participating in hazing practices will be subject to disciplinary action at the discretion of the principal/or designee, who will determine the level and severity of the discipline action to be taken including detention, suspension and/or removal from the team or school activity. Student leaders (team captains, club officers, etc.) are expected to discourage and report hazing to their coach, teacher, and/or administration. (Definitions of Hazing, 2007)

Not only have schools increasingly adopted antihazing rules, but also forty-two states have passed laws aimed at preventing hazing in educational settings and the workplace.

Forms of Hazing

Hazing comes in many styles, ranging from mild teasing and silly antics (such as dressing in foolish costumes or chanting childish verses) to brutal physical torture.

Three baseball players were suspended and charged with battery for overpowering a sophomore player and cutting his hair.

A cheerleader recalled that before she could cheer at football games or even try on her uniform, she had to get through "Hell Night." This so-called "squad tradition" required her to dress in skimpy pajamas and parade around the mall on a Friday night eating dog food. She said, "It was embarrassing, but it was a school tradition" (Bloom, 2003).

Five seventh-grade football players were bruised from a paddling by eight eighth-grade players. The father of an eighth-grader said, "Isn't no big deal."

Following a hazing ritual for new high-school-choir members, a boy reported, "I was beaten with a two-by-four, and left welts across my rear, and I was hit about four times. I was then covered in human waste, Crisco oil, peanut butter, things were shoved down my pants."

Fourteen girls were dropped from a field hockey team after they subjected younger players to sexual-simulation acts and other demeaning experiences.

Thirteen high-school football players were suspended after a junior-varsity player was beaten up in the varsity locker room. The youth was treated for fluid in his lungs and later quit school.

A student who suffered learning disabilities had newly joined the high-school wrestling team when he was hazed by teammates in a series of attacks—smashed against the wall, stuffed into a locker, hog-tied, and sodomized with a plastic knife. On one occasion he suffered a serious knee injury and needed counseling for emotional trauma. Eight participants in the assaults were arrested; seven were expelled from school. A team member told police that "both the wrestling and the basketball coaches at the school saw the victim hog-tied and did nothing" (Actual hazing cases, 2005).

A graduate of a private boarding school recalled that "the seniors liked to take 9th graders out of their beds in the middle of the night. The seniors would wear panty hose over their heads so you couldn't see who they were. They would drag you down to the hockey rink—which was very isolated—and you would be covered in honey and then with feathers. It was meant to frighten, intimidate, and humiliate. The faculty did nothing to discourage this kind of mal-treatment" (Kennedy, 2007).

Apparently the most effective stimuli behind efforts to eliminate hazing in schools are news-media reports of shocking attacks on initiates to such school organizations as athletic teams and clubs. For instance, at Mepham High School on Long Island (New York), the 2003 football season was canceled after players admitted to sadistically hazing fellow teammates. At the school's summer football camp, two thirteen-year olds had been abused by older players four or five times a day throughout the five days of camp in the woods of Pennsylvania.

Broomsticks dipped in mineral ice, a kind of liquid heat, golf balls, pine cones, and toothbrushes, were all pushed into the boys' rectums. All the while, older players watched and laughed. They had bags of ice and they were bashing it all over [one boy's] body until the bags broke. They bashed him in his head, over his back, his legs, his arms. A grand jury report later described how they used duct tape to pull off the children's pubic hair, how they forced him and another boy they sodomized to kick each other in the groin, and then threatened to beat and kill all of them if they told anybody. (Van Sant, 2004)

Following a grand-jury report, the coaches who had been in charge of the camp were dismissed from their teaching positions. Three of the older players confessed in juvenile court to their part in the hazing. One was put on probation, another was sent to a boot camp, and the third was placed in a detention center.

SEXUAL ANNOYANCES

Two additional types of behavior that schools have banned in recent years are *sexual harassment* and *excessive displays of affection*. The former annoys people who are targets of sexual attention. The latter annoys such bystanders as school administrators, teachers, parents, and sexually conservative students.

Sexual Harassment

Sexual harassment consists of unwelcome approaches of a sexual nature. Harassers can be students, teachers, administrators, or support staff (janitors, bus drivers, secretaries, counselors). The victims of harassment are usually students, but sometimes they are school personnel, as in the case of a principal making unwanted sexual advances to a teacher.

Harassment can be verbal (comments about a person's body, sexual remarks or accusations, jokes or stories involving sex acts), physical (grabbing, rubbing, flashing, mooning, touching, pinching in a sexual way, sexual intercourse), or visual (display of naked pictures or sex-related objects, obscene gestures).

Legally there are two forms of sexual harassment—*quid pro quo* and *hostile environment*. The quid-pro-quo variety (in Latin the expression means exchanging "this for that") consists of a harasser offering to trade one thing for another. For example, in the exchange's positive form, a male teacher promises a high-school girl a grade of *A* for the semester if she allows him to hug her. Or, in its negative form, a sixteen-year-old boy threatens to beat up a fourteen-year-old boy if the younger schoolmate doesn't allow the older one to fondle the younger one's genitals.

Hostile-environment harassment consists of unwelcome sexual touching, comments, or gestures that make a person feel uncomfortable or unsafe at school, or that prevents a person from engaging in or profiting from a school activity.

> Diana's school soccer team coach is constantly telling her sexual jokes and making suggestive comments. During practice, he whistles and winks at her when she runs by him. Diana told the coach that his behavior makes her uncomfortable, but he responded by saying that she needs to learn how to accept compliments. Recently, he showed her a calendar of bikini-clad female athletes and told her she is sexy enough to pose for such a magazine. She is thinking of quitting the soccer team just to avoid the coach.
>
> Luis gets constant attention from a particular group of girls in his high school. They send him sexually explicit notes, blow kisses at him, and rub up against him in the hallway. They wait for him when he gets off the school bus and when he gets out of class. They always seem to show up wherever he is. Someone keeps calling his house, asking for him and then hanging up, and Luis is sure it's those girls. He has even seen them drive by his house in the afternoon. At first, he thought it was funny, but it's starting to embarrass and frustrate him. He's started to avoid going out so he won't have to see them, and he's pretended to be sick a few times so he didn't have to go to school (Sexual harassment, 2007).

For a behavior to qualify as sexual harassment, it must be unwanted by the receiver of the attention. Hence, it is not harassment when a girl enjoys having a boy wink at her, tell an off-color joke, or put his arm around her waist. Such acts, when welcomed by the recipient, are considered to be flirting.

Excessive Displays of Affection

The liberal sex standards that evolved in America after the 1960s were accompanied by students exhibiting more public displays of affection at school— embracing, kissing, and passionately caressing. A particular irritant for school personnel is *dirty dancing* or *freak dancing* (*freakin'*), which consists of couples groping each other's sexual regions and grinding their groins together during school-sponsored dances. As such behavior has increased, the acronym PDA (public displays of affection) has become the popular label for the practice.

Teachers and administrators often feel that sexually suggestive antics distract students from their studies, disrupt the smooth flow of the learning program, and embarrass sexually conservative classmates. Thus, in recent times many schools have adopted formal rules about physical expressions of attraction. The nature of rules can vary markedly from one school to another. As the following examples illustrate, regulations range from general statements to lists of specific prohibited acts.

Fredonia (New York). Students are expected to conduct themselves as responsible young adults. Public displays of affection are inappropriate in an educational setting.

Grant District 110 (Illinois). Our policy doesn't mention hugs. [The term *hugs*] is pretty ambiguous so our professional staff can review each case and make a decision.

Lubbock (Texas). Public display of affection is prohibited on the campus at Lubbock High School. Students are subject to disciplinary action for public displays of affection.

Percy Julian Middle School (Chicago). "Extreme hugging" is banned because it causes hallway traffic jams, and students are often late getting to class. So students may hug as long as they don't block traffic.

Los Alamos (New Mexico). In order to maintain a respectful atmosphere on campus, students are to refrain from overt public displays of affection while on school grounds and at school events. This includes sitting on laps, groping, lengthy kissing, etc. If a student has a question as to what is appropriate, he or she may discuss it with an administrator. High-school staff will intervene when displays of affection are inappropriate.

Casper (Wyoming). Students at Natrona County High School's spring prom are required to sign a pledge stating that they will not consume alcohol or illegal drugs before or during the dance and they accept the rule that "freak dancing, lap dancing, bumping, grinding, thrusting, dirty dancing, and any dancing that involves excessive physical contact" is prohibited.

Chesapeake (Virginia). Students are to refrain from any public display of affection that would offend others. A student committee determined that the following actions are unacceptable: (a) kissing on the lips, (b) sitting on another's lap, (c) licking, (d) hugging/holding from behind (front to back). Consequences may range from a parent contact, detention, suspension, or referral to the Office of Pupil Discipline.

The PDA issue has been highly controversial, partly because students, parents, and school personnel so often disagree among themselves about which specific actions should be banned and why.

A seventh-grade girl, sent home for embracing a classmate at Prattville Junior High School (Alabama), complained, "I think it's kind of stupid. I mean it's not like we're doing anything wrong. It's just a hug."

A Fossil Hill (Texas) eighth grader, who was chided by a teacher for holding hands with her boyfriend, said, "I can understand how a 25-minute hug or making out in the hallway would be PDA, but I don't see how holding hands is. You hug your parents or little brother or sister and it doesn't lead to things" (Chavez, 2007).

In defense of his district's ban on displays of affection, the superintendent of the Mascoutah (Illinois) schools said, "We feel students come to school to learn, and we feel that an environment that discourages inappropriate public display of affection is in keeping with the highest standards we could have as a community and as a school district."

The president of StoppingSchoolViolence.com said, "I see nothing wrong with hugging. If the teachers could tell the difference between good touch and bad touch, and whether someone is bullying or horse playing, that would go much farther" (Bonisteel, 2007).

The executive director of the Texas Association of Secondary School Principals said, "I don't know where you draw the line. It just has to be done in such a way that people are using common sense. It's a fine line administrators have to walk" (Chavez, 2007).

Prior to 1999, few schools had formal sexual harassment or PDA policies. However, a Supreme Court decision that year (*LaShonda Davis v. Monroe County Board of Education*) found school districts liable for financial damages in instances of peer sexual harassment. That case concerned a fifth grader who had been repeatedly harassed by a fellow student in a school district that ignored the problem. And the court warned that general, broadly worded policies alone would not protect schools from lawsuits. Thus, school districts began formulating more precise rules concerning which sorts of sex-related student behavior would be permitted on school property. By 2008, many districts had decided that establishing strict no-exception PDA regulations was the safest way to avoid the problem of deciding which displays to permit and which to ban. Thus, *no-touching-at-all* policies have increasingly been adopted, thereby outlawing hugs, handshakes, handholding, and high fives.

SUGGESTIONS FOR SCHOOL PRACTICE

The events reviewed in this chapter imply that school authorities would be wise to issue formal policies about bullying, hazing, sexual harassment, and displays of affection. Without such regulations and their consistent implementation, students are at risk for physical/psychological harm and sexual exploitation. At the same time, teachers, administrators, and school-board members are at jeopardy for lawsuits.

Because of significant differences among communities and their schools, it seems unreasonable to expect that a single set of rules can be devised to satisfy the needs of all schools. Thus, each community—and perhaps each school in certain communities—will need to formulate its own set of policies. This means that school officials face the task of creating three sets of rules—one set for bullying and hazing, another for sexual harassment, and a third for displays of affection. The following description illustrates one process officials might adopt for preparing and implementing such policies.

1. A staff member is assigned to survey the Internet for other school systems' policy statements about the particular issue at hand. The survey involves entering words or phrases into a search engine (such as Google, Ask, Live Search, or Yahoo!Search) to derive sources of information about the issue. The following are samples of relevant expressions to enter for the three fields of interest.

   For bullying and hazing: *school bullying, school hazing, bullying defined, hazing defined, anti-bullying, anti-hazing, student handbooks, student behavior rules,* and *student conduct.*

   For sexual harassment: *school sexual harassment, school sex, school sexual exploitation, school sexual abuse,* and *sex in school.*

   For displays of affection: *public displays of affection, school displays of affection, school hugging, school sexual behavior.*

2. The staff member prints a selection of different schools' regulations from the Internet search that bear on the issue under consideration (bullying/hazing, sexual harassment, or displays of affection).

3. A committee is formed to offer suggestions about what should be included in the school system's policy statement about the issue. Committee members are selected to represent the perspectives of the people most intimately affected by the policy. For example, the committee may include a member of the board of education, an administrator from the school district's central office, a school principal, one or two teachers, one or two students, and one or two parents. Each committee member is asked to consult the staff member's Internet –results' summary and propose which elements from that material should be in the school system's regulations. Each committee member performs this task alone, and then casts his or her opinion as a written recommendation.

4. The staff member compiles the committee members' recommendations and writes a summary that identifies (a) those policies supported by all or most of the members and (b) those on which members disagreed.

5. The summary is sent to the committee members, who are invited to a meeting at which the group discusses the controversial items in the summary, thereby giving members an opportunity to offer reasons in support of their preferences. Following the discussion, the members are asked to vote on each controversial item in order to show how they now feel about which items should be included in the policy statement and which should not.

6. The staff member writes a new summary of the committee members' opinions, based on the outcome of the discussion, showing the extent of consensus regarding the policy. In the new summary, the staff member suggests how any remaining differences among committee members might be resolved.

7. The new summary is provided to the school district's board of education, the body that serves as the ultimate authority for policy making. The board may seek the advice from the district superintendent's office.

8. The board of education tentatively adopts a policy statement that is either the new summary intact or a revision endorsed by the board.

9. The tentative policy is announced publicly, and people are invited to respond to it either in writing or orally at a board of education meeting.

10. With the responses to the tentative policy in mind, the board of education issues a final version of the policy that will be printed in a student handbook that includes regulations governing students and staff members' behavior.

Finally, it seems apparent that policy statements about bullying/hazing, sexual harassment, and displays of affection are most helpful to students, parents, administrators, and teachers when the statements identify precisely which acts are permitted and which are not. Such vague expressions as "unseemly displays of affection will not be tolerated" are not very helpful and lead to confusion, dispute, and inconsistent implementation.

Music

The two kinds of music most often prohibited in schools are religious compositions and morally offensive songs. Conflicts over these prohibitions are analyzed in the following pages under three headings: (a) religious music, (b) morally offensive lyrics, and (c) suggestions for school practice.

RELIGIOUS MUSIC

As noted in Chapter 7, the passage relating to religion in the first amendment to the U.S. Constitution contains two parts: "Congress shall make no law respecting an establishment of religion, or prohibiting the free exercise thereof." As explained earlier, the first part is referred to as the *establishment clause* and the second as the *free-exercise clause*. Ever since the 1790s, the establishment portion has usually been interpreted in courts to mean there should be strict separation between religion and the secular government. Ergo, because public schools are government institutions, religion does not belong in schools. Consequently, school personnel have been challenged to devise ways of both recognizing students' rights to practice the religion of their choice and, at the same time, not promote (establish) a particular faith.

Despite the apparent separation of church and state implied in the amendment, traditions from colonial times continued strong in public schools after the first amendment's adoption in 1791. Earlier in the mid-seventeenth century, following the introduction of public schooling in Britain's American colonies, the "opening exercises" at the beginning of the school day included Protestant hymns. During the Christmas and Easter seasons, school choirs featured Christian music. And the desirability of Christian music in schools would be further supported by Catholic immigrants who arrived in large numbers after the mid-nineteenth century.

However, a changing social climate in America in the mid-twentieth century lead dissident groups to challenge the continuation of Christian music in public schools. Immigration from non-Christian nations turned the United States into an increasingly multireligious nation. At the same time, there was an increase of both (a) "casual" Christians who did not actively promote their faith and (b) the nation's small number of nonreligious citizens. By the close of the twentieth century, an estimated 15 percent of the populace were atheists, agnostics, secular humanists, or simply nonbelievers who objected to religious proselytizing in public schools. As a result, from the 1960s onward, a growing number of lawsuits challenged the legality of religious music in schools.

Over the past four decades, several federal court cases about religious music in schools have resulted in conflicting rulings—some of them favoring and others censoring performances of Christian music. And because the U.S. Supreme Court has never issued a definitive ruling about the matter, the legal status of such music continues to be rather murky, as reflected in the following four cases.

The Sioux Falls Incident

The 1977 Christmas-season program at an elementary school in Sioux Falls (South Dakota) resulted in a parent filing a lawsuit (*Foley versus Sioux Falls School District*) on the grounds that the program was replete with religious material that violated the U.S. Constitution's first amendment. The Sioux Falls school board responded by issuing a set of rules that would govern future holiday programs. The rules stipulated that:

- The only holidays that could be observed were ones that had both a religious *and* secular purpose, so holidays with only a religious purpose could not be celebrated in schools.

- Music, art, literature, and drama having a religious theme or basis could be included in the school curriculum only if "presented in a prudent and objective manner and as a traditional part of the cultural and religious heritage of the particular holiday."

- Religious symbols could be included as teaching aids or resources and only if "such symbols are displayed as an example of the cultural and religious heritage of the holiday and are temporary in nature." (Heaney, 1980)

When the case was argued in a federal district court, the judge declared that the 1977 Christmas program had, indeed, breached the first amendment's separation of church and state. In addition, the court stated that the new rules adopted by the Sioux Falls board of education were reasonable and, if diligently followed, would be in keeping with the first amendment's intent. Thus, the court found in favor of the school district. However, the plaintiff—Foley— was dissatisfied with the decision, claiming that the rules still fostered "an excessive government entanglement with religion," so he took that case to the U.S. Eighth Appeal Court where the two judges who heard the case sustained the district court's judgment.

Although the rules permit the schools to observe holidays that have both a secular and a religious basis, we need not conclude that the School Board acted with unconstitutional motives. It is accepted that no religious belief or non-belief should be promoted by the school district or its employees, and none should be disparaged. The Sioux Falls School District recognizes that one of its educational goals is to advance the students' knowledge and appreciation of the role that our religious heritage has played in the social, cultural, and historical development of civilization. (Heaney, 1980)

In effect, religious music whose *principal* or *primary* effect neither advanced nor inhibited religion was deemed constitutionally acceptable. Christmas programs could legally be conducted in the future if they met the test of the school district's rules.

However, the appeal court's judges did not consider their ruling in *Florey versus Sioux Falls* to be a definitive judgment that would settle the "entanglement" issue in all such cases.

We simply hold—on the basis of the record before us—that the policy and rules adopted by the Sioux Falls Board of Education, do not violate the [Constitution's] First Amendment. (Haeney, 1980)

Although the U.S Supreme Court has never issued a definitive ruling on matters of religious holidays in schools, the Court did let stand the *Foley versus Sioux Falls* decision that recognition of holidays may be constitutional if the purpose is to provide secular instruction about religious traditions rather than to foster a particular religion. Thus, *Foley versus Sioux Falls* has continued to serve as the primary—though admittedly vague—guide in such matters.

The Salt Lake Incident

When Rachel Bauchman was enrolled as a student at West High School in Salt Lake City, she joined an a-capella choir directed by Richard Torgerson. However, Rachel, as a Jew, was offended when the preponderance of the choir's musical selections were Christian religious songs, and the places in which the choir performed included such Christian venues as the Church of the Madeleine, the First Presbyterian Church, and the Mormon Temple Square. When Torgerson rejected Rachel's pleas to have religious music dropped from the choir's repertoire, Rachel's mother filed a lawsuit in federal district court, charging that the U.S. Constitution's establishment clause was being violated because Torgerson "selected songs for the religious messages they conveyed . . . [and] selected religious sites for Choir performances with the purpose and effect of publicly identifying the Choir with religious institutions" (Brorby, 1997).

However, the district court rejected the Bauchmans' claim and found in favor of Togerson and the school district. When the Bauchmans took the case to the Tenth U.S. Circuit Court of Appeal, the three justices who heard the arguments supported the district court's ruling. They decided that the school system, through its choir director, had not violated the Constitution's prohibition against the government's endorsing a religion. In December 1997, the judges wrote that

> We believe a reasonable observer [would recognize that the] Choir represents one of Salt Lake City's public high schools and is comprised of a diverse group of students; many of the Choir's songs have religious content—content predominately representative of Judeo-Christian beliefs; in contrast to a church choir, this Choir also performs a variety of secular songs; the Choir's talent is displayed in the diverse array of songs performed and in a number of different public (religious and nonreligious) settings, all of which reflect the community's culture and heritage. Certainly, any given

observer will give more or less meaning to the lyrics of a particular song sung in a particular venue based on that observer's
individual experiences and spiritual beliefs. However, the natural
consequences of the Choir's alleged activities, viewed in context
and in their entirety by a reasonable observer, would not be the
advancement or endorsement of religion. Ms. Bauchman's complaint therefore fails to support a claim that the Choir curriculum
or Choir activities have a principal or primary effect of endorsing
religion. (Brorby, 1997)

The Everett Incident

In preparation for the June 2006 graduation exercises at Henry M. Jackson
High School in Everett (Washington), the seventeen members of the school's
wind ensemble chose *Ave Maria* (*Hail, Mary*) as the composition they would
play. It would be solely an instrumental rendition without the words of the
song. However, prior to the ceremony, the Everett school superintendent,
Dr. Carol Whitehead, vetoed *Ave Maria* on the ground that it might be seen
as promoting the Catholic/Christian religion. In response to the superintendent's rejection, a girl who played alto saxophone in the ensemble—Kathryn
Nurre—filed a lawsuit against Dr. Whitehead, charging that the superintendent's decision violated students' first amendment right of free speech. The
suit was supported by the Rutherford Institute, a conservative legal foundation
based in Charlottesville (Virginia) that handles hundreds of cases each year
that involve questions of religious freedom and free speech.

The following reactions to the incident from members of the public reveal
the varied opinions people expressed about the event.

> I heartily applaud Kathryn Nurre for filing a lawsuit against her
> school's superintendent.... [This] is another ridiculous example
> of "allow no state-sponsored religious teaching" at a school event.
> More students and their families should stand up against the en-
> croachment of their freedoms and rights against those public ser-
> vants who seek to impose their own anti-Christian views. (Hartsock,
> 2006)

> I wholeheartedly support the separation of church and state. For
> example, I believe we should revert to the pre-1954 version of the
> Pledge of Allegiance that doesn't contain "under God." But as a
> music educator, I cannot condone the suppression of art and

artistic expression. It is the position of the National Association for Music Education that the study and performance of religious music within an educational context is a vital and appropriate part of a comprehensive music education. The omission of sacred music from the school curriculum would result in an incomplete educational experience. (Geiger, 2006)

Ave Maria is a religious song; a Catholic/Christian song praising the mother of Jesus. That was its sole purpose by composers of the various versions. Personally, I love the music. As a Jew, I can choose to ignore the words and just enjoy the music for its beauty. But the key word here is "choose"—[so] I would never want [*Ave Maria*] forced upon me in a government-sponsored or school function. (Cohen, 2006)

The lawsuit was argued in a federal district court, with the ruling announced in late September 2007. The court found in favor of the school district by declaring that the superintendent was not violating the student's right to free speech by banning *Ave Maria*. The presiding judge wrote that "prohibition of the performance of *Ave Maria* was based on the decision to keep religion out of graduation as a whole, not to discriminate against a specific religious sect or creed," so the content restriction was permissible (Beckwith, 2007).

Miscellaneous Incidents

Other religious-music episodes in recent years illustrate the sorts of controversies that continue to occur. Most incidents concern schools' Christmas celebrations.

An order issued by the Woodland (Illinois) School District prohibited the playing of music on school bus radios. Several parents charged that the purpose of the order was to ban Christmas carols, so the parents' attorney sent the following letter to school officials.

Your order that no Christmas carols may be played under these circumstances constitutes an illegal suppression of the rights of our clients' children under the Free Exercise Clause of the First Amendment to the United States Constitution. It also reflects illegal hostility directed against Christianity. Respectfully, demand is made that you immediately rescind this order and allow Christmas carols to be played in the buses along with other music. (Kovacs, 2004)

The school superintendent responded that "I could care less if it's Christian, country or classical music. Playing radios on the bus will distract drivers from hearing students, and students from hearing instructions from the driver. It's absolutely ludicrous to think we're preventing Christmas music on the bus. It's totally safety [that concerns us]—absolutely nothing else" (Kovacs, 2004).

The issue was settled by leaving the decision about playing music on bus radios to the discretion of individual bus drivers.

The Egg Harbor (New Jersey) school board removed *Silent Night* from an elementary school holiday program after a parent complained; then the board reinstated the song after the complaint was withdrawn. The holiday program included songs celebrating Hanukkah and Kwanzaa (School's ban, 2004).

To avoid violating the Constitution's establishment clause, the organizers of a holiday program at Ridgeway Elementary School in Dodgeville (Wisconsin) renamed the Christmas-time festival "Winter Program" and reworded the carol *Silent Night* to form the following secular version: "*Cold in the night, no one in sight, winter winds whirl and bite, how I wish I were happy and warm, safe with my family out of the storm.*" A spokesman for Liberty Counsel, a law firm dedicated to defending Christian causes, objected to the school's action: "The law is clear—Christmas is constitutional. When a public school intentionally mocks Christian Christmas songs by secularizing their content, they cross the line from a neutral position, which the Constitution requires, to a hostile position, which the Constitution forbids" ("Silent Night," 2005).

Most, but not all, banning of religious music focuses on the year-end holiday season. When Rossford (Ohio) High School scheduled an anti-drug assembly, program planners intended to feature a local rock band, *Pawn*. But when the school's attorneys discovered that many of the band's songs referred to God and Jesus, they told the superintendent that the songs were inappropriate. Thus, the superintendent cancelled the program because "There is some controversy, and I'd rather err on [the side of caution]" (Ban the Christmas, 2004).

In summary, the issue of permitting religious music in public schools continues to be highly contentious. When controversies have led to lawsuits, jurists have typically applied the *reasonable-person* standard: "Would a 'reasonable person' feel that a religious musical composition appeared to endorse a particular religion?" The problem with such a standard is that people can have very different interpretations of what constitutes "reasonable."

MORALLY OFFENSIVE LYRICS

The term *moral*, as intended in the following discussion, refers to *the socially correct ways that people should behave toward each other*. And moral's opposite—*immoral*—means behavior considered improper and thereby offensive. It is also the case that the meaning of *moral* can be extended to beings in spirit form, such as God, Jesus, Moses, and Mohammad. Therefore, transgressions aimed at revered prophets and invisible spirits can qualify as immoral as readily as offenses against humans.

Particularly important for understanding bans on music is the fact that the sorts of behavior encompassed by the expression *moral* often change with the passing of time, so that singing songs that were acceptable in schools at one time may be deemed unacceptably offensive at a later time, and vice versa. In addition, the media through which students gain access to offensive songs can change as well.

Changing Standards with the Passing of Time

As mentioned in previous chapters, the 1960s in America served as a social-standards watershed. The decade's newly introduced morality featured "free love," rebellion against authority, "if it feels good, do it," and the exploration of unconventional emotional states through the use of an expanding cornucopia of illicit drugs—marijuana, cocaine, LSD, heroin, and more. Each of these themes was celebrated in songs of the day and over the following decades. The changes also produced a generational divide, with youths often adopting the new standards while their parents still subscribed to traditional views of morality. Thus, social changes posed problems for schools, whose personnel tried to maintain long-standing values at the time that increasing numbers of students embraced newly popular values.

Consequently, conflicts arose over what music should (a) be performed during assembly programs, school plays, and school dances and (b) listened to on tape recorders and radios during recess and lunch periods. There were arguments about imagined hidden meanings in the lyrics of the most popular rock-and-roll performers of the day, as in the Beatles' tune *Yellow Submarine*.

Did the line "We all live in a yellow submarine" refer to yellow LSD pills that were popular at the time? And in the Beatles' song *Hey, Jude*, was the intravenous use of drugs implied in the passage "Hey Jude, don't make it bad; take a sad song and make it better. The minute you put it under your skin, then you begin to feel better." So it was that songs whose suspicious lyrics reflected an unwelcome new-age morality could be banned in schools.

Another moral value that matured in the mid-twentieth century and affected music in schools concerned long-accepted allusions to ethnic minorities, particularly blacks. In an effort to eliminate epithets in songs that African-Americans considered denigrating, schools started to eliminate well-known songs from choral programs and music classes or to sanitize old favorites by removing objectionable expressions. For example, words like *massa, darkeys,* and *Niggas* were excised from such Stephan Foster (1826–1864) classics as *Swanee River, Away Down Souf, My Old Kentucky Home,* and *Ring, Ring de Banjo.* So, during recent decades, compassion for the feelings of ethnic minorities has led to the banning from schools of songs that appear to make sport of ethnic groups. Humorous lyrics that were welcomed in the past have been declared politically incorrect and dropped from school performances. Songwriter Irving Berlin's Jewish ditties (*Jake, Jake, the Yiddisher Ball Player* and *Cohen Owes Me Ninety-Seven Dollars*) that were popular in the early 1900s would be banned today. So would his *Latins Know How, When You Kiss an Italian Girl,* and *Oh, How That German Could Love.*

Beginning in the 1970s and accelerating into the twenty-first century, the music most often banned in schools has been hip hop's *rap.* Hip hop started as a cultural movement in the early 1970s after a disk jockey from Jamaica, Clive Campbell, assumed the stage name Kool Herc and settled in Kingston New York's West Bronx where, during his broadcasts, he chanted improvised rhymes against a background of rhythmic recordings. Such chanting—labeled *rapping*—was incorporated into an evolving hip-hop culture that celebrated distinctive jargon, styles of dress, dancing (*break dancing*), social values, and graffiti art on public structures (buildings, subways, bridges). Although hip-hop has been most intimately associated with African–American urban life, its rap stars have included individuals from other ethnic groups as well. One of the most popular rappers, Marshall Bruce Mathers III, is a white youth who rapped under the pseudonym Eminem. Millions of compact discs and videos have been sold around the world by rappers bearing such names as *50 Cent, Wu-Tang Clan, The Notorious B.I.G., Geto Boys, The Dogg Pound, Tupac Shakur, Gravediggaz, Cypress Hill, Lords of Acid, Black Crowes,* and *Blues Traveler.*

Hip-hop culture and its rappers have split into several types. The type considered most objectionable, when judged by traditional social standards, is known *gangsta rap* because it celebrates violence—murder, mayhem, obscenity, sexual abuse, ethnic hatred, the denigration of women, and the killing of police officers. Religion is mocked in such lyrics as "The pope smokes dope, and God is high on mescaline" (Marijuana lyrics, 2007). Fearing that *gangsta rap* was giving hip-hop culture a commercially damaging reputation, one of the chief promoters of rap, Russell Simmons, in 2007, urged recording companies and radio stations to outlaw any songs that included three words often featured in rap music—*bitch, ho* (a ghetto version of *whore*), and *nigger*. And because the values promoted by *gangsta rap* depart so radically from the values taught in schools, the gangland variety of hip-hop culture is the kind that school personnel and parents have most vehemently condemned.

But in opposition to people who denounce *gangsta rap*, hip-hop's defenders have argued that

> A rap song about a murder is not a murder, a heavy metal song about suicide is not self-annihilation. The cross-dressing Marilyn Manson is not a seducer. When he snarls at the Church, he's not burning a cross. As MIT's Henry Jenkins told Congress, kids know that pop culture performers are putting on an act, playing a part—a part that offers a sublimated outlet for the audience's anger at authority or ambivalence about sexuality or organized religion. . . . Whatever you think of what kids are watching, listening to or saying, they have a Constitutional right to it. And curtailing anyone's rights threatens everyone's rights. (Casino, 2007)

New Media Bring More Offensive Lyrics

Beginning in the mid-1980s, an ever-expanding succession of electronic inventions increased the complexity of educators' efforts to monitor the music students listen to at school—cell phones, handheld computers, and music players (iPods) that enabled students to store hundreds of tunes which they could hear privately by means of a tiny earphone. Thus, by the early years of the twenty-first century, a student equipped with an iPod could listen to songs without anyone knowing if the lyrics were acceptable to school personnel. Furthermore, youths could place their music videos on the Internet by means of such social-networking Web sites as MySpace, FaceBook, and YouTube. Therefore, students using school computers that were connected to the Internet could surreptitiously hear songs and view video clips whose contents were forbidden in schools. Alternatively, youths could use their own cell phones that offered Internet access to enjoy outlawed songs and videos during school hours.

Typical of objectionable material on YouTube is a video that includes images of a drug syringe, a bare female buttocks, and ghostly faces that accompany such lyrics as "She's like heroin, sipping through a little glass. I'm looking for some help, I need someone to save her ass." Or in another video, a crudely photographed fake fight between two teenagers is linked to lyrics that suggest, "If you got bad news, you wanna kick them blues—cocaine. She don't lie, she don't lie, she don't lie—cocaine."

In summary, the sources of unacceptable songs available to students have expanded dramatically over the past three decades because of advances in digital technology. Such developments have posed new challenges for schools that seek to reduce students' access to objectionable lyrics and their accompanying video images.

SUGGESTIONS FOR SCHOOL PRACTICE

Religious music and morally offensive lyrics are separate problems that call for their own solutions.

Decisions about Religious Music

Because most controversies about religious music in schools occur during the year-end holiday season, Charles C. Haynes of the first amendment Center has proposed that

> The solution is for the school to plan programs in December that include sacred music, but aren't dominated by it. Let the performers (and the audience) know that the choral selections were made for aesthetic and educational reasons, not to promote religion. And make sure that a variety of traditions and cultures are represented— not just in December, but throughout the school year.
>
> Before planning December holiday concerts or other activities in a public school, choral directors and administrators should ask themselves three simple questions:
>
> 1. Do we have a clear educational purpose? Under the First Amendment, learning about religious holidays is an appropriate educational goal—celebrating or observing religious holidays is not.

2. Will any student or parent be made to feel like an outsider by the concert or activity? Most parents and students are fine with learning about religious traditions—as long as the school's approach is academic, not devotional. It is never appropriate for public schools to proselytize.

3. Is our overall curriculum balanced and fair? December shouldn't be the only time sacred music pops up in the curriculum. Students should learn about religious music from various traditions at other times of the year. (Haynes, 2003)

Decisions about Morally Offensive Lyrics

One approach to coping with objectionable songs in schools consists of five steps: (a) defining the kinds of lyrics that are unacceptable and why those kinds are banned, (b) specifying the measures to be used in controlling students' access to offensive songs, (c) identifying who will be responsible for implementing the policy, (d) announcing the plan to staff members, students, and parents, and (e) establishing procedures for dealing with people who object to the policy and its implementation.

Defining unacceptable lyrics. A list of words and phrases can be compiled along with the conditions under which such words are considered offensive. One condition can be that a person uttered the expression with the *intent to do harm*, such as to denigrate a classmate, an ethnic group, or a religion. Another condition can be that the word is liable to *incite violence*. A third is that the expression is *customarily interpreted as obscene*.

Ways of controlling access to offensive lyrics. The invention of the Internet, cell phones, and iPods has made control particularly difficult. Some schools set up rules governing the use of computers and personal digital devices, then expect students to obey the rules. Other schools install software on school computers that blocks access to selected Web sites, such as YouTube and MySpace. Still other schools ban cell phones, handheld computers, and iPods from the campus, or at least from classrooms.

The kinds of punishment that will be applied for infractions of the offensive-lyrics policy should be specified so that students understand the risk they take if they disobey the rules.

Identifying who will implement the policy and how. A decision is made about who is authorized to report violations of the policy (teachers? principals? bus drivers? secretaries? cafeteria workers?), about who confronts students who violate the rules, and who decides what sanctions are imposed for infractions.

Disseminating the plan. A description of the unacceptable-songs policy is distributed to school personnel, students, and parents.

Coping with complaints. A procedure is established for responding to people who object to the policy and its methods of implementation. The procedure defines who is responsible for responding and the steps to be taken to resolve complaints.

Vandalism

Vandalism is the act of intentionally destroying or damaging property belonging to an institution, to a group, or to an individual other than oneself. The vandalizing of schools is nothing new, for there have always been people bent on damaging school property—motivated by vengeance, ill will, avarice, or a perverse spirit of adventure. The incidence of school vandalism has increased in recent decades, rousing school authorities and the police to adopt more effective measures to curb the trend.

Although it is apparent that school vandalism is widespread, the exact amount of destruction and its cost are unknown because many incidents are not reported, particularly when the damage is relatively minor—a few broken windows, slashed bus tires, rude words scrawled on a sidewalk, eggs smashed on a cafeteria wall. Even though the precise expense of vandalism is not known, it is clear that by the early years of the twenty-first century, the annual cost of school vandalism exceeded $1 billion, a marked increase over the estimated $460 million in 1978 (Vandalism, 2005).

A U.S. Department of Justice summary of vandalism studies reported,

> [t]hose who vandalize or break into schools are typically young and male, acting in small groups. Vandalism and break-ins are most common among junior high school students, and become less frequent as students reach high school.... Many vandals have

done poorly academically, and may have been truant, suspended, or expelled. As is typical of many adolescents, students who vandalize and break into schools have a poor understanding of their behavior's impact on others, and are more concerned with the consequences to themselves.

Offenders are no more likely to be emotionally disturbed than their peers who do not engage in the behavior, nor are they any more critical of their classes, teachers, or school in general. While the majority of students do not engage in vandalism, they do not generally harbor negative feelings toward those who do. In other words, "vandalism is a behavior that students can perform without the risk of condemnation by other students."

Youth who lack full-time parental supervision during after-school hours have been found to be more involved in all types of delinquency than students whose parents are home when they return from school. (Johnson, 2005)

In this chapter, issues of vandalism are addressed under these three topics: (a) forms of vandalism, (b) the treatment of perpetrators and victims, and (c) suggestions for school practice.

FORMS OF VANDALISM[1]

Instances of destruction can be divided among nine classes that identify

- what has been harmed—(a) structures, (b) equipment, (c) living things;
- the nature of the harm—(d) disfigurement, (e) graffiti, (f) computer hacking; and
- methods or instruments used—(g) arson (h) noxious substances, (i) explosives.

Structure Damage

Much of the ruin wrought by vandals is to school buildings, with damage costs ranging from a few hundred dollars to millions.

[1] The contents of this chapter are drawn heavily from Chapter 8 in *Violence in American Schools* by R. Murray Thomas. Copyright © 2006 by R. Murray Thomas. Reproduced with permission of Greenwood Publishing Group, Inc., Westport, CT.

Four teenagers were caught by police in the early evening at Gibbs High School in St. Petersburg (Florida) where the four had broken into a construction site and started-up three fork lifts and a front-loader tractor with which they smashed a portable classroom. They were charged with trespass and criminal mischief. (Four juveniles, 2004)

At night vandals opened a fire hydrant in front of Conant High School in Hoffman Estates (Illinois) and plugged up a storm drain so that a flood of water ran under the school's locked doorways and soaked 40,000 square feet of classroom carpeting and corridor flooring. The damage was estimated at $100,000. (Vandals at Conant, 2005)

Thieves who stole an auto from a garage behind a residence drove the car through the front doors of nearby Southwest High School in Lincoln (Nebraska). The impact damaged 16 glass panels, four heavy metal doors, and railings at a cost of around $25,000. (Vanderford, 2005)

Equipment Damage

Frequent targets of vandals are such items of school equipment as buses, computers, desks, file cabinets, musical instruments, science-laboratory supplies, shelves of books, wall maps, and trophy cases.

Two boys, ages 9 and 10, were caught running away from Danville (New Hampshire) Elementary School after an alarm went off during the pair's Sunday afternoon rampage that caused $100,000 damage to school equipment. When asked why they had attacked the school, the boys said they wanted to "have a little fun."

The demolition began with the pair pelting the school building with eggs and smashing windows with rocks, then forcing open the front door and spending the next two hours moving from room to room, damaging everything in sight. The destruction included:

- Broken classroom and door windows, with shards of glass strewn across floors
- Chairs and desks smashed beyond repair
- Phones ripped from the wall
- A can of soft drink poured into copying machines

- 50 computers destroyed
- Paint splattered on walls of an art room
- Medicine cabinets broken open in the nurse's room
- The new gymnasium and several classrooms sprayed by fire extinguishers
- Glass fragments spread across the outside garden that pupils had planted.

School officials said, "Because the offenders are under age, it's not certain what penalty in New Hampshire they may face, if any, other than possibly having do some 'community service.'" The boys' parents "expressed regret." (Perry, 2001)

During the night, vandals slipped through a gap in a chain fence to gain access to the school-bus parking lot in North Royalton (Ohio) where they slashed 50 tires on 25 buses. Because the vandals could only reach the outside tires of the dual-tire rear wheels of the buses, drivers were still able to make their morning round of delivering 3,800 students to school. The slashed tires were replaced at a cost of $14,000. (O'Malley, 2004)

A surveillance camera tape-recorded the activities of six boys, ages 12 to 16, as they spent five hours on a Sunday afternoon breaking into vending machines, smashing windows, upsetting voting machines, and ransacking more than 30 rooms in a Detroit (Michigan) elementary school. The tape enabled police to identify the six and arrest them for breaking and entering and for malicious mischief. (Grant, 2004)

Schools in Thompson (Connecticut) were forced to close for a day so that workers could clean the town's 24 school buses whose seats and windows had been sprayed with fire-extinguisher powder during the night. Not only had the vandals emptied the buses' extinguishers during the attack, but they had also broken or stolen onboard security cameras. (Stacom, 2005)

Damage to Living Things

Some vandals include animals or plant life among their targets.

Two 15-year-olds, who bragged at their high school about their weekend escapade of destruction at Weibel Elementary School in

Fremont (California), were arrested for vandalism that included re-moving a three-foot-long pet orange-and-black corn snake from its cage and burning it to death in the kindergarten class's microwave oven. The youths had entered the school through an unlatched win-dow, spread paint on walls, and knocked over hundreds of library books, causing an estimated $1,000 damage. The pair were sus-pended from school for five days and returned to the custody of their parents. (Rubenstein, 2001)

Citizens of Valley Center (California) were outraged to learn that 11 graduating seniors had broken into the high school's quadrangle and, using a chainsaw, felled seven ornamental trees. As a result, school authorities banned the 11 from participating in graduation exercises, and plans were laid for obtaining payment for the dam-age. The school superintended said, "If I could have my way, every one of the kids involved would have to personally get a job and earn every cent it will cost to put things right again. Unfortunately, I have no way of enforcing the manner in which reparations will ultimately be made." (Carr, 2004)

A pair of juveniles broke into JLS Middle School in Palo Alto (Cal-ifornia), and killed a pet hamster in addition to scribbling graffiti on the walls, spraying fire extinguisher powder, smashing musical instruments, and altering computer files. (Two juveniles, 2004)

Disfigurement

Damage can include disfiguring a building, walkway, bus, auto, billboard, picture, furniture, computer, or other object by scratching it or splattering it with paint, garbage, or staining liquids.

As a prank after a Saturday night dance at Granger High School in Murray (Utah), a group of students threw eggs against the house of the head football coach. When the coach came out of the house, the students drove off in a truck, but the coach was able to see the license number and discover the truck's owner. When school convened the following Monday, the coach confronted the youths and pinned one against the wall. The coach was reprimanded for that act because, as a school official explained, "A district employee is allowed to intervene physically with a student in order to prevent physical harm to another person. Other than that, they shouldn't intervene physically." (Westley, 2005)

Carpets in the library at East Elementary School in Craig (Colorado) needed refurbishing after juveniles doused them with cans of chocolate syrup and fire-extinguisher dust. The two boys who had broken into the school over the weekend were later caught by police who had identified the pair through personal articles they had inadvertently left at the scene of the crime. The boys faced charges of criminal mischief, theft, and burglary. Colorado law required that individuals convicted of criminal mischief have their driver's license revoked. Or, if a teenager did not yet have a driver's license and later applied for one, that license would be suspended for six months to a year after the youth's sixteenth birthday. (Currie, 1999)

Graffiti

Graffiti is a special kind of disfigurement consisting of unauthorized inscriptions, words, figures, or designs that are painted, drawn, marked, etched, or scratched onto any surface of public or private sites. Schools are among the favorite targets of graffiti's creators. Tools used for sketching graffiti's illicit phrases and symbols include paint-spray cans, felt-tip markers, paint-and-brush, pens, pencils, chisels, knives, or even a finger on a dirty wall, window, or school bus. The most popular instrument in recent years has been the paint-spray can because of its several advantages. It contains the medium (paint) and applicator (spray can) in one relatively small container, making it easily concealed and transported. Spray paint sticks to most surfaces, and varied effects can be produced (thin lines, wide lines, large masses) with different sized nozzles.

Graffiti is often employed as a weapon in confrontations between groups or individuals over their ethnic, sex-preference, social-class, or religious differences.

Over a weekend, courtyard windows and walls at San Francisco's A. P. Giannini Middle School were spray-painted with swastikas, racial insults targeting various ethnic groups, and sexual obscenities aimed particularly at women. School-district officials reported that, whereas graffiti at schools was frequent (the district's paint crew spent 40% of its time removing graffiti), racial affronts were uncommon. (The ethnic composition of the middle school's 1,291 students was 59% Asian-American, 10% White, 9% Latino, 6% African-American, and the remaining 16% of mixed or unknown heritage.)

An English teacher who had been at the school for 15 years felt that the swastikas were intended for him. "I happen to be Jewish, so it's personal. I felt like turning around and walking away. This is the most extensive graffiti I've seen. I've been tagged before, but it was nothing with such hateful venom in it. It's very, very disturbing."

The school staff took up a collection to raise $300 as reward money for anyone who would provide information leading to the arrest of the culprits. (Marech, 2005)

Students' conflicts over heterosexual versus homosexual orienta-tions were at the center of a graffiti incident at Howell (Michigan) High School where four students, armed with spray-paint canisters, sprayed over the words "God hates fags" that had been written on a rock in front of the school; then they substituted the word "Love." But the four did not stop there. They also spray-painted "Love" 50 times around the flagpole and on nearby sidewalks and benches. In keeping with the school's code of conduct, officials suspended the four from school. But in protest to the suspension, more than 350 students staged a sit-down demonstration in front of the school, claiming that the punishment was too harsh. At the same time, two-dozen counter-protesters, with the word STRAIGHT painted on their chests, taunted the crowd of demonstrators. The school principal defended the suspensions by saying, "Although the word 'love' is a beautiful message, instead of using sidewalk chalk that we could wash out, they used spray-paint." The district director of operations estimated that sandblasting the sidewalks to remove the graffiti would cost several thousand dollars because "Concrete is an unforgiving surface." (Howell students, 2005)

Threats against African-Americans and the letters KKK were scrawled alongside smeared feces on the wall of a boys' bathroom at Franklin High School in Elk Grove (California). (Hume, 2005)

Officials at Barnstable High School in Hyannis (Massachusetts) forbid students from bringing backpacks to school after a messages

scrawled on a restroom wall warned that people were going to die
the following day. (Cassidy, 2007)

In graffiti cases, school officials are faced with the task of deciding what
sanctions should be applied to students who deface buildings.

> The Katy (Texas) Independent School District intended to send a
> sixth-grade girl to an alternative school for four months for writing
> "I love Alex" on a school gymnasium wall with a baby-blue Sharpie
> pen. (Eriksen, 2007)

> Five Kauai (Hawaii) high school seniors were banned from walking
> with their classmates during the graduation ceremony after they
> admitted to painting graffiti on campus buildings. In response, they
> put posters up around school saying they were sorry and agreed to
> put their artistic skills to use by painting new lines on the parking
> stalls in the student parking lot. (School bans 5, 2005)

Occasionally graffiti is considered to be socially acceptable and of sufficient
artistic quality to be retained as a decorative addition to a school.

> As a graduation prank, seniors at Montpelier (Vermont) High
> School sneaked into the school over a holiday weekend to paint
> a large celestial mural on 170 ceiling tiles in the school's main
> lobby. When the principal returned to school following the holiday,
> he was astonished at the sight, then tried to decide how to cope with
> "a case of vandalism that's really quite beautiful. I think everyone
> agrees that it's beautiful. We're enjoying it right now, and we don't
> plan on removing it or eliminating it." School authorities declined
> to discipline the seniors or press charges against them for entering
> or for vandalizing school property. (School won't erase, 2005)

Computer Hacking

The damage caused by hackers includes (a) obtaining personal information about students or staff members and using that information to cause
harm to those individuals, (b) stealing tests that are stored in files, (c) trans-
ferring funds out of financial accounts, (d) altering information, such as students' grades or records of misconduct, and (e) inserting false information,
such as honors, certificates, or degrees supposedly earned by students or staff
members.

A 16-year-old sophomore at Harrison High School in Kennesaw (Georgia) was suspended from school for 10 days for having used a school-library computer to illegally enter the school-district's private network and copy students' and staff members' social-security numbers, phone numbers, and addresses. (Torres, 2003)

Three students who disliked the grades they had earned in courses at Oak Lawn (Ilinois) High School cracked into the school's record files on several occasions to change their own and others' marks. They entered the school computer system through a program called Parent Portal, designed to enable parents to find information about their own son's or daughter's grades and attendance record. Normally, individuals could only read such information, not alter it. However, the three youths learned how to change the contents of files, then used that knowledge to improve more than 30 grades—raising *failures* to *passings* and B's to A's. The three operated from computers both at home and at school until a teacher exposed their scheme. Officials suspended the students from school for 10 days and denied them further use of school computers. (Napolitano, 2005)

Arson

Arson is the crime of setting fire to property with the intent to do damage. Buildings—including school buildings—are the type of property most often targeted by arsonists. Other types of school property that vandals set afire are books, furniture, file-cabinet contents, office machines, science equipment, and athletic gear. Of the various forms of vandalism, arson usually is the most costly for a school district.

The U.S. Department of Homeland Security reported in 2005 that 61 percent of all school structure fires were the result of arson, with 70 percent of those fires occurring in high schools. "Children under the age of 18 started 41,900 fires, causing an estimated 165 civilian deaths, 1,900 civilian injuries, and $272 million in direct property damage. Seventy-eight percent of fires occur during the school week and 22 percent on weekends. Typically, fires are started in school bathroom trash cans, locations that present children with a place to set a fire and areas that are normally without constant adult supervision" (Brown, 2005).

Two fires at a 370-student Washington, DC, charter school caused $2-million of damage to the main office, two classrooms, and an auditorium. A 15-year-old student at the school was arrested for starting the first fire, while authorities sought to discover who had set the second blaze. (Wilbur, 2005)

Clouds of smoke billowing through Harriet Tubman Elementary School in Washington, DC, caused 445 pupils and 87 staff members to evacuate the building while fire fighters extinguished a blaze in a boy's bathroom. The fire had been set by a 10-year-old boy who had ignited rolls of toilet paper that quickly filled the building with smoke. The boy was subsequently enrolled in a juvenile-fire-setters program conducted by the fire department. (Wagner, 2005)

Noxious Substances

Both physical and psychological damage can result from vandals using toxic or offensive substances to harm property or people.

A 16-year-old at Cordoza High School (Washington, DC) was arrested for stealing mercury from a science laboratory and releasing it at the school. He was arraigned on five charges—dumping a hazardous material, conspiracy to commit dumping, cruelty to children, theft, and receiving stolen property. A 15-year-old involved in the case was charged with dumping hazardous materials. The Environmental Protection Agency warned that mercury, even in small amounts, can be a health hazard if it is in a confined area. Thus, officials closed the school four days in order to decontaminate the building. (Cauvin & Haynes, 2005)

During a summer training camp for cheerleaders, four girls from Keller (Texas) High School received a pizza from members of a rival team, then covered the pizza with human feces and reported that the pizza had been sent to them in that condition by the rival team. However, investigators discovered that the Keller cheerleaders themselves were responsible for the prank. The camp organizers sent the four home, where the girls faced the prospect of being dropped from the cheerleading team and being enrolled in the school district's disciplinary alternative high school. (Cheerleaders, 2005)

Explosives

Among the most feared instruments that vandals use in their attacks on property and persons are homemade explosive devices such as pipe bombs and Molotov cocktails.

The typical pipe bomb is a metal pipe packed with explosive material—gunpowder, TNT, or a combination of such chemicals as chlorate and sugar. Sometimes the packing includes small, sharp metal objects, such as nails or screws. A fireworks fuse or any military-grade cord is inserted into a hole drilled in the side of the pipe so the bomb can be detonated. Or an electrical timing device can be attached to the pipe to set the bomb off at a predetermined moment. The two ends of the pipe are sealed with steel or brass caps. When the bomb explodes, it splatters metal fragments across the landscape.

A Molotov cocktail or benzene torch consists of a glass or plastic bottle partly filled with a flammable liquid, usually gasoline or alcohol (methanol, ethanol). The mouth of the bottle is plugged tightly shut with a cork or plastic stopper; then a cloth rag is tied tightly around the mouth. "The weapon is used by first soaking the rag in a flammable liquid immediately prior to using it, lighting the rag, and throwing the bottle at the target. The bottle shatters on impact, spilling the flammable liquid over the target, which is then ignited by the burning rag" (Molotov cocktail, 2005).

Incidents of vandals using explosive devices in schools have assumed a variety of forms.

> In a Kansas City high school, a bomb that exploded in a locker sent 11 students to the hospital. A California elementary school was closed after ten bombs, in the form of fireworks strapped to aerosol cans, were found in the building. A Nevada middle-school student brought a pound of ammonium nitrate to school. Eight boys placed two homemade bombs in a Minnesota elementary school. (Bombs and school security, 2005)

> At Sherwood High School in Sandy Spring (Maryland), $10,000 in damage resulted from vandals throwing Molotov cocktails into a computer laboratory. (Chellappa, 2004)

> Perhaps the most elaborate use of explosives for committing violence in schools occurred in the 1999 Columbine High School episode in Colorado. Before two youths started their shooting spree at the school, they had placed two backpacks containing explosive

devices at a street intersection some distance from the school. The backpacks were set to go off as a diversionary tactic to draw police and fire personnel away from the school. The diversion did succeed prior to the boys' launching their attack at the school. In addition to the guns they wielded, the two had brought with them a large assortment of homemade bombs which they distributed both inside and outside the school building as their attack progressed. Only after the attackers had killed 13 schoolmates, wounded 23, and shot themselves were the police and bomb experts able to search the premises for explosives. Their task took an entire week during which investigators checked 1,952 student lockers and 700 backpacks for weapons. The search yielded 30 bombs that had exploded during the attack and 46 unexploded devices as well as bombs that the two youths had planted with timing devices in their own autos in the parking lot. (Bomb survey, 2000)

In the immediate wake of the Columbine killings, bomb scares in schools rose dramatically. One Maryland school district suffered more than 150 bomb threats and fifty-five associated arrests in a single year. Although the incidence of bomb threats gradually subsided as the years passed, the danger of vandals setting off explosive devices is ever present.

TREATING VANDALS

The options available for treating vandals include warning students, conferring with their parents, assigning them to detention, suspending or expelling them, removing privileges, and placing them on probation. For particularly serious or heinous vandalism, students can be sent to jail or prison. An additional penalty requirement, especially suitable in serious vandalism cases, is that students or their parents pay restitution for the damage done.

Which type of treatment is chosen in a case of vandalism can depend on a variety of variables in the case, including the vandal's age and apparent motives, the type and extent of damage, the potential effect the treatment will have on the student's educational progress, and the estimated likelihood that the treatment will deter the vandal from committing future misdeeds.

Age was an important factor in Salina (Kansas) where police were unable to take two girls into custody because the law prohibited the arrest of anyone under age 10. The girls, ages 6 and 7, had littered the art room in Heusner Elementary School with 34 containers of tempera paint, several jars of glitter glue, and other art supplies. Broken crayons were spread across the floor, and a jar of body lotion was poured on a desk. (Girls trash, 2005)

Students or their parents can be required by state law, local law, or school policy to pay the costs of intentional damage that students caused to school property. In cases that involve only minor damage, some schools allow restitution in the form of working off the expense by such assignments as cleaning the school, painting over graffiti, or contributing community service in place of paying for the damage.

An example of a state law governing school vandalism is the Alaska statute that requires students or their parents to pay up to $15,000 of school property damage resulting from a student's intentional destruction. The $15,000 limit was imposed so that the cost to families with limited financial means would not be unduly burdensome. Where individual cases warranted charging parents more, a court could exceed the $15,000 limit. When more than one family was involved in a vandalism incident, each family could be liable for as much as $15,000 (Meyer, 2003).

The code-of-conduct for secondary-school students in Beaufort County (South Carolina) informed parents that if their son or daughter destroyed or defaced school property, parents would be required to pay for the damage. In order to render the warning more specific after a Bluffton High School student spray-painted profanity on walls and lockers in a men's bathroom, district officials set prices for different types of damage. The price for the bathroom spray-painting incident was $300. For such minor episodes as students writing on walls with marker pens, students were required to make amends by repainting the walls. (Knich, 2005)

Seniors who engaged in vandalism activities at Marshwood High School in Eliot (Maine) were required to pay for damage they had committed in what they said was a graduation-week prank. The amount of the cost that each would bear was adjusted by authorities to the role each had played in the prank. The largest amount—$5,300—was charged to the youth who had sprayed fire-extinguisher powder in the high school gymnasium, which resulted in school officials postponing the senior-class assembly. Twelve other seniors were punished for toilet-papering the gymnasium and lobby. All of them were required to pay $60 to $70 each, and they were banned from senior-class activities except the graduation ceremony. (Jacques, 2005)

SUGGESTIONS FOR SCHOOL PRACTICE

Would-be vandals are less likely to attempt risky ventures if they know that police officers are patrolling the halls, that teachers keep cell phones handy, that surveillance cameras are located around the campus, or that students are subject to metal-detector searches when they enter school.

Precautionary measures that might usefully be adopted by schools include the following:

- Installing woven-wire fencing and locked gates, deadbolt locks on doors and windows, door and window shutters, and doors that open freely only from inside.

- Banning matches, lighters, or smoking materials from school property.

- Ensuring that no combustible items are stored near the outside of buildings.

- Trimming or removing shrubbery that is close to buildings or that obstruct the view of the building from the street; planting thorny bushes and unclimbable trees near entry points.

- Placing intruder alarms, motion sensors, heat sensors, and glass-break sensors at key passageways to different parts of the school building and in areas where valuable equipment and records are stored.

- Storing high-value audio-visual equipment and computers in rooms with high-quality locks. Removing signs that indicate the location of expensive equipment.

- Bolting computers to office and laboratory desks.

- Equipping storage areas with smoke detectors linked to the fire department.

- Posting warning signs that tell what activities are permitted in particular sites and tell who has permission to enter those sites.

- Imprinting the school's name or logo on all computers, television sets, DVD players, and cameras can deter vandals who had hoped to sell the equipment.

- Illuminating building exteriors, such as by installing lighting fixtures that are activated by visible motion.

- Focusing video cameras on places that vandals might enter the school.

- Establishing regular security patrols.

- Setting up a 24-hour vandalism hotline for people living near schools.

- Creating an evening activity program for youths who loitered around schools.

There is no consensus on whether well-lit school campuses and building interiors or "dark" campuses are superior in terms of crime prevention. Obviously, lighting adjustments alone are not effective deterrents, but in combination with other responses, both approaches have shown positive results. Well-lit campuses and buildings make suspicious activity more visible to observers, and also may offer some protection to custodial staff and others who may legitimately be on campus after dark. On the other hand, a "lights out" policy makes it more difficult for potential intruders to manipulate locks and hinges at entry points, and if intruders do enter the building, observers can easily spot any lights that should not be on. (Johnson, 2005)

The need to guard school property from harm can also appropriately be balanced against the emotional climate in which children and youths are expected to enjoy learning. Students often complain of feeling oppressed when their school resembles a jail—metal-detector screening, clothing searches, video cameras in hallways. Thus, schools in which instances of vandalism are rare can go light on instituting visibly repressive protection methods. Some regulations created to reduce vandalism have been deemed unduly restrictive by the courts. For example, a federal judge abolished a New York City law that ordered the arrest of youths ages eighteen, nineteen, and twenty who carried "graffiti instruments" (spray paint and broad-tipped markers). The judge ruled that the law imposed "unreasonable conditions on a limited class of individuals" (Lueck, 2007).

On the assumption that potential vandals will often be deterred from carrying out their plans if they know the actual risk involved, officials are well advised to inform students, staff members, and parents of their school's anti-vandalism provisions—what acts are considered to be vandalism and what penalties vandals can expect. Media for conveying such information include student-conduct handbooks, newsletters to parents, assembly programs for students, classroom discussion sessions, video-illustrated presentations at parent meetings, segments of television and radio news broadcasts, and newspaper articles.

Drugs, Alcohol, and Tobacco

For obvious reasons, schools have always outlawed illicit drugs and alcohol. "Doped" and "stoned" students do not make efficient learners. Nor do teachers serve as efficient instructors or positive role models for students if the teachers' minds are muddled with drugs and drink.

The high incidence of students using illegal drugs and alcohol has been a serious problem since the 1960s. And by 2008, there was a question about whether progress was being made in combating the spread of drugs in schools. The Monitoring-the-Future (MTF) annual surveys suggested that the use of illicit drugs by students had dropped significantly over the past decade. In contrast, Center on Addition and Substance Abuse (CASA) studies reported a recent rise in the availability and use of drugs among middle-school and senior-high students.

The aim of the MTF surveys has been to collect data on past-month, past-year, and lifetime drug use among students in grades eight, ten, and twelve. The results of the 2006 study showed that since the peak years of drug abuse in the mid-1990s there were decreases at all three grade levels in the *any-illicit-drug* category. By 2006, any drug use had fallen by 37 percent among eighth graders since the peak year in 1996. The peak year for tenth and twelfth graders was 1997. By 2006, *past-year* use had fallen by 25 percent among tenth graders and by 14 percent among twelfth graders. Combining all three grades, *past-month* abuse for any illicit drug had dropped by 23 percent between 2001 and 2006 (National Institute, 2006).

However, according to the CASA studies, the percentage of middle-school students who reported that drugs were used, kept, or sold in their schools had risen from 19 to 31 percent of schools between 2002 and 2007. For senior-high students, the ready availability of drugs had advanced from 44 percent of the surveyed schools to 61 percent over the same five-year period (Snider, 2007). In high schools, 80 percent of students said they saw schoolmates who were drunk or were using, dealing, possessing, or under the influence of illegal drugs (Nyhan, 2007). In schools where drugs were prevalent, students were four times more likely to smoke cigarettes, five times more likely to use marijuana, and six times more likely to get drunk at least once a month than were students in schools less affected by drugs (Hernandez, 2007).

Part of the discrepancy between the MTF and CASA outcomes is perhaps accounted for by differences between the two studies in the kinds of questions asked of survey respondents and in the way the data were reported. For example, while MTF results showed a marked decrease in the use of *any illicit drug*, the researchers found variations between types of drugs used, such as marijuana and cocaine. Between 1992 and 2005, the *past-month use* of marijuana increased from 12 to 20 percent among high-school seniors, from 8 to 15 percent among tenth graders, and from 4 to 7 percent among eighth graders. Reported *past-month-use* of marijuana by high-school seniors peaked in 1978 at 37 percent and declined to its lowest level in 1992 at 12 percent. In contrast, the *past-month-use* of cocaine by high-school seniors peaked in 1985 at 6.7 percent, up from 1.9 percent in 1975. Cocaine use declined to a low of 1.3 percent in 1992 and 1993. In 2005, 2.3 percent of high-school seniors reported past-month cocaine use (National Institute, 2006).

The availability in schools of behavior-altering substances varies from one type of drug to another. The 2006 MTF study showed the percents of high-school seniors who reported that it was easy to obtain the following substances: marijuana 84.9 percent, amphetamines 52.9 percent, cocaine 46.5 percent, barbiturates 43.8 percent, crack 38.8 percent, LSD 29 percent, heroin 27.4 percent, crystal methamphetamine 26.7 percent, tranquilizers 24.4 percent, PCP 23.1 percent, and amyl/butyl nitrites, 18.4 percent (National Institute, 2006).

Therefore, despite some confusion about recent trends in the popularity of illegal drugs and alcohol, the evidence clearly shows that such substances in schools are the cause of serious problems for students' welfare and for the efforts of school personnel to conduct successful learning programs.

Whereas objections to drugs and alcohol have been founded primarily on those substances' ill effects on students' ability to think clearly and to learn efficiently, the case against tobacco has been different. Until recent years, cigarettes, cigars, pipes, and chewing tobacco were somewhat tolerated, at least in high schools. Cigarettes were considered a nuisance not welcomed in classrooms, but faculty members—and occasionally older students—were permitted to smoke in designated areas, such as in a lounge or outside the building. Unlike drugs and alcohol, cigarettes did not addle the brain and thereby did not seriously interfere with learning. Instead, tobacco products were frowned on for being messy—potential fire hazards whose smoke irritated nearby persons' eyes and lungs. Then in the final decades of the twentieth century, a host of scientific evidence attested to tobacco's role in causing mouth, throat, and lung cancer as well as heart disease and strokes. Consequently, since that time the use of tobacco in schools and at school functions (sporting events, picnics, dances) has been prohibited at a rapidly increasing rate. A typical school regulation about tobacco products is the one included in the Brighten High School (Tennessee) student handbook.

> Since Tennessee law makes the purchase, possession, or use of cigarettes illegal for anyone under the age of 18, the use of tobacco in any form by any student is prohibited. The Tipton County Board of Education prohibits smoking and the possession of tobacco products on all school campuses. Violations of the above policy will result in disciplinary action taken against the offender which could be in the form of corporal punishment and/or short or long term suspension. The rules apply during lunch, during any school activity, and during the school day. They also apply during the trip to and from school for those who ride a bus. A citation will be issued to violators. (Tobacco use, 2007)

In the following pages, trends in the banning of drugs, alcohol, and tobacco are traced through a series of five topics: (a) illegal drugs, (b) prescription and over-the-counter products, (c) alcohol, (d) tobacco, and (f) suggestions for school practice.

ILLEGAL DRUGS

The term *illegal drugs* is used in this chapter to mean substances that are either proscribed by law or are available only by means of a prescription from a medical doctor. Such illicit substances that students have found attractive include marijuana, cocaine, hallucinogens, methamphetamine, and steroids.

Marijuana

Marijuana is a mind-altering (psychoactive) mixture of dried shredded leaves, stems, seeds, and flowers of the hemp plant (Cannabis sativa), usually smoked as a cigarette (joint) or in a pipe (bong). Ingesting marijuana gives users a feeling of euphoria and well-being. Other forms of cannabis that also affect mood and thought patterns are sinsemilla, hashish, and hash oil. Street names for marijuana include *pot, grass, aunt mary, boom, chronic, dope ganja, gangster, grass, herb, kif, mary jane, reefer, skunk,* and *weed.*

The use of marijuana is highly controversial, with the drug's very vocal advocates arrayed against its staunch critics. Proponents of cannabis—such as members of National Organization for the Reform of Marijuana Laws (NORML)—argue that the drug is the third most popular recreational substance in America (behind alcohol and tobacco). "Some 20 million Americans have smoked marijuana in the past year, and more than 11 million do so regularly despite harsh laws against its use.... According to the prestigious European medical journal, *The Lancet,* 'The smoking of cannabis, even long-term, is not harmful to health.... It would be reasonable to judge cannabis as less of a threat... than alcohol or tobacco'" (NORML, 2007a).

Marijuana's advocates not only promote the drug for recreational uses but also as a medical treatment for pain relief, control of nausea and vomiting, and appetite stimulation. In addition, cannabis has been recommended for treating glaucoma, a disorder resulting from undue fluid pressure within the eyeball. Since 1996, the twelve states that have passed laws permitting the medical use of marijuana include Arkansas, California, Colorado, Hawaii, Maine, Montana, Nevada, New Mexico, Oregon, Rhode Island, Vermont, and Washington (Medical marijuana, 2007). Those states have generated a curious state/federal conflict. Whereas, purveyors of marijuana for medicinal use can operate legally under state laws, such operations can be shut down by federal agents as they enforce the federal prohibition against marijuana trafficking.

In opposition to the supporters of marijuana, the drug's critics—such as agencies of the United States Government—charge that the short-term effects of marijuana use include problems with memory and learning, distorted perception, difficulty in thinking and problem solving, loss of coordination, increased heart rate, and anxiety. As for the drug's role as a medicine, marijuana was included among substances judged to have no significant medical benefit under the Controlled Substances Act of 1970. That rejection of cannabis as a medicine was endorsed by the U.S. Supreme Court in 2001. The Glaucoma Foundation has disapproved of using cannabis to reduce eyeball pressure because

> hemp products are less effective than safer and more available medicines. The high dose of marijuana necessary to produce a clinically relevant effect on IOP [intraocular pressure] in the short term requires constant inhalation, as much as every three hours. The number of significant side effects generated by long-term oral use of marijuana or long-term inhalation of marijuana smoke make marijuana a poor choice in the treatment of glaucoma. (Glaucoma Foundation, 2007)

In response to claims that marijuana is harmless, critics point out that marijuana was involved in 242,200 of the 816,696 drug-related cases arriving in hospital emergency rooms. And even some advocates of marijuana—such as the members of NORML—warn that the drug can be dangerous under certain conditions. Thus, NORML has issued a set of *Principles of Responsible Cannabis Use*, which stipulate that (a) cannabis products should not be given to children ("young people"), (b) adults should not drive a car or operate machinery when under the influence of cannabis, and (c) cannabis should not be used when it impairs one's health or the rights and welfare of other people (NORML, 2007b).

In summary, the question remains unsettled regarding the conditions under which cannabis products are harmful to users and to other people who are in contact with users. But in virtually all schools, marijuana and similar forms of the hemp plant are banned.

Two of the problems that marijuana poses for schools are those of school personnel using cannabis and students advertising their marijuana habit.

School personnel users. With cannabis so widespread in America, it is hardly surprising that teachers and administrators are among the users. And when those individuals have apparently functioned adequately in their jobs, there is the problem of deciding what should be done about them when their drug habit is exposed.

> Sheriff deputies who raided the home of a 33-year-old Spanish-language teacher from Largo High School in Pinellas County (Florida) discovered five full-grown marijuana plants in a bedroom

closet, 11 seedlings in a bedroom, and some harvested marijuana in another closet. The teacher told authorities that he grew the hemp plants for his own personal use and did not try to sell the drug to students. He was arrested on a felony charge of manufacturing a controlled substance. (Raghunathan, 2007)

A 41-year-old Vernonia (Oregon) elementary-school principal retained his job, even after being cited at a state park for possession of marijuana. The Vernonia schools superintendent said that the accused had his "full support" and would stay on as principal of Washington Grade School and Mist Elementary School after admitting to a Clatsop County sheriff's deputy that he had been smoking pot. The superintendent said, "It was an unfortunate mistake and a poor choice to make. But I've had a meeting with [the principal], and he's planning on making things better, making things right." (Austin, 2007)

A 57-year-old cooking teacher at Braddock Senior High in Dade County (Florida) was arrested after he received in the mail a package containing 11 grams of marijuana. An alert postal employee had smelled marijuana from an envelope addressed to the teacher. When a postal inspector, along with state and federal agents, delivered the package to the teacher's address, he agreed to let them open the envelope and search his home. Not only did the envelope contain marijuana, but the agents also found in the house a bottle with marijuana, a small plastic baggie of marijuana, a pipe, and cigarette papers. The teacher was charged with possession of marijuana and drug paraphernalia. (Ovalle, 2007)

Students advertising their marijuana habit. Parents, school staff members, and segments of the general public are distressed at students openly sharing their marijuana experiences and interests.

The 2007 high-school yearbook in the Colorado mountain town of Conifer featured photos of students smoking marijuana and drinking beer—photos that drew the ire of parents and school administrators. Students were pictured holding a bong and exhaling smoke in a section labeled "Health—addicted addictions." Three female students—all named—held up citations for underage drinking in a second photo titled "Regrets and mistakes."

When the student editor of the yearbook was questioned, she said, "The point of the yearbook entirely is to cover what happens in the year. You'd be surprised at how many children at Conifer High School smoke pot. I wanted to push more for a deeper side of Conifer, which, for a lot of students, is drugs and alcohol."

The teacher who supervised the yearbook's preparation wrote a letter to parents explaining, "It wasn't my intent or my students' intent to portray such a negative tone in their attempt to cover all aspects of a students' life and some of the very difficult choices they face. My [student] editor and I have discussed at length and have agreed that there was no balance on the pages that are of concern and that some elements are completely inappropriate. These issues detract from the many wonderful things that are included in this book." (Colo, prep, 2007)

A study of Internet blogs, public chat rooms, message boards, and other [W]eb sites that attract teens revealed that about 2% of the posts specifically mentioned drugs or alcohol. Many teens' messages . . . traded information about using illicit substances without getting hurt or caught. Some debated drug legalization and the drinking age. Others told of partying experiences that involved sexual liaisons while they were drunk or high on drugs. An official from an addiction treatment center said that the Internet's misinformation about drugs is "staggering. What kids used to learn about drugs on street corners, they now learn online. [The Internet] erases geographic and social boundaries. Kids who live in remote areas can develop a camaraderie online of drug-abusing kids. They can share stories about drug experiences." (Leinwand, 2007)

Cocaine

Cocaine, a drug made from the leaves of the coca plant, functions as both a stimulant of the central nervous system and an appetite suppressant. It can be used in several forms—(a) as a fine powder that is insufflated (sniffed, snorted, blown), (b) as crystals (crack) that are melted and their vapor smoked through a pipe or metal tube, or can, (c) as leaves that are chewed or brewed into a tea, or (d) as a liquid injected into the blood stream with a hypodermic needle. Slang terms for the drug include *blow, coke, dust, lines, powder, rock* (crack), *snow, sneeze,* and *toot*. Ingesting cocaine produces what addicts say is an intense sense of happiness and increased energy. Because cocaine is addictive, its use can easily become a habit difficult to break.

The National Clearing House for Alcohol and Drug Information warns teenagers that cocaine

> causes a short-lived high that is immediately followed by opposite, intense feelings of depression, edginess, and a craving for more of the drug. . . . People who use cocaine often don't eat or sleep regularly. They can experience increased heart rate, muscle spasms, and convulsions. If they snort cocaine, they can also permanently damage their nasal tissue. Using cocaine can make you feel paranoid, angry, hostile, and anxious, even when you're not high. Cocaine interferes with the way your brain processes chemicals that create feelings of pleasure, so you need more and more of the drug just to feel normal. People who become addicted to cocaine start to lose interest in other areas of their life, like school, friends, and sports. Cocaine use can cause heart attacks, seizures, strokes, and respiratory failure. People who share needles can also contract hepatitis, HIV/AIDS, or other diseases. (National Clearing House, 2007)

In its frequency of use by students, cocaine is a distant second to the most popular illicit drug, marijuana. Among high-school seniors in 2005, 44.8 percent reported having ever used marijuana/hashish, 8.0 percent reported having ever used cocaine, and 1.5 percent reported having ever used heroin (National Institute, 2006).

Problems with cocaine in schools range from the primary grades through high school.

> A first-grade boy at Forrest Hills Elementary School in Tampa (Florida) discovered a packet in the pocket of his jacket and handed the packet to his teacher, who turned the parcel over to narcotics detectives. The narcotics agents determined that the bag contained 89 grams of crack/cocaine. The boy said he had no idea of how the crack ended up in his pocket. (89 grams, 2007)

> A 7-year-old girl brought 18 pink plastic packages containing a white powder to her second-grade class in a Philadelphia school and passed the bags to classmates so they could taste the contents. The powder turned out to be cocaine. One girl who ate some of the powder was taken by her mother to a hospital for treatment after the child "started shaking and she couldn't stop shaking." (Bags of cocaine, 2006)

Two seventh-grade boys in a New Mexico middle school were arrested for selling cocaine to schoolmates. Two other students were suspended from school for knowing about the drug sales but failing to report the incidents to school authorities. (Police say, 2007)

A star 18-year-old basketball player at Scott County (Kentucky) High School was arrested for trafficking in a controlled substance when he came to school with 1.6 grams of rock cocaine that he planned to deliver to a customer. The cocaine was broken into five small pieces that the youth had carried in his shoe. (Ogawa, 2007)

As in the case of marijuana, school personnel can be involved in cocaine use.

The principal of Van Buren Middle School in Tampa (Florida) was sentenced to 364 days in the county jail after he had tried to buy $20 worth of crack cocaine from an undercover narcotics agent in the school office while classes were in session. The court also ordered him to complete a drug-treatment program while in jail. Following the year in jail, he would need to perform 200 hours of community service, forfeit his teaching license, and be subject to probation for an additional three years. School officials reported that the man had been highly respected as a principal ever since he entered the school district in 1991. (Principal arrested, 2007)

Two recent events that might help schools' campaigns to curb cocaine trafficking were a study of cocaine users and the invention of a low-cost electronic cocaine sensor.

Researchers at Johns Hopkins University concluded that the decrease in cocaine use in the United States over two decades—1979–2002—was chiefly among people with the greatest amount of formal education. The lead author of the study explained that, "Much like smoking, people with a better understanding of the impact cocaine has on health are more likely to modify their behavior. Better educated individuals also may have more resources and access to health care services, such as drug treatment programs" (Cocaine use, 2007). Thus, raising the educational level of the school population—particularly through health-education classes—might well have a positive effect in reducing cocaine addition.

The ability of officials to quickly identify substances that contain cocaine was advanced in 2006 by the invention of a handheld electronic sensor that immediately recognizes cocaine, thus making time-consuming laboratory analyses unnecessary (Gallessich, 2006).

Hallucinogens

Substances that qualify as hallucinogens cause changes in a person's perception of reality so that users often report seeing images, hearing sounds, and experiencing sensations that seem real, but are merely illusions. In the past, plants and fungi that contained hallucinogenic qualities were ingested—mushrooms, peyote (a spineless cactus), ergot (a fungus that grows on rye and other grains), Virola bark resin, and various beans and seeds. However, today the effective chemicals in those natural substances are created synthetically to provide a higher potency.

Three representative hallucinogens are described in the following paragraphs to illustrate typical effects those drugs have on users—LSD, PCP, and psilocybin mushrooms. Additional hallucinogens that produce similar effects are DMT (Dimethyltryptamine), mescaline (peyote), AMT (alpha-methyltryptamine), Foxy Methoxy (5-methoxy-N, N-diisopropyltryptamine), MDMA (Ecstasy), and ketamine.

Results of the 2006 Monitoring-the-Future survey indicated that 3.4 percent of eighth graders, 6.1 percent of tenth graders, and 8.3 percent of twelfth graders reported use of one or more of those substances at sometime in their life. In 2005, the percentages had been slightly higher among eighth and tenth graders (3.8 percent and 5.8 percent) and lower among twelfth graders (8.8 percent) (Johnston, O'Malley, Bachman, & Schulenberg, 2006).

LSD. Lysergic acid diethylamide or LSD—a major hallucinogenic drug discovered in 1938—is referred to by such street names as *acid, blotter, dots, mellow yellow,* and *window pane.* It is synthesized from lysergic acid, which, in its natural state, is found in ergot. In 2006, approximately 1.6 percent of eighth graders, 2.7 percent of tenth graders, and 3.3 percent of twelfth graders surveyed had used LSD on at least one occasion. In addition, 40 percent of eighth graders, 60.7 percent of tenth graders, and 69.3 percent of twelfth graders believed that using LSD regularly was a "great risk."

> The effects of LSD are unpredictable. They depend on the amount of the drug taken; the user's personality, mood, and expectations;

and the surroundings in which the drug is used. Usually, the user feels the first effects of the drug within 30 to 90 minutes of ingestion. These experiences last for extended periods of time and typically begin to clear after about 12 hours. The physical effects include dilated pupils, higher body temperature, increased heart rate and blood pressure, sweating, loss of appetite, sleeplessness, dry mouth, and tremors....If taken in a large enough dose, the drug produces delusions and visual hallucinations. (Hallucinogens, 2007)

Users refer to their experience with LSD as a "trip" and when it is a frightening experience it is called a "bad trip." These experiences are long; typically they begin to clear after about 12 hours. Some LSD users experience severe, terrifying thoughts and feelings, fear of losing control, fear of insanity, death, and despair. (Addiction health services, 2007)

Sometimes children's encounters with LSD are unintentional, the result of pupils failing to be wary of substances offered to them by schoolmates. For example, three fourth graders at Haddon Elementary School in Los Angeles were taken to a hospital emergency room after falling ill from sucking breath-freshener capsules that a classmate had found on the way to school and had shared with friends. Investigators discovered that LSD had been injected into the capsules (LSD sickens, 1998).

PCP. Phencyclidine or PCP is a bitter-tasting white crystalline powder sold on the illicit drug market in tablets, capsules, and colored powders. It can be snorted, smoked, or drunk in water or alcohol. For smoking, it can be applied to a leafy material, such as mint, parsley, oregano, or marijuana. Street names for PCP include *angel dust, boat, tic tac,* and *zoom.*

PCP's effects can be felt within minutes of its ingestion and can last for many hours. Those effects can involve rapid breathing, increased blood pressure and heart rate, heightened temperature, nausea, blurred vision, dizziness, and decreased awareness of what is going on. High doses can cause convulsions, coma, and death. PCP is addictive, leading to psychological dependence, extreme cravings, and compulsive drug-seeking behavior. Among high-school seniors surveyed in 2006, 2.2 percent reported using PCP at sometime during their life.

In 2004, an estimated 8,928 drug-related cases treated in U.S. emergency hospital rooms involved PCP, while LSD contributed to 1,953 visits.

Miscellaneous hallucinogens were involved in another 3,445 cases (Hallucinogens, 2007).

Psilocybin. Some varieties of mushrooms grown in South America, Mexico, and the United States contain the chemical psilocybin, which is absorbed by a mushroom eater's mouth and stomach lining. Ingesting psilocybin often leads to a mixture of pleasant feelings, confusion, hilarity, a sense of being closely connected to nature and the universe, highly enhanced colors, and visions of animated organic shapes. The effects of psilocybin are usually experienced within twenty minutes of ingestion and can last for six hours.

When psychedelic mushrooms are eaten in a hostile environment, by an inexperienced person, or in an unexpectedly high dose, a *bad trip* may result—with the "trip" accompanied by vomiting, muscle weakness, drowsiness, and panic. An example of a bad trip is the experience of a seventeen-year-old student at Argyle (Texas) High School who was hospitalized after falling unconscious at school. The police who investigated the incident discovered that the youth had become intoxicated on mushrooms in a fellow student's car. The ailing youth was jailed for public intoxication, and the owner of the car faced a felony charge of possessing a controlled substance (Fielder, 2007).

Methamphetamine

Methamphetamine is a white or yellow powdered substance that can be taken orally, injected, snorted, or smoked. On the street, it is referred to as *chalk, crank, croak, crypto, crystal, fire, meth, tweek, white cross,* and *glass* (if meth's rock form is chipped, the chips resemble glass shards).

When users have smoked or injected meth, they experience a delightful "rush" or "flash" for a few minutes. Snorting or swallowing meth produces euphoria—a psychological "high" but not a rush. Following the rush, "there is typically a state of high agitation that in some individuals can lead to violent behavior. Other possible immediate effects include increased wakefulness and insomnia, decreased appetite, irritability/aggression, anxiety, nervousness, convulsions, and heart attack" (Methamphetamine, 2007).

> Meth is addictive, and users can develop a tolerance quickly, needing larger amounts to get high. In some cases, users forego food and sleep and take more meth every few hours for days, "binging" until they run out of the drug or become too disorganized

to continue. Chronic use can cause paranoia, hallucinations, repetitive behavior (such as compulsively cleaning, grooming, or disassembling and assembling objects), and delusions of parasites or insects crawling under the skin. Users can obsessively scratch their skin to get rid of these imagined insects. Long-term use, high dosages, or both can bring on full-blown toxic psychosis (often exhibited as violent, aggressive behavior). This violent, aggressive behavior is usually coupled with extreme paranoia. Meth can also cause strokes and death. (Methamphetamine, 2007)

According to the Monitoring-the-Future survey, the abuse of methamphetamine decreased among tenth graders from 2005 to 2006 (2.9 to 1.8 percent for past-year use; 1.1 to 0.7 percent for past-month use). The percent of twelfth graders who saw harm in trying crystal methamphetamine ("ice") increased from 54.6 percent in 2005 to 59.1 percent in 2006 (Johnston, O'Malley, Bachman, & Schulenberg, 2006).

Steroids

Anabolic-androgenic steroids were first synthesized in the 1930s and since then have been used therapeutically to stimulate bone growth and appetite, induce male puberty, treat some types of male impotence, and help counter body-wasting in such disorders as cancer and AIDS. Because anabolic steroids increase muscle mass and physical strength, they are frequently used by athletes to enhance strength or physique. However, serious health risks accompany long-term or excessive doses of steroids. Harmful effects include trembling, liver or kidney tumors, cancer, jaundice, high blood pressure, cholesterol imbalance (increased low-density lipoprotein and decreased high-density lipoprotein), severe acne, and dangerous changes in the structure of the left ventricle of the heart. Young adolescents who use steroids before their bodies fully mature may permanently stunt their height. Overuse of steroids by men can result in testicle shrinkage, reduced sperm count, infertility, baldness, breast development, and greater risk of prostate cancer. Overuse by women can stimulate the growth of facial hair, male-pattern baldness, menstrual-cycle changes, and a deepened voice (National Institute on Drug Abuse, 2007).

During the 1990s, steroid use by high-school athletes rose dramatically, more that doubling between 1991 and 2003, as "more than 6% of 15,000 students surveyed admitted trying steroid pills or injections. At the same time, less than 4% of the nation's high schools were testing for steroids" (Livingstone, 2005).

Throughout the first decade of the twenty-first century, vigorous efforts have been mounted to prevent the use of anabolic steroids at all levels of competitive sports—professional, college, high school, and middle school. At an increasing pace, schools are testing athletes for steroid use, a practice encouraged by a U.S. Supreme Court 2002 ruling that allowed mandatory drug tests for middle- and high-school students who participate in extracurricular activities. By 2006, the campaign to reduce the abuse of steroids in high schools was apparently having an effect, as the proportion of twelfth graders who considered steroid use risky had increased from 56.8 percent in 2005 to 60.2 percent in 2006 (Johnston, O'Malley, Bachman, & Schulenberg, 2006).

In 2006, New Jersey became the first state to introduce statewide steroid testing of high-school athletes, with the program limited to approximately 10,000 youths who competed in post-season tournaments. Five percent (500) of that total would be randomly tested each year. The first year's cost was estimated at $50,000 (Bell, 2006).

The nation's largest statewide testing began in the autumn of 2007, when more than 20,000 Texas high-school athletes were liable for testing through a program paid for by a $3-million fund. Any athlete who measured positive for steroids would serve a thirty-day suspension from sports. A second failed test would result in a one-year ban, and a third would permanently end the youth's high-school competitive-sports career (Trotter, 2007).

PRESCRIPTION AND OVER-THE-COUNTER PRODUCTS

Prescription drugs and easily purchased products intended for other purposes are among the substances students use to achieve extraordinary psychological sensations.

Most Americans take drugs prescribed by doctors for the intended medical purposes, but an estimated 20 percent of the population has used prescription narcotic painkillers, sedatives, tranquilizers, and stimulants for nonmedical reasons. Students—mostly adolescents—are within that 20 percent. The abuse of prescription drugs has been increasing as doctors prescribe more drugs for more health problems than ever before and as Internet online pharmacies make it easy, even for students, to get drugs without a prescription. The 2004 Monitoring-the-Future survey found that 9.3 percent of twelfth graders reported using the Vicodin (pain suppressor) without a prescription in the past year, and 5.0 percent reported using OxyContin (pain suppressor), making those medications among the most commonly abused prescription drugs by adolescents. The use of such opioids, central nervous system (CNS) depressants, and stimulants can alter brain activity and lead to addiction.

> Abuse of prescription drugs to get high has become increasingly prevalent among teens and young adults. Past year abuse of prescription painkillers abuse now ranks second—only behind marijuana—as the Nation's most prevalent illegal drug problem. While overall youth drug use is down by 23% since 2001, approximately 6.4 million Americans report non-medical use of prescription drugs. New abusers of prescription drugs have caught up with the number of new users of marijuana. (Vallance, 2007)

> Abuse of Vicodin was 3.0% among 8th-graders, 7.0% among 10th-graders, and 9.7% among 12th-graders in 2006, remaining stable but at relatively high levels for each grade. Despite a drop in past-year abuse of OxyContin among 12th-graders in 2006, abuse among 8th-graders nearly doubled since 2002 (from 1.3% in 2002 to 2.6% in 2006). (National Institute, 2006)

Household products that students can obtain even more easily than prescription drugs are either (a) nonprescription medications sold over the counter or (b) items intended for uses other than human consumption.

A prime example of the abuse of nonprescription medicines is DXM (dextromethorphan), an ingredient in many nonprescription cough syrups, tablets, and lozenges. When used according to medicine-label directions, these cough suppressants are safe and effective. However, when ingested in large doses, they produce effects ranging from distorted visual images at low (approximately 2 ounce) doses to a sense of complete dissociation from one's body at doses of 10 ounces or more, with those effects typically lasing for six hours. At parties, teens mix excessive amounts of cough suppressant with alcohol or cola to produce a *player's potion* that can lead to brief euphoria and often unconsciousness.

The practice of inhaling the gases of household items in order to generate mind-altering sensations is referred to as *huffing, bagging,* or *glading.* Typical items are paint thinners, spray paints, glue, dry-cleaning fluids, gasoline, correction fluids, felt-tip-marker fluids, deodorant and hair sprays, vegetable oil

sprays for cooking, and fabric-protector sprays. Street parlance for such products includes *poor man's pot* and *air blast*. Among students questioned as part
of the 2006 Monitoring-the-Future survey, 29.2 percent of eighth graders,
40.1 percent of tenth graders, and 51.2 percent of twelfth graders reported
using inhalants at some time in their lives.

ALCOHOL

With the use of liquor so widespread in American society, it should come
as no surprise that alcohol has been the schools' most frequently abused
substance.

A survey of 4,390 high-school seniors and dropouts on the U.S. West Coast
in the late 1990s revealed that (a) one in every six respondents averaged at
least one alcoholic drink every other day, (b) one quarter of those surveyed experienced a drinking-related problem (missing school, feeling sick) on at least
three occasions during the previous year or suffered a more serious problem at
least once, such as getting into a fight or being arrested, and (c) one quarter had
engaged in two or more high-risk drinking activities (combining alcohol with
other drugs, getting drunk) several times the previous year (Ellickson, 1998).

A 1990 nationwide Youth Risk Behavior Survey reported that among students in grades nine throughtwelve, over 88 percent had consumed alcohol in
their lifetime, and 58.6 percent had at least one drink during the thirty days
preceding the survey. More than one-third (33.6 percent) had first consumed
alcohol before age twelve, and 92 percent drank for the first time before age
eighteen (Centers for Disease Control, 1991). A 1997 study in Alaska revealed
that nearly 40 percent of high-school students had their first drink before age
thirteen (Schumacher, 1997). Then the early years of the twenty-first century
saw a gradual decrease in teenage alcohol use. Thus, a national study in 2006
would report that 72.7 percent of American high-school seniors had used alcohol sometime during their lives, and 66.5 percent had done so in the past
year (Johnston, O'Malley, Bachman, & Schulenberg, 2006).

Several sorts of damage can result from teens' alcohol abuse. Drinking
can decrease their sense of responsibility, leading to frequent absence from
school, failure to complete assignments, bad marks, damaged social relationships, unsavory reputations, reduced prospects for future success, shame, and
a diminished self-image. Alcohol abuse increases the incidence of teenage
accidents, suicide, violent behavior, high-risk sex, and emotional problems.

A variety of influences have contributed to alcohol consumption among adolescents.

- *Parental examples.* One of the most important factors influencing youths' drinking behavior is the model set by parents and other admired adults. When parents drink, their offspring generally conclude that drinking is acceptable behavior. Especially if parents offer a sip of beer, wine, or vodka to their underage children, the children will take up drinking before the legal age of twenty-one. In contrast, children of parents who view alcohol use as morally wrong, or children who believe their parents would be extremely upset about their imbibing in liquor, are less likely to experiment with alcohol and illicit drugs.

- *Legality.* Unlike such substances as marijuana and cocaine, the sale and consumption of alcohol is not only legal but also aggressively encouraged by liquor producers. Although federal law requires that youths abstain from drinking (at least in public) before age twenty-one, such prohibition is not taken seriously by many teens. More than half (54 percent) in the CARA survey said that legal restrictions have no effect on their decision to drink (Gara, 2005).

- *Internet information exchange.* An investigation of 10 million Internet online messages by teenagers during 2006 showed that adolescents' experiences with alcohol were a frequent topic of discussion. "The study's analysis of alcohol messages found that teens mentioned hooking up and having sex while drunk, being drunk at parties, getting help for a friend who drinks too much and drinking until getting sick. The most popular drinks mentioned in the messages were beer and vodka" (Leinwand, 2007).

- *Mass-Communication media.* Movies, television programs, magazines, and billboards appear to exert a strong influence over young people's attitudes about alcoholic beverages.

The CASA survey revealed that 43 percent of twelve-to-seventeen-year olds saw three or more R-rated movies (restricted to adults) each month in theaters or on home videos. Those teenagers were five times more likely to drink alcohol than were teens that watched no R-rated movies in a typical month.

Research reports show that exposure to alcohol advertising shapes young adolescents' attitudes toward alcohol, their intentions to drink, and underage drinking behavior. Alcohol advertising appeared during all 15 of the top teen television shows in 2002. Alcohol advertisers spent $990 million (22% more) for TV ads in 2002 and placed 39% more alcohol ads on TV than in 2001. Twenty-two percent of the alcohol ads aired on TV in 2002 were more likely to be seen by youth 12-20 years of age than adults. These 66,218 ads were also more likely to be seen by youth ages 12-20 than by young adults ages 21-34. (Marin Institute, 2007)

A national study published in January 2006 concluded that greater exposure to alcohol advertising contributes to an increase in drinking among underage youth. Specifically, for each additional ad a young person saw (above the monthly youth average of 23), he or she drank 1% more. For each additional dollar per capita spent on alcohol advertising in a local market (above the national average of $6.80 per capita), young people drank 3% more. (Center on Alcohol Marketing, 2007)

- *Drug-infested schools.* In the CASA study, students who reported drugs being available in their schools were twice as likely to drink alcohol as those who said drugs were not available. The number of students attending schools where drugs are present rose from 44 to 62 percent for high-school students and from 19 to 28 percent for middle-school students between 2002 and 2005 (Gara, 2005).

Finally, in view of the pervasive consumption of alcohol in America and its widespread use among adolescents, what should be the goal of campaigns against alcohol abuse? The traditional aim has been to completely wipe out the use of illegal drugs and alcohol.

Efforts in the United States to decrease drug use have focused on preventing initiation or otherwise eliminating consumption. While this strategy has yielded significant reductions in the onset of illicit drug use, it has obviously had minimal impact on teen alcohol use. That a single strategy differently affects alcohol and illicit-drug use should not be surprising, given the different positions of these two kinds of behavior within adolescent culture. . . . [Research evidence has suggested that] alcohol use and misuse were more strongly associated with social activities such as dating and partying than with delinquent and related behaviors such as theft, burglary, and running away from home. The opposite was true of hard-drug, cannabis, and cigarette use. If efforts to reduce the ill effects of teen alcohol use are to be successful, they must take into account its key characteristics—its prevalence and its social context. (Ellickson, 1998)

In effect, teaching *responsible alcohol use* rather than—or in addition to— teaching *complete avoidance* may be a more appropriate aim of abuse-prevention efforts than the traditional focus on entirely eliminating teenage drinking.

TOBACCO

Schools have a variety of reasons for banning tobacco products. Not only are cigarettes a fire hazard, but (a) discarded butts contribute to the trash on school property, (b) nicotine is the number one entrance drug into other substance-abuse problems, and—most important—(c) cigarettes and cigars pose a serious health risk for both smokers themselves and people nearby.

Some youths seek to avoid the harm of smoking by adopting *smokeless tobacco* (chewing tobacco and snuff). However, those substances, when stashed in the mouth, involve their own hazards. Habitually chewing tobacco can cause (a) cracking and bleeding lips and gums, (b) receding gums that eventually cause teeth to fall out, (c) increased heart rate, high blood pressure, and irregular heartbeats that raise the risk of heart attacks and brain damage from a stroke, and (d) cancer of the mouth.

From 1990 until 1999, around 70 percent of American teens had smoked cigarettes at some period in their life. That figure had dropped dramatically to 54 percent by 2005. A further decrease between 2005 and 2006 was reported for tenth graders (from 38.9 to 36.1 percent) and twelfth graders (from 50 to 47.1 percent (National Institute, 2006).

> The prevalence of *current cigarette use* increased from 27.5% in 1991 to 36.4% in 1997 and then declined significantly to 23.0% in 2005. The prevalence of current *frequent cigarette use* increased from 12.7% in 1991 to 16.8% in 1999 and then declined significantly to 9.4% in 2005. (Centers for Disease Control, 2006)

An important factor credited for the declining popularity of smoking among teenagers was the dramatic rise in the price of cigarettes. A pack that cost 38 cents in 1970 would cost $3.26 in 2000. In addition, federal and state governments, public-health agencies, and schools launched programs to inform students and the general public of the health risks of smoking. At the same time, the places in which people were permitted to smoke were curtailed so that smoking increasingly became a shameful habit rather than the symbol of maturity and sophistication that it had represented in the past.

Tobacco companies met the challenge to their business in three ways. They first attacked the validity of research that exposed the health dangers of smoking. But when the evidence of health dangers became so overwhelming that the companies could no longer dismiss it, they announced their own antismoking campaigns. However, a study of 1,700 middle-school students' exposure to those efforts "found that tobacco manufacturer Philip Morris' youth anti-smoking campaign was making students more likely to smoke" (Jones, 2007). In parallel with those campaigns, tobacco industry expenditures on cigarette advertising and promotion rose from $5.7 billion in 1997 to $15.2 billion in 2003 (Centers for Disease Control, 2006).

In summary, attempts to reduce the popularity of tobacco products among students were succeeding during the first decade of the twenty-first century, even in the face of renewed efforts by the tobacco industry to attract youths to smoking.

SUGGESTIONS FOR SCHOOL PRACTICE

Three ways that schools can endeavor to reduce students' use of illegal drugs, alcohol, and tobacco are to (a) issue drug-policy regulations, (b) introduce drug and alcohol testing, and (c) include more drug education in the curriculum.

Drug-Policy Regulations

For the convenience of students and their parents, the school's drug policy can be described in a handbook that each student receives. The policy statement is most helpful if it specifies the exact substances that are banned and tells the precise consequences students can expect if they violate the ban. The following are two summaries of student-handbook statements. The first example lists the consequences for each type of rule infraction. The second lists the consequences from which officials may select as punishment for any sort of rule violation, including breaches of drug, alcohol, or tobacco policies.

Washington Township High School in Sewell (New Jersey). The student handbook states that any student who possesses, consumes, or is under the influence of alcohol or controlled substances (marijuana or other dangerous drugs) or any student who possesses drug paraphernalia will be subject to the following disciplinary measures:

First offense, suspended for a minimum of five school days.

Second offense, suspended for a minimum of ten school days and a possible board-of-education expulsion hearing.

Any student who tests positive for drugs must obtain a letter from a physician attesting to the student's physical, mental, and emotional ability to return to school. A violator must attend a counseling intake session and follow all recommendations that may include becoming involved in an out-of-school counseling program before readmission to school. If the administration deems necessary, a referral to the Child Study Team will be made to determine the student's eligibility and need for special education programs. The student will be monitored by a counselor upon return to school. All offenses are cumulative over a student's high school tenure. (Washington Township, 1999)

Olentangy High School in Lewis Center (Ohio). The handbook stipulates that students shall not possess, use, transmit, conceal, make arrangements to sell or purchase, or use narcotics, alcohol, or drugs immediately prior to or during school or a school function. Look-alike drugs and drug paraphernalia are included. Tobacco, in any form, shall not be carried or used by any student on school property or at school events. Paraphernalia used for tobacco products is prohibited. Per Senate Bill 218, administrators will refer violators of the tobacco policy to the juvenile court. As a response to infractions of any of the above rules, officials can choose to subject violators to one or more of the following consequences: (a) after-school or morning detention, (b) Saturday or Wednesday School, (c) in-school detention, (d) suspension-alternative program, (e) out-of-school suspension, (f) court referral, (g) expulsion, (h) compensatory payment of damages, (i) loss of bus privileges, (j) loss of credit for assigned work or tests, and/or (k) assigned work related to the offense. (Olentangy High School, 2007)

Drug and Alcohol Testing

At a growing rate, schools have been testing students to determine if they had used prohibited substances.

After the U.S. Supreme Court in 1995 declared that drug testing of student athletes was permissible under the Constitution, schools began adopting drug testing, however at a very slow pace, primarily because of the substantial costs involved. By 2003, only 13 percent of America's schools had testing programs (Colgate, 2003).

Four common drug-testing methods depend on samples of urine, saliva, hair, or sweat (patch). Urinanalysis reveals drug use for the previous two or three days for most drugs and slightly longer for chronic marijuana use. Saliva and sweat tests detect substances ingested during the previous twenty-four hours. Hair-sample analysis can detect drugs ingested over the previous several months.

Four alcohol-testing techniques involve the analysis of breath, blood, urine, or saliva samples. Breath testing can be either by chemicals or an electronic device. In the chemical test (Breathalyzer), a student exhales into a balloon with one continuous breath. The balloon's mouthpiece is attached to a glass tube. The alcohol content of the exhaled air is shown by the number of the tube's bands that changed from yellow to green. When using an electronic device, the student blows into a mouthpiece or straw, and the device displays the person's alcohol blood level.

School drug and alcohol testing is quite controversial. Proponents of testing suggest that it catches students who are presently on drugs and deters others from using drugs for fear of punishment, such as expulsion from school. Critics say testing violates students' privacy rights and gives schooling a prison-like atmosphere.

> Although some officials would like to see a policy of mandatory testing of every student, most drug screenings require parental consent. Most schools require that there be probable cause or reasonable suspicion before requesting a drug test. If a teacher notices a student who appears aloof or has red and glassy eyes, he or she may request a drug test. More common than random or suspicion-based high school drug testing is the testing of high school athletes. In nearly every school district, students who wish to compete in school sports must sign a release for a drug screening. This has become common in schools because of statistics showing that male high

school athletes have a greater risk of drug abuse. These facts, accompanied by the fear of injury during competitions, have fueled the debate and existence of drug testing among athletes. (Sofsian, 2005)

Curriculum Provisions

A further method of combating drug, alcohol, and tobacco abuse is that of enlarging the role of drug education in the curriculum. The most obvious place for such expansion is in health-education classes. Units of study that concern substance abuse can also be added to other subject-matter areas, such as in courses titled *Modern American History, Social Problems, Applied Chemistry, Current Literature, Economics, Life Skills, Job Preparation,* and the like.

Weapons

Firearms and explosives have never been permitted in schools. Nor have swords, daggers, switchblades, and hunting knives, except on special occasions. However, pocketknives, fingernail files, arts-and-crafts X-acto knives, and cardboard-box openers were often permitted prior to the 1999 episode known as *the Columbine killings*. But the Columbine episode would serve as a turning point that separated a period of more lenient views regarding tools and instruments in schools from the period of no-tolerance that would dominate the 2000–2008 era.

THE COLUMBINE EFFECT

Shortly before lunchtime on April 20, 1999, two teenage boys—armed with sawed-off shotguns, a semi-automatic rifle, a semi-automatic pistol, and pipe bombs—walked into Columbine High School in Littleton (Colorado), where they killed thirteen people (twelve students, one teacher) and wounded twenty-three more before shooting themselves to death. In the days following the incident, authorities found journals and videos that the two shooters had prepared, with plans for the school attack and a neighborhood massacre, and, "if they were unable to escape from the United States, [they would hijack] an airplane which they would then crash into New York City" (Columbine, 2005).

Over the years following the Columbine killings, aftereffects of the event appeared in the form of motion pictures (*Bowling for Columbine* in 2002, *Elephant* in 2003), books (*Hey, Nostradamus!* in 2003, *Years of Rage* in 2005), and music videos (*Alert Status Red* in 2004) (Columbine, 2005). There was also evidence that the Columbine episode continued to influence teenagers who would engage in deadly weapon violence. For example, youths fascinated with the Columbine massacre included the sixteen-year-old on Minnesota's Red Lake Indian Reservation, who, in March 2005, shot to death five students, a school security guard, and a teacher before killing himself. Two days later, in a suburb of Buffalo (New York), a fifteen-year-old boy was arrested, accused of plotting to blow up his high school. Authorities reported that he had purchased bomb-making materials, including gunpowder, primers, ball bearings, and pipes that were already bored out. In a search of the boy's home computer, officials found downloaded autopsy reports about the Columbine killers. Earlier in the school year, the youth had written an essay for his English class suggesting that the Columbine killers' actions had been their form of rebelling against an oppressive environment (Thompson, 2005).

So it was that the Columbine episode became the prototype shooting disaster in America's schools, and other youths who admired the Columbine pair's success would subsequently plan—and sometimes carry out—their own escapades of killing.

The Columbine tragedy stimulated wide-scale speculation about reasons for the teenagers' rampage and about how such events might be prevented in the future. Many schools adopted zero-tolerance policies toward students who bore weapons or threatened violence. Other schools established antibullying policies on the assumption that the pair of killers in the Columbine case had been goaded into their brutal act by months of taunting by schoolmates.

NEW SCHOOL RULES

During the decade before the Columbine incident, federal and state governments had already been passing legislation that limited people's access to firearms. For instance, within a year after U.S. President Bill Clinton in 1994 called for zero tolerance of guns in schools, forty-seven states enacted laws or policies complying with the U.S. Education Department's mandatory suspension of gun-carrying students (Newman, 1995). So the effect of the Columbine episode was to hasten schools' adoption of weapons' no-tolerance rules. The typical nature of such rules can be illustrated with legislation in two states and policy statements in seven school districts.

States' School-Weapons Laws

Washington State legislation stipulates that

(1) It is unlawful for a person to carry onto, or to possess on, public or private elementary or secondary school premises, school-provided transportation, or areas of facilities while being used exclusively by public or private schools:

(a) Any firearm;

(b) Any other dangerous weapon as defined in RCW 9.41.250 (sling shot, sand club, or metal knuckles, or spring blade knife, or any knife the blade of which is automatically released by a spring mechanism or other mechanical device, or any knife having a blade which opens, or falls, or is ejected into position by the force of gravity, or by an outward, downward, or centrifugal thrust or movement);

(c) Any device commonly known as "nun-chu-ka sticks," consisting of two or more lengths of wood, metal, plastic, or similar substance connected with wire, rope, or other means;

(d) Any device, commonly known as "throwing stars," which are multi-pointed, metal objects designed to embed upon impact from any aspect; or

(e) Any air gun, including any air pistol or air rifle, designed to propel a BB, pellet, or other projectile by the discharge of compressed air, carbon dioxide, or other gas.

(2) Any such person violating subsection (1) of this section is guilty of a gross misdemeanor. If any person is convicted of a violation of subsection (1)(a) of this section, the person shall have his or her concealed pistol license, if any, revoked for a period of three years. Anyone convicted under this subsection is prohibited from applying for a concealed pistol license for a period of three years. The court shall send notice of the revocation to the department of licensing, and the city, town, or county which issued the license.

Any violation of subsection (1) of this section by elementary or secondary school students constitutes grounds for expulsion from the state's public schools.... An appropriate school authority shall promptly notify law enforcement and the student's parent or guardian regarding any allegation or indication of such violation.

Upon the arrest of a person at least twelve years of age and not more than twenty-one years of age for violating subsection (1)(a) of this section, the person shall be detained or confined in a juvenile or adult facility for up to seventy-two hours. The person shall not be released within the seventy-two hours until after the person has been examined and evaluated by the county-designated mental health professional unless the court in its discretion releases the person sooner after a determination regarding probable cause or on probation bond or bail. (Washington State Legislature, 2007)

State law in Georgia defines weapons as

Any pistol, revolver, or any weapon designed to propel a missile of any kind, or any dirk, bowie knife, switchblade knife, ballistic knife, any other knife having a blade of two or more inches, straight-edges, razor, razor blade, spring stick, metalknucks, blackjack, any bat, club, or other bludgeon-type weapon, or any flailing instrument consisting of two or more rigid parts connected in such a manner as to allow them to swing freely, which may be known as a nun chucks, nun chuck, nunchaku, shuriken, or fighting chain, or any disc, of whatever configuration, having at least two points or pointed blades which is designed to be thrown or propelled and which may be known as a throwing star or oriental dart, or any weapon of like kind, and any stun gun or taser. (Murray County, 2004)

Individual Schools' Weapons Rules

There are marked differences among schools in the specificity of their rules governing weapons and in the objects that are forbidden.

Cocopah Indian Tribal Schools (Arizona): "No weapons of any kind."

Nogales High School (La Puente, California): The dress code prohibits "Clothing, jewelry or other accessories which may be used as a weapon, or which may be a safety hazard to the wearer or others, such as heavy chains, wallet chains, key rings with chain attached, two-finger rings, neck chains (links 1/4 inch or greater)."

Walker Junior High School (La Palma, California): "Weapons include real or fake knives of any shape or size, real or fake guns, and similar type items or any other dangerous objects. Bringing weapons or dangerous objects to school OR holding them for someone may result in expulsion from the school district and arrest. This includes 'Look-alike' items. Jokes and threats about these things at school will not be tolerated and may result in expulsion and arrest."

Virginia Beach (Virginia) *High Schools:* "Carrying or possessing firearms or other dangerous weapons, including look-alikes, is prohibited. Using, distributing, selling, lighting or discharging an explosive device, including fireworks, on school property violates Virginia law and School Board policy. Legal authorities may impose imprisonment and/or fines for guilt. Possessing and using laser lights to potentially cause harm, injury, or irritation violates the Code of Student Conduct. Expulsion recommendation and police notification are mandatory for these offenses."

Norfolk (Virginia) *Public Schools:* "A student shall not possess, handle, or transmit a knife, razor, ice pick, explosive, sword, cane, machete, firearm, look-alike/toy gun, mace (or similar substance), pellet or air rifle, pistol, or other object that reasonably can be considered a weapon, or wear clothing or jewelry with slogans, symbols, or pictures depicting weapons, gangs, or criminal activity. Violation of this rule may result in suspension or expulsion. The rule does not apply to normal school supplies such as pencils or compasses or other objects unless they are used as weapons."

Hillsdale (California) *High School:* "Any student who assaults another student, or who carries an instrument construed to be a weapon, or who brings to school a blade of any size, will be recommended for expulsion. A weapon is defined as any object which can be used to hurt another person or which causes that person to believe that he/she will be harmed in some way. We include in the gun category any imitation or replica (e.g., a toy pistol, pellet gun, forced air gun, starter pistol, or paint ball gun). It makes no difference whether the gun is loaded or unloaded, or whether it can be fired or not. Additionally, every blade, regardless of its size, will be viewed as a weapon, including any pocket knife, penknife, Swiss Army knife, or other utility blade."

Colorado School for the Deaf and Blind: The expression *"dangerous weapon"* means:

a. A firearm, whether loaded or unloaded, or a firearm facsimile that could reasonably be mistaken for an actual firearm.

b. Any pellet, BB gun or other device, whether operational or not, designed to propel projectiles by spring action or compressed air.

c. A fixed blade knife with a blade that measures longer than three inches in length or a spring loaded knife or a pocket knife with a blade longer than three and one-half inches.

d. Any object, device, instrument, material, or substance, whether animate or inanimate, used or intended to be used to inflict death or serious bodily injury including, but not limited to slingshot, bludgeon, brass knuckles, or artificial knuckles of any kind. In accordance with federal law, expulsion shall be for no less than one full calendar year for a student who is determined to have brought a firearm to school in violation of this policy, unless the student's Individualized Education Program (IEP) team determines that the student's behavior is a manifestation of the student's disability. The superintendent may reduce the length of this one-year expulsion requirement on a case-by-case basis. If the student's IEP team determines that the student's behavior is a manifestation of the student's disability, the student may be removed to an appropriate interim alternative educational setting for up to 45 school days."

ILLUSTRATIVE CASES

School weapons episodes can vary in the types of instruments they involve, the settings in which episodes take place, the participants, the factors precipitating the events, and the consequences experienced by participants. Diverse combinations of those variables are illustrated in the following cases. The first seven events are based on reports for the 2005–2006 school year by the National School Safety and Security Services (2007).

As she walked to her high school in San Leandro (California), a 14-year-old girl was shot three times in the back and killed by a boy (a non-student between 16 and 18 years old) who had jumped out of a car, shot the girl, and then killed himself in an apparent murder-suicide. Police confirmed the two had known each other.

A girl at an Irmo (South Carolina) high school summoned the school's security officer to the school parking lot, saying she was afraid that a 19-year-old male non-student there might shoot her. As the officer approached, the 19-year-old aimed a pistol at him, whereas the officer responded by firing a bullet into the hood of the 19-year-old's car, causing the youth to drop the pistol and surrender.

A 55-year-old female first-grade teacher in Moulton (Alabama) died of irreversible brain damage suffered when she was beaten by a 15-year-old high-school boy who, police believed, had pummeled her unconscious with his fists before stealing money from her purse. The attack came after 4:00 pm while the teacher was alone in the classroom doing administrative work.

In Jacksboro (Tennessee), a 15-year-old freshman boy shot and killed an assistant principal, then shot the principal and another assistant who were hospitalized for their wounds.

A school police officer in San Antonio (Texas) shot and killed an 18-year-old male who allegedly attempted to run down the officer as he attempted to stop the suspect and another male from stealing a car in a middle school parking lot.

A 16-year-old Garden Grove (California) high school boy, involved in a fight near the school's athletic fields, was shot and later died at the hospital. Observers reported that gang members had jumped in to assist the youth in the fight when a member of the opposing gang drew a gun and shot the boy. Six gang members were arrested in connection with the murder.

In Conway (South Carolina), a 24-year-old man stabbed an 18-year-old high school girl in a school parking lot as students were arriving at school. Apparently the two had some type of dating relationship.

When the Baraboo (Wisconsin) high school principal tried to wrestle a gun from a 16-year-old student, the gun fired and killed the principal. At the boy's trial, the prosecutor charged that the youth had brought a revolver and shotgun to school with the intention of murdering the principal, who had recently suspended the 16-year-old twice. However, the boy's attorneys contended that the youth suffered from attention-deficit disorder, was abused at home, and endured endless teasing at school while the principal and teachers did nothing to stop the taunting. The prosecutor responded by saying the 16-year-old himself was a bully who had invited suspension by harassing schoolmates. The jury convicted the youth of first-degree intentional homicide. (Teen says, 2007)

A 13-year-old middle-school student in Lake Alfred (Florida) threw two homemade bombs into the livestock area of the school campus. Each bomb consisted of a plastic soda bottle filled with water and chemicals. The boy was arrested on a charge of throwing a destructive device intended to cause harm. (*Violence in Our Schools*, 2005)

In the morning before school, a 16-year-old student at Lamar High School in Arlington (Texas) brandished a pair of two-foot-long swords as he approached a group of fellow students. When he slashed a 14-year-old freshman's face, the screams of the crowd alerted an unarmed security guard who rushed to the scene, tackled the sword-wielding youth, and held him on the ground until help arrived. The assailant was arrested and taken to jail, while the injured 14-year-old was sent to the hospital for stitches to repair the cut he had suffered. (Douglas, 2005)

The sight of a moving red dot on a corridor wall at the high school in Hastings, (Minnesota) alerted a teacher to a boy brandishing what appeared to be a small double-barreled pistol. When the teacher took the 14-year-old to the principal's office, the boy said that the simulated derringer pistol was a laser pointer that had been part of his Halloween costume. He had brought the fake gun to school to show his friends. Under the school's strict no-weapons policy, the youth could face a yearlong expulsion because, as the Hastings police chief explained, even replicas of weapons were not acceptable in schools. (Schoepf, 2004)

A 15-year-old student at Independence High School in San Jose (California) was attacked in front of the school by five members of a street gang and stabbed seven times in the back with a screwdriver. One member of the gang was arrested for the attack. (*Violence in Our Schools*, 2005)

Responding to an anonymous tip, police arrested a 17-year-old in Rosemead (California) for filling marker pens with an explosive that would detonate when the pen caps were removed. A search of the boy's home revealed explosive materials and books describing how to fashion homemade weapons. The youth admitted placing altered pens at different locations near Rosemead High School, where three unsuspecting passers-by picked them up, opened them, and suffered injuries when the devices exploded. The 17-year-old said he planted the pens as an act of revenge for his having been expelled from school. (Thermos, 2005)

A Hamden (Connecticut) father—enraged over his daughter's suspension from the Sacred Heart Academy softball team for breaking team rules—pummeled the softball coach in the head and chest with a baseball bat. The father was cited for first-degree assault and reckless endangerment, charges that could result in a prison sentence of up to 20 years. (Eagan & Gonzalez, 2005)

A fourth-grade girl at Philadelphia's Benjamin Franklin Elementary School was arrested for attempting to poison her teacher by pouring a mixture of fingernail polish, nail-polish remover, and hand lotion into the teacher's coffee mug during class. The teacher did not use the mug and only learned about the incident from the parent of another girl who had witnessed the act. The arrest charge against the 10-year-old included aggravated assault, possession of an instrument of crime, simple assault, and reckless endangerment of another person. School officials suspended the child from school for five days while a disciplinary hearing was held. The girl faced expulsion to an alternative school for difficult pupils. (Dean, 2005)

Not only are actual weapons prohibited in schools, but threats to use weapons are also punishable.

A 15-year-old who attended Pahrump Valley High School (Nevada) was the first student to board the school bus one Monday morning. He stepped into the bus, held a newly sharpened samurai sword over the head of the woman driver, and ordered her off the bus. According to the boy's plan, he hoped to use the bus the following day as his get-away vehicle after setting off shotgun shells to ignite propane tanks behind the school and blow up the school building. (Paul, 2002)

At the end of the school day at Rhoades Elementary School in Wayne Township (Indiana), two boys—ages 10 and 11—shouted that there was a bomb in the building. After the school was evacuated, a search of the building failed to produce any explosives. The shouters were taken into custody and charged in juvenile court with false reporting and disorderly conduct. False reporting would qualify as a felony if filed against an adult. In a letter sent to all parents of children at

Rhoades Elementary, school officials explained, "You never know if it's a threat or it's a rumor. Our policy is to investigate all threats and take appropriate action." An executive from the Indiana Association of Public School Superintendents warned, "You can't make jokes or comments like that. It's like boarding an airplane nowadays—the things you once said aren't funny anymore." (O'Neal, 2003)

A message scribbled on the wall of a girls' bathroom at Martha's Vineyard Regional High School (Massachusetts) read "On Dec. 12th 'I' will pull a Columbine." A search of students' lockers by the police failed to provide clues about who had written the threat. However, officials reported that they did have a list of suspects as a result of handwriting analyses and of videotapes from security cameras that photographed students entering and leaving the bathroom on the day that the scrawled threat appeared. (Stearns, 2003)

As the foregoing examples demonstrate, some devices are violent by their very nature and thus generally banned from schools. Such is the case with guns, explosive devices, knives, swords, and daggers. Other instruments, by their nature, are intended for peaceful purposes but can on occasion be used as dangerous weapons—razors, pens, pencils, keys, sticks, and more. Thus, school personnel are obliged to be alert not only to the presence of actual weapons but also to the likelihood that angry students might use such common school items as pencils, pens, or tools to harm others.

The widespread publicity given to shootings might suggest that guns are the main weapons used in school violence. However, an FBI survey covering the five-year period 2000–2004 revealed that, in more than 558,000 campus-related crimes, knives were the most commonly used instruments. Nearly 11,000 incidents involved a blade, compared to 3,400 that involved a firearm. The survey also reported that the largest number of teenagers arrested for crimes at school were from the 13 – to 15-year-old age group, accounting for 38 percent of those arrested, more than seventy-six males. Year after year, October was the month in which the most crimes occurred (Shapira, 2007).

CONTROVERSIAL DECISIONS

The implementation of no-tolerance practices has not gone unchallenged. Periodically episodes arise that attract criticism of the school authorities who are responsible for applying zero-tolerance policies. Here are four such cases.

> Administrators at Payne Junior High School in Chandler (Arizona) suspended a 13-year-old boy for five days because he drew a sketch of "what looked like a gun." School officials said such behavior posed a threat to classmates. The boy's parents responded by charging officials with overreacting to a drawing that was no more than "a harmless doodle" that did not show blood, bullets, or injuries, nor did it target any human. The student's mother complained, "The school made him feel like he committed a crime. They are doing more damage than good." The five-day suspension was then reduced to three days. (Ariz. school, 2007)

An 11-year-old girl was suspended from school for ten days because she had brought a Tweety-Bird key chain to class. The chain was 9 inches long. Earlier in the year, school officials had pointed out to students several items that they considered weapons and that were banned from school. Those items included chains that were at least two-feet long. At the time, officials had explained that anyone caught with such an item would be automatically suspended. As the girl was being sent home, she said, "It's only a little chain, and I don't think it can really hurt anyone." However, the 11-year-old was punished according to the school's zero-tolerance weapons policy. But subsequent complaints from the American Civil Liberties Union (ACLU) and newspaper and television media caused the school district to dismiss the suspension. (Better safe, 2001)

A 16-year-old honor student in Greenville (South Carolina) was expelled from Eastside High School for using a knife with a four-inch blade to cut out plastic nametags for a Youth-in-Government club meeting. The girl had retrieved the knife from her car to use as she and fellow club members were in the school library preparing for the meeting. When the student's parents filed a lawsuit against the school district, the judge reversed the expulsion because district officials had failed to produce any evidence of how long the blade was or that the girl "possessed or used [the knife] with the intention of inflicting bodily harm or death." At the original expulsion hearing, the school principal had said she would have handled the episode differently if she had not been forced to apply the district's no-tolerance policy. (Walton, 2003)

A second-grader in Alexandria (Louisiana) was expelled for bringing her grandfather's gold-plated pocket watch to school—a watch that had a tiny knife attached. (Cauchon, 1999)

Critics of zero-tolerance policies have assailed the U.S. Congress, state legislatures, and local school boards for allowing no room for exceptions to the automatic application of no-tolerance rules—exceptions that authorities could make after considering extenuating conditions in particular cases.

SUGGESTIONS FOR SCHOOL PRACTICE[1]

The proposals described in this section concern (a) information for students and parents, (b) the employment of school security guards, (c) ways to control who enters a school, (d) metal detectors for revealing hidden weapons, (e) video cameras to record events in sensitive areas of a school, (f) crime-prevention roles for students, and (g) revised school designs.

Which measures a given school will adopt depends on such variables as (a) the frequency of weapons problems in the past, (b) the level of crime and disorder in the surrounding community, (c) the expense—in terms of money and personnel—of the various safety procedures, and (d) how much officials want the school to resemble a prison rather than a pleasant, welcoming site of learning opportunities. The following are among the more popular safety practices recently adopted by American schools.

Informing Students and Parents

Students can hardly be expected to abide by schools' weapons rules if those rules are not explained to them at the outset of the school year. Furthermore, students' parents have a right to know what those expectations are. Thus, school authorities are wise to describe specifically which instruments are considered dangerous weapons, why they are regarded as dangerous, and what consequences students face if they breach weapons rules. This description can appropriately be included in the school's student handbook or in a letter sent to parents.

---

[1] The final section of this chapter draws heavily on Chapter 2 from *Violence in America's Schools* by R. Murray Thomas. Copyright © 2006 by R. Murray Thomas. Reproduced with permission of Greenwood Publishing Group, Inc. Westport, CT.

Security Guards

More schools each year are employing professionally trained security guards whose tasks include (a) patrolling the school and surrounding campus before, during, and after classes are in session, (b) supervising the operation of video surveillance cameras, alarm systems, and metal detectors, (c) detaining students and visitors who are suspected of carrying weapons, (d) stopping fights, and (e) alerting the police to security problems.

There continues to be controversy over the question of whether it is better for security guards to be unarmed rather than to carry a pistol, stun gun, or baton.

A stun gun or Taser is a device that fires

> a pair of pronged darts that latch onto clothing or skin and send a 50,000-volt shock into the body in five-second bursts, which overrides the subject's central nervous system, causing uncontrollable contraction of the muscle tissue and instant collapse. The darts are attached to wires, which can reach up to 21 feet. People who have been "tased" report extreme, debilitating pain. (Stelzer, 2005)

Stun guns are in widespread use by police and, in some school districts, are carried by officers assigned as security personnel in schools. Because some people have died after being stun-gunned, parents and school personnel often object to equipping security guards with Tasers. In early 2005, a fourteen-year-old Chicago boy went into cardiac arrest after being "tased"; and the Miami, Florida, police revised their stun-gun policy after officers stunned both a six-year-old boy in a school office and a twelve-year-old girl truant who was trying to escape (Jacksonville police, 2005; Stelzer, 2005).

A typical baton is a steel stick used for hitting an assailant. Some batons, like telescopes, can be extended to a length of 16 or 24 inches. Others, like a stun gun, emit an electrical charge that momentarily shocks an assailant into a helpless state.

Two advantages claimed for arming security guards are that (a) the sight of a gun in a guard's holster deters potentially dangerous students or visitors from misdeeds and (b) if an armed offender actually fires his or her weapon, a guard can immediately stop further assault by shooting the offender. Proponents of the practice of arming guards contend that, in such cases as the Red Lake massacre cited in Chapter 1, fewer lives would be lost if guards carried weapons.

The first victim in the Red Lake incident was an unarmed guard who tried to stop the youth who did the killing. However, critics have claimed that having gun-toting police patrolling school corridors casts a depressing jail-like aura over what is supposed to be a friendly, appealing setting in which students spend much of their time.

Security guards can be trained and supervised by the school system itself, or else the system can contract out such services. The author of a study of security-guard practices in six large school systems (Atlanta, Baltimore, Montgomery County [Maryland], Philadelphia, St. Louis, Washington, DC) concluded that

> [w]e noted a greater level of professionalism, diligence, and a strengthened security posture at the schools using in-house security services. . . . An in-house security-guard force provides for a more professional working environment and. . . . tends to be much more manageable. Further, the [school system] benefits more from its own in-house comprehensive security training and does not have to rely on training from an outside source that might not understand the rules and regulations unique to their school jurisdiction. (Andersen, 2005)

School districts have been cautioned to obtain bids from several companies if they plan to contract out their security services. The Washington, DC, public schools, in failing to obtain competitive bids, overpaid a security contractor by $11.4 million (McElhatton, 2004).

Entry-Control Techniques

The likelihood of deadly violence is obviously reduced if procedures are in place to prevent weapons from being brought onto school grounds. Such entry-control procedures include

> Placing a guard at the campus entry gate to check the identification of auto drivers and passengers; requiring students and staff to have a vehicle parking sticker in order to park on the campus.
>
> Limiting the number of doors through which people can enter the school, with greeters at those doorways watching for signs

of weapons; locking other exterior doors to prevent access from outside; labeling those doors inside: "For emergency exit only—Alarm will sound if opened."

Informing students and visitors that anyone walking around the campus during class hours will be (a) challenged for a pass or student identification card and (b) subject to search or scanning by a metal detector.

Ensuring that when a student is suspended or expelled, his or her identification card is confiscated, and—in large schools—making that student's picture available to the school's security staff. (Green, 1999)

Metal Detectors

Particularly in high-crime neighborhoods, schools have increasingly employed portal, scanner, and x-ray metal detectors as entry-control devices.

A *portal* metal detector is a doorway-like framework through which students, staff members, and visitors must pass as they enter the school. Any object a person wears or carries that will conduct electricity—and particularly such metal items as handguns or knives—sets off an alarm (noise or flashing light) as the person walks through the frame. Then the operator of the detector must discover whether the sensed object is a weapon or, rather, is a benign piece metal, such as a belt buckle or coin.

A *scanner* is a hand-held, battery-operated device that looks rather like a cell phone with an antenna or wand attached. The scanner operator, by moving the wand around and close to a student's body, can rather accurately locate sources of electrical-conductive material that are in or on the student's clothing or body. When the scanner senses such an item, it makes a squealing noise, alerting the operator to discover whether the item is something that could serve as a weapon.

If a school is attempting to do a complete screening of students each morning, the hand-held metal detector will more likely be used as a supplement to portal metal detectors. . . . Hand-held detectors allow the security staff to more accurately locate the source of an alarm on a student's body, after a student has already walked through a portal system and caused an alarm. (Green, 1999)

An x-ray detector reveals the shape of objects in such containers as bookbags, backpacks, briefcases, handbags, and boxes without the need to open the containers. When the shape of an object suggests that it might be an illegal item (gun, knife, or explosive), the package can be opened to determine whether it is, indeed, a potential weapon.

Although metal detectors generally do their job well, their use is accompanied by three bothersome problems. First, they slow the process of students and staff members entering school, particularly if scanners are used. Second, it is expensive to train and pay personnel to operate detector systems efficiently. Third, the use of detectors adds to the penitentiary-like atmosphere of a school—an atmosphere that students and teachers can find unpleasant.

Despite their usefulness, metal detectors are not foolproof. As a report for the school board in Dade County, Florida, observed: "Students become creative. They pass weapons in through windows to friends, hide knives and other sharp instruments in shoes and in a girlfriend's hair. They manage to find creative ways to bring weapons to school" (Constitutional Rights Foundation, 2005).

The installation of metal detectors has not always been greeted with universal student approval.

> At the outset of the fall-2005 semester at New York's DeWitt High School, security guards explained to groups of returning students that metal detectors had been installed. Therefore, when students arrived at school each day, they would need to line up, remove metal from their pockets, take off belts, and walk through a metal detector. Their bags would be also be scanned by an X-ray machine, and no one would be allowed to leave the building at lunchtime. In response to the new regulations, the students circulated a protest petition and skipped classes to join a 1,500-strong peaceful march two miles to the Department of Education where they could meet the administrators who had agreed to hear their objections to the new security procedures. During the hearing, student representatives voiced their grievances. Then school officials pointed out why tighter security seemed needed—DeWitt Clinton's crime rate was 60% higher than that of any other New York school of similar size, and the school had suffered 13 major crimes during the previous school year. Although officials were unwilling to undo any of the new security measures, guidance counselors agreed to meet with students to determine if any changes could reasonably be made. (Santos, 2005)

Video Surveillance Cameras

Like metal detectors, video cameras in classrooms, corridors, entryways, and school buses have become more popular as school officials have sought better methods of monitoring students and visitors' behavior. But the adoption of video surveillance has been relatively slow as a result of concerns about (a) the costs of video arrangements (from $75,000 to $100,000 for a 16-camera system) and (b) video cameras' potential for violating individuals' right to privacy. By early 2005, only 191 of New York City's 1,356 public schools had camera systems. However, all twenty-five schools currently under construction and all future New York schools would be equipped with cameras (Lombardi, 2004).

Video cameras can serve several useful purposes. They enable school personnel at a remote location—such as the main office—to see events that occur at the fifteen or twenty or thirty sites of cameras around the school. Students' and visitors' awareness that cameras are recording their movements helps deter them from weapons violence. And the resulting magnetic-tape records of events are useful for identifying offenders and for judging their actions. Even when taped images are a bit blurred, offenders often confess their misdeeds when shown pictures of the incident. In court cases or school hearings, such tapes contribute evidence toward a just judgment of what happened.

However, video surveillance is accompanied by fears of unreasonable privacy invasion. In response to such fears, school boards sometimes establish rules governing the use of video cameras. Consider the guidelines suggested by the Information and Privacy Commission in Ontario (Canada).

> Video cameras should only be installed in identified areas of schools where video surveillance is a necessary and viable detection or deterrence activity.
>
> Equipment should never monitor the inside of areas where students and staff have a reasonable expectation of privacy (such as clothing-change rooms and washrooms).
>
> Students and staff should be fully notified about the video surveillance program through clearly worded signs. Schools should not use hidden cameras.
>
> Strict controls are needed to ensure the security and the integrity of the recorded images.

Retention periods need to be set [for the recording tapes]. We rec-
ommend that tapes that have not been used as part of an investigation should be erased after not more than 30 days. (Cavoukian,
2003)

Crime-Prevention Roles for Students

Probably the best protection against weapons violence comes from students'
willingness to discover and report the presence of weapons in school or to
report schoolmates' attack plans.

The National Crime Prevention Council has suggested the following ways
students can contribute to a safe school environment.

Refuse to bring weapons to school and refuse to keep silent about
those who carry weapons.

Report any threats or crimes immediately to school authorities or
police.

Report suspicious behavior or talk by other students to a teacher or
counselor at your school. You may save someone's life.

Learn how to manage your own anger effectively. Find out ways
to settle arguments by talking it out, working it out, or walking
away rather than fighting.

Help others settle disputes peaceably. Start or join a peer-mediation
program in which trained students help classmates find ways to
settle arguments without fists or weapons.

Set up a teen court in which youths serve as judge, prosecutor,
jury, and defense counsel. Courts can hear cases, make findings,
and impose sentences, or they may establish sentences in cases
where teens plead guilty. Teens feel more involved in the process
than in an adult-run juvenile justice system.

Start a school crime watch. Consider including a student patrol that
helps keep an eye on corridors, parking lots and groups, and a
way for students to report concerns anonymously.

Become a peer counselor, working with classmates who need support and help with problems.

Create a welcoming environment for students. Get to know new
students and those who are unfamiliar to you. (Menard & Martindale, 2005)

More school systems are introducing programs in which students are taught alternatives to violence for coping with their conflicts with classmates or school staff, and teachers are being trained to spot violence-prone children and to intervene when violence escalates (Carter, 2003).

At a growing rate, school officials have urged students, staff members, and parents to use crime-watch hotlines for reporting evidence of weapons violence. For example, police in Fort Worth (Texas) praised students at Southwest High School who had used a hotline to report a classmate's bringing a gun to school (Kovach, 2004).

Revised School Designs

Security concerns have become high-priority considerations in architects' school designs. For example, when Supai Middle School in Scottsdale (Arizona) was razed and rebuilt in 2002, it was constructed in a courtyard style that required visitors to enter through the office. Previously, visitors could wander around campus without reporting to the office. Under a similar plan, as the aging elementary school in Tualatin (Oregon) was replaced in 2004, the new school consisted of a single building, with the office by the main door so the staff could control who came and went. In contrast, the old campus had several buildings, allowing people to go directly to classrooms and avoid the office. To cope with the problem of having multiple buildings to monitor, officials at Sandy High School in the Oregon Trail School District installed a 32-camera surveillance system. And the new high school in Clackamas (Oregon) was built to optimize clear lines of sight through corridors, avoiding small alcoves and places with blocked views; a door-locking system enabled the staff to put the entire 2,000-student school on lockdown within seconds (Lopez, 2005).

Officials also make schools safer when they

> Enclose the campus with a robust fence that forces people to consciously trespass, rather than allowing uninhibited, casual entry.
>
> Install classroom doors that teachers can lock from either the inside or outside.
>
> Ensure that the school building and classroom areas can be locked off from the gym and other facilities that are used during off hours.
>
> Provide a dropoff/pickup lane for buses only.

Build single-stall bathrooms to reduce bathroom confrontations and problems.

Add secure skylights that allow light in but are less vulnerable to entry than typical windows.

Minimize the number of flat roofs from which an assailant could fire a gun.

Locate buildings and other student gathering areas back from streets, driveways, or parking areas by at least 50 feet.

Install security alarms in administrative offices and rooms containing high-value property, such as computers, VCRs, shop equipment, laboratory supplies, and musical instruments. (Green, 1999)

People

The people banned from schools include troublesome intruders, troublesome staff members, and troublesome students. Each of these types subsumes several subtypes. For example, troublesome intruders include child molesters, sex offenders, members of street gangs, religious proselytizers, and peddlers of commercial products. Troublesome staff members can be thieves, sex offenders, religious zealots, and incompetents. Troublesome students include sex offenders, gang members, the chronically disrespectful, and perpetually unproductive learners.

TROUBLESOME INTRUDERS

The word *intruders* refers to people who are neither students nor staff members in a school. Therefore, even though the parent of a student may be well known to teachers or a principal, the parent still qualifies as an intruder under the definition used here.

Child Molesters and Sex Offenders

Sex offenses against children or youths can assume various forms, including seduction, rape, fondling, exhibitionism (abusers displaying their sexual parts to pupils), pornography (abusers photographing undressed pupils or showing pupils pictures of naked people or ones engaged in sexual intercourse), voyeurism (secretly watching or photographically recording the appearance of a pupil in a location that that the pupil could logically expect to be private), and prostitution (employing a pupil to engage in sex acts).

Because sex predators are prone to frequent schools and playgrounds, states and local communities have laws banning convicted offenders from schools and limiting how close to schools offenders can reside. Those limits vary from one state to another. In California, it is illegal for convicted molesters to live within a tenth of a mile (528 feet) of a school. In Illinois, the distance is 500 feet (about a block and a half) and in Kentucky 1,000 feet.

States also provide publicly available lists of sex offenders, enabling school personnel to identify convicted molesters who may live in their district. Thus, when visitors to a school sign the visitors' register with their true name, they can be identified and refused admission. To make this system more reliable, such places as Manhattan Beach (California) Middle School have installed electronic scanners that view each visitor's driver license and, if the license information matches records of offenders stored in the scanner, the message "possible offender" flashes on a screen. That message is sent by e-mail to the school principal and the police department (Scanner alerts, 2007).

Street-Gang Members

Street gangs in the United States are hardly a recent invention. They have existed since early days, especially when immigrants moved into neighborhoods dominated by people of their own ethnic heritage, and they formed gangs to protect their interests in the face of attacks by competing ethnic groups. However, the rapid increase in gangs, their violent acts, and their threat to safety in schools are mainly phenomena of the past three decades.

Members of street gangs typically

- Are from a particular ethnic group.
- Are predominantly males (90 percent).
- Adopt distinctive dress styles, colors, tattoos, insignia, jewelry, and mottos.
- Consider a particular street or neighborhood their "turf," which they guard against invaders and often mark out with graffiti.

- Are likely to use and peddle illicit drugs.

- Carry weapons—guns, knives, and clubs—at least part of the time.

The thousands of gangs in the United States vary widely in numbers of members. Some gangs—such as the Crips and Bloods based in Los Angeles, or the Folk Nation and People Nation based in Chicago—have hundreds of members in other communities throughout the nation. At the other extreme of size, many gangs consist of a mere handful of members whose turf may be limited to a single block on a city street.

The incidence of gangs in schools is somewhat related to the size of the community, with the frequency of gangs increasing as the population approaches 50,000. The largest number of students reporting the presence of gangs in their schools appeared in cities with populations between 100,000 and 249,999 (54 percent), followed closely by areas with populations between 250,000 and 999,999 (53 percent). "Students in areas with populations of 1 million or more were slightly less likely to report gangs (51%). Even in the smallest jurisdictions (populations smaller than 1,000), 23% of students reported gangs in their schools" (Howell & Lynch, 2000).

Most schools try to keep nonstudent gang members from entering buildings, grounds, playfields, and parking lots so as to prevent potential violence and the spread of drugs and alcohol. The task of enforcing the ban on nonstudent gang members usually falls to school security officers—to the armed police who have been hired by schools at a rapidly increasing rate in recent years.

Religious Proselytizers

As explained in Chapter 7, during colonial times America's public schools routinely included daily Christian religious lessons, prayers, Bible reading, and the singing of hymns. This tradition continued after the founding of the United States, even though the first amendment to the nation's Constitution was interpreted to mean no religion should be taught in public schools. However, by the latter years of the twentieth century, lawsuits were being filed to prevent schools from teaching religion. The judicial decisions issued in those cases provided the guidelines used today for determining the role religious instruction may play in public schools.

Permissible instruction. First, consider what schools may legally do regarding religious instruction.

School districts may release students during school hours for religious in-struction away from the campus, although districts are not required to do so. If a school does provide a released-time program, teachers and other staff mem-bers cannot encourage or force students to participate. School funds may never be used in any way to support a released-time program, nor can a religious group rent school facilities for instructional sessions.

Any school that permits noncurricular clubs (ones not associated with the school's regular study program) must accord religious groups the same priv-ileges available to secular clubs. Religious clubs may meet during the period within the school day that was set aside for extracurricular activities. Schools may prohibit people from the community from attending student clubs. How-ever, they must apply this rule equally to all types of clubs.

A school can teach units of study referred to as *comparative religion*, whose aim is to describe the beliefs and practices of different faiths without portraying any of the faiths as more desirable or more believable than any other. Not only may a regular teacher be in charge of instruction, but also visiting speakers may participate if they agree to give objective accounts of their belief system without implying that their faith is better than anyone else's.

Prohibited instruction. Next, consider what sorts of religious workers are barred from public schools. Strangers (such nonstaff members as priests, ministers, imams, rabbis, or other religious advocates) are not permitted to use class time for proselytizing, that is, for teaching about their religion in a manner designed to convert students to their faith.

In 1989, a coalition of seventeen religious and educational organizations issued a set of principles for distinguishing between *teaching about religion* in public schools and *religious indoctrination*. Teaching about religion means that

- The school's approach to religion is academic, not devotional.
- The school strives for student awareness of religions, but does not press for student acceptance of any one religion.
- The school sponsors study about religion, not the practice of religion.
- The school exposes students to a diversity of religious views; it does not impose any particular view.
- The school educates about all religions; it does not promote or denigrate any religion.
- The school informs students about various beliefs; it does not seek to conform students to any particular belief. (Risinger, 1993)

Peddlers of Commercial Products

Commercial vendors of supplies and services to schools are banned after evidence reveals they have engaged in illegal practices. School staff members sometimes conspire with vendors to swindle schools, as illustrated in the following examples.

> The superintendent of Maryland's second-largest school district was arrested on 16 counts of misconduct, including mail and wire fraud. In a jury trial, prosecutors charged the superintendent with receiving $145,000 in kickbacks for school contracts that he directed to a friend's company or to a software supplier that employed the superintendent's girlfriend. (Mistrial declared, 2007)

> The Wake County (North Carolina) School District was robbed of at least $3.8 million by a gang of five conspirators. Two of the gang were school-district employees—the director of transportation and his "quality-control assistant" responsible for ensuring that all purchase orders were genuine. Two others were officials of the auto-parts company that provided services and equipment for the district's buses and other vehicles. The fifth member was the boyfriend of one of the auto-company officials.

> The main devices the conspirators used to defraud the schools were false purchase orders sent to the auto-supply company. Investigators discovered that near the end of the fiscal year in 2003 and 2004, the school district's transportation department had issued to the auto-parts company 2,535 false invoices totaling more than $3.8 million. Each invoice was for less than $2,500, which was the maximum amount allowed for orders that would not require competitive bids.

> The largest amount of stolen money was banked by the auto company. Lesser amounts were used by members of the gang to buy luxury items for their own use—trucks, campers, motorboats, golf carts, automobiles, widescreen television sets, computers, exercise equipment, storage units, and more. The five individuals arrested for fraud were required to relinquish items they had bought with the stolen money. The auto-supply company was forced to return $1.3 million to the school district that the company had labeled "a prepayment for future parts" and to return $100,000 in supplies belonging to the school system. The five defendants faced charges of conspiracy and obtaining property by false pretenses, felonies

that could result in prison sentences of three to five years. (Hui, 2005)

TROUBLESOME STAFF MEMBERS

The term *staff member* refers to anyone who works at a school, whether as a paid employee or as an unpaid volunteer. Thus, everyone holding the following positions is considered to be a staff member—principal, assistant principal, business manager, teacher, counselor, secretary, coach, teacher's aide, cafeteria employee, custodian, bus driver, gardener, school board member, and the like. Individuals in any of these positions can prove troublesome when they assume the role of thief, sex offender, religious zealot, or incompetent worker. The troubles they cause lead to their being banned from further employment in schools.

Thieves

School personnel sometimes take advantage of their positions of trust by stealing school money or equipment. When caught, they not only lose their jobs but are usually fined and/or sentenced to jail also. The people who most frequently misappropriate funds are those in charge of the distribution of money or of the assignment of contracts to suppliers of services and products. The most egregious cases can involve very large sums of money.

> A woman who had served as the monitor for 17 Washington, D.C., charter schools from 2003 to 2006 pleaded guilty to theft and tax evasion after authorities discovered she had stolen $800,000 that was intended for services to students. Throughout her tenure, she had illegally steered school contracts to friends or kept the money herself. She excused her actions as the result of "poor judgment" and was sentenced to 35 months in prison. (Ex-D.C. charter school, 2007)

> The founder of one of California's largest charter school networks was indicted on 113 felony counts of misappropriation of public funds, grand theft, and tax evasion for embezzling millions of dollars of public-school funds so as to enrich his family and friends.

His theft led to the bankruptcy and collapse of the charter-school network. (Charter school chief, 2007)

In what one New York State official described as "the largest, most remarkable, most extraordinary theft" from a school system in American history, members of the Roslyn School District's administrative staff stole over $11-million of school funds over a six-year period. The five individuals indicted for fraud included the superintendent of schools, a companion with whom he lived, the assistant superintendent of finance, and two other central-office employees. When questioned by prosecuting attorneys, the superintendent admitted embezzling $2-million that he used for "vacations, meals, dry cleaning bills, furniture, dermatology treatments, car loans, real estate investments, and personal expenses averaging about $20,000 a month in some years." Angry members of the community who attended his court hearing believed the superintendent was less than contrite in his statement of apology to the judge in which "he seemed to portray himself as one of his own most deeply wounded victims." He had said, "During the past year and a half I have reflected daily on the mistakes I made in the last few years after a 35-year outstanding career in public education. These egregious errors have irreparably damaged, if not destroyed, my career in public education. I cannot adequately explain the pain my errors have caused me.... I only hope and pray that someday the Roslyn community will remember the good I did for the district as well as find it in their hearts to forgive me for my mistakes." (Vitello, 2005)

Sex Offenders

Sexual misconduct by school personnel can cover the same range of offenses as that of the intruders mentioned earlier, with the most common transgressions being inappropriate touching and seduction. Fondling and seduction are particularly apt to occur in classes that provide close contact between teacher and student in informal settings. Thus, sexual abusers are more often music, art, and drama teachers or athletic coaches than ones who conduct formal classes in mathematics, science, language arts, and social studies.

The 30-year-old wife of Brighton (Colorado) Collegiate High School's former principal was arrested and fired after having a sexual liaison with one of her students during a camping trip that she chaperoned. She was sentenced to 45 days in jail and five years probation. (Barge & Moreno, 2007)

After pleading guilty to two counts of felony child seduction, a popular theater-arts teacher at Broad Ripple High School in Indianapolis (Indiana) received a one-year jail sentence for having oral sex with a 16-year-old girl from his theater class. A yearlong relationship between the two had begun with a kiss in a darkened school auditorium.

Things progressed to fondling in his truck and then sexual encounters at his home. In interviews with detectives, the girl said she was confused several times by the relationship, which included daily phone calls, e-mail, and instant messaging with [the teacher]. Despite assurances that he loved her, eventually she broke off their encounters.

In addition to the jail term, the teacher was required to register as a sex offender and to pay $2,100 for the victim's counseling sessions that had resulted from the victim's need to cope with the distress of guilt and shame from the affair. (Corcoran, 2005)

Between mid-2004 and the close of 2005, at least twenty-five cases nationwide involved female teachers molesting students (Koch, 2005). In nearly all instances, women teachers had sex with boy students, which raised the question of whether men teachers who were charged with sexually abusing girls received more drastic punishment from courts than did women teachers who molested boys. In other words, was there a double standard by which men were treated more harshly than women—and, in particular, more harshly than attractive young women?

News media brought the question of fairness to public attention in late 2005 through reports that a 25-year-old female teacher in Florida, instead of being sentenced to a jail term for her sexual act with a 14-year-old boy, was placed on three years' house arrest to be followed by seven years of probation. She had been charged with two counts of lewd and lascivious battery and one count of lewd and lascivious exhibition for engaging in sexual intercourse with the student in the back seat of a sport utility vehicle that another teenager was driving. Critics estimated that if a male teacher had committed the same offense with a girl student, a judge would have sent him to jail. (Koch, 2005)

Religious Zealots

Teachers who violate the constitutional first-amendment ban on teaching religion in public schools continue to be a perennial source of controversy.

The most publicized conflicts in recent years have concerned teaching about human beginnings—whether, in science classes to teach Darwin's theory of evolution or the Bible's version of creation (or its modern variant, *intelligent design*), or perhaps to teach both. A crucial court decision in 2005 derived from a case in Dover (Pennsylvania) that concerned the school board's requiring biology teachers to read to their classes a statement that cast doubt on Darwin's theory and recommended that students read a book that supported creationism. The statement said,

> [t]he Pennsylvania Academic Standards require students to learn about Darwin's theory of evolution and eventually to take a standardized test of which evolution is a part. Because Darwin's theory is a theory, it continues to be tested as new evidence is discovered. The theory is not a fact. Gaps in the theory exist for which there is no evidence. A theory is defined as a well-tested explanation that unifies a broad range of observations. Intelligent design is an explanation of the origin of life that differs from Darwin's view. The reference book "Of Pandas and People" is available in the library along with other resources for students who might be interested in gaining an understanding of what intelligent design actually involves. (Court rejects, 2005)

When the biology teachers refused to read the disclaimer to their students, a member of the Dover High School's administration did so.

Then eleven parents who were distressed over the school board's statement filed a lawsuit, *Kitzmiller versus Dover Area School District*. The ensuing trial drew nationwide publicity, and the case ended when the presiding judge ruling against the school board. He explained,

> [w]e have addressed the seminal question of whether ID [intelligent design] is science. We have concluded that it is not, and moreover, that ID cannot uncouple itself from its creationist, and thus religious, antecedents. (Cavanagh, 2005)

In effect, creationism, in whatever guise it might assume, should continue to be banned from science classes.

Sometimes teachers who are particularly devout Christians have rejected their school's approved science curriculum and have sought to teach creationism in place of Darwinism. Such was the point of contention in the 1994 case of *Peloza versus Capistrano Unified School District*.

> John E. Peloza, a high-school biology teacher in Capistrano (California), refused to abide by the school district's requirement that Darwin's evolution theory be taught in biology classes. When school officials ordered him to teach evolution, he filed a lawsuit charging that the school district had illegally (1) insisted that he teach evolution, (2) infringed on his right of free speech by prohibiting him from talking with students about religion during the school day, and (3) injured his reputation as result of defamatory statements made to and about him. (Fletcher, 1994)

However, in both a district court and in the court of appeals that subsequently heard the case, Peloza's suit was dismissed as having insufficient merit. If he wished to keep his job, Peloza would still be required to teach Darwinism and to avoid expressing his religious beliefs to students during school hours.

When students claim that teachers have pressed religious beliefs on them in class, a question can arise over what, exactly, the teacher had said. Thus, a Kearny (New Jersey) High School youth—in order to avoid possible error or ambiguity about a teacher's utterances—audio recorded his eleventh-grade history-class instructor's telling the class that evolution and the Big Bang theory were not scientific, that dinosaurs were aboard Noah's ark, and that only Christians could go to heaven. The recordings from eight class sessions were then provided to school officials as evidence that the thirty-eight-year-old teacher often preached Christian doctrine. On one occasion the instructor had urged students to embrace Jesus as their savior and added,

> [i]f you reject his gift of salvation, then you know where you belong. He did everything in his power to make sure that you could go to heaven, so much so that he took your sins on his own body, suffered your pains for you, and he's saying, "Please, accept me, believe." If you reject that, you belong in hell. (Kelley, 2006)

Reactions to the incident from the community were mixed. Some people praised the youth for exposing the history teacher's preaching. Others condemned the student, and he received one death threat. The Rev. Barry W. Lynn, executive director for Americans United for Separation of Church and State, said,

> [t]his is extremely rare for a teacher to get this blatantly evangelical. He's really out there proselytizing, trying to convert students to his faith, and I think that's more than just saying I have some academic-freedom-right to talk about the Bible's view of creation as well as evolution. (Kelley, 2006)

As a result of the episode and its widespread publicity, school officials stated that they would "monitor" the teacher's future conduct in class, and they outlawed any further recording of what teachers say in class.

Incompetent Workers

Teachers are the most difficult kind of school employee to dismiss for incompetence. In nearly every school system, teachers must serve an initial probationary period—usually three years—during which they can be fired without any stated reason. After probation, teachers are usually accorded *permanent status*, a somewhat limited kind of tenure. The task of terminating permanent-status teachers is laborious and costly, because school officials are bound by rules that are part of the contracts negotiated with teachers unions. The rules have been established to protect skilled teachers from arbitrary dismissal by vindictive and unscrupulous principals, superintendents, or school-board members. But the rules can be so strict, and the costs of pursuing cases through the courts can be so high, that in such places as New York City the task of getting rid of unsatisfactory teachers is—as the schools chancellor has complained—"almost impossible." According to John Stossel,

> [t]he regulations are so onerous that principals rarely even try to fire a teacher. Most just put the bad ones in pretend-work jobs, or sucker another school into taking them. (They call that the "dance of the lemons.") The city payrolls include hundreds of teachers who have been deemed incompetent, violent, or guilty of sexual misconduct. Since the schools are afraid to let them teach, they put them in so-called "rubber rooms" instead. There they read magazines, play cards, and chat, at a cost to New York taxpayers of $20 million a year. (Stossel, 2006)

In California and most other states, a permanent-status teacher cannot be dismissed until district officials meticulously document poor performance over time, formally declare the intention to dismiss the teacher, and give the teacher a period during which to improve (such as three months). If improvement has been insufficient, the case can move to an arbitration committee or civil court, followed by further appeals if either party in the case—teacher or school—is dissatisfied with the committee or court decision. This arduous process can take years and many thousands of dollars to complete.

Hence, unsatisfactory teachers can be banned, but the task of dismissing them is so demanding that incompetents are rarely removed.

TROUBLESOME STUDENTS

Teachers, principals, counselors, bus drivers, and cafeteria employees find many students troublesome—particularly in middle schools, since the greatest incidence of trouble making is found in the thirteen- to fifteen-year-old age group. However, the only students that are sufficiently bothersome to invite expulsion from school are usually sex offenders, gang members, thieves and vandals, the chronically disrespectful, and the perpetually unproductive.

Sex Offenders

Sex molestation by students can assume diverse forms—unwelcome remarks, stalking, fondling, seduction, and rape.

Students who are sex offenders confront schools with a special problem. Whereas, no one questions the banning of strangers and staff members who molest children or youths, student offenders are another matter. People who are concerned about the right of children and youths to become educated often puzzle over the wisdom of simply ousting student sex offenders from schools. On one hand, other students need to be protected from the danger of being molested, so the banning of known offenders helps provide that protection. On the other hand, it is the right of all children to better their life chances through education, so they deserve to attend school. Thus, school officials are obliged to decide whether a convicted molester should continue to attend their school or be banned. Moreover, if banned, where should the offender go to continue his or her education.

In arriving at a decision, officials can usefully consider the risk level assigned to the offender by the court in which she or he was tried for past offenses. The meanings of the levels are

Level 1: low risk of repeat offense

Level 2: moderate risk of repeat offense

Level 3: high risk of repeat offense and a threat to public safety exists.

The court may have added a further designation to the risk-level rating— *sexual predator, sexually violent offender,* or *predicate sex offender.*

> *Sexual predator* means a person convicted of a sexually violent offense and who suffers from a mental abnormality or personality disorder that makes him or her likely to engage in predatory sexually violent offenses.

> *Sexually violent offender* means a person convicted of a sexually violent offense.

> *Predicate sex offender* means a person convicted of a sexually violent offense following a previous conviction for such an offense.

Some state sex-offender-registers inform school districts or individual schools whenever convicted molesters are about to enroll in their schools, but other registers fail to send such information. As a result, school personnel can find themselves facing an awkward decision, as in a case at Belgrade (Montana) High School, where officials suddenly discovered that two convicted rapists—one age nineteen, the other age fifteen—had been attending their school. The nineteen-year-old had been at Belgrade High for three years and was now just one semester short of graduating. The board of education expelled the nineteen-year-old because he had been convicted of a serious offenses he could be a risk to other students, he had not completed sex-offender treatment, and he could not be supervised in school. But school officials did arrange for the youth to earn the equivalent of a high-school diploma (a General Educational Development certificate) through off-campus study. As an assistant principal explained,

> I'd like to see him get an education. He needs to get an education and I know that he has some ambitions in life that he'd like to

pursue and I think he has a right to do that. [But] just not in our
school setting. (Belgrade school board, 2007)

The fifteen-year-old sophomore in the case was allowed to return to Belgrade
High if he met specified behavior conditions (Sullivan, 2007).

One way that officials often solve their problem of what to do about a
convicted sex molester is to transfer the offender to a different school. That
different school may be one designed for delinquents—youths who have committed crimes of various sorts. Or the transfer can be to a regular public or
private school. But in either case, the transfer now puts the alternative school's
students at potential risk of being molested. What measures, then, should be
adopted in the alternative school to protect its students? One approach involves
telling the school's personnel about the offender's past (so that staff members
can monitor the newcomer's actions) but not informing schoolmates or their
parents (in order to protect the offender from prejudicial treatment by fellow
students). However, this solution may be rejected by parents who believe they
should know the nature of the classmates with whom their children are obliged
to consort. Difficulties that can result from such a solution can be illustrated
by an incident at Gig Harbor (Washington) High School.

> Four boys were assigned a three-day suspension from school for
> distributing fliers with pictures and descriptions (home addresses,
> personal information) of two convicted sex offenders who were at-
> tending Gig Harbor High. One of the offenders was a 16-year-old
> Level-2 molester convicted of "indecent liberties using force." The
> four suspended youths had discovered their two schoolmates' sex-
> offense records on an Internet website operated by the Washington
> Association of Sheriffs and Police Chiefs. The site provided infor-
> mation about Level-2 and Level-3 offenders, including their current
> addresses. The principal told newspaper reporters that the suspen-
> sions had been for harassment and unauthorized use of school
> equipment to print the fliers. One of the suspended youths com-
> plained, "I don't fully understand why I got suspended for some-
> thing I felt was right," and he added that school officials should
> have taken the initiative to notify parents that their kids attended
> classes alongside convicted sex offenders. (Champaco, 2007)

School personnel can usefully recognize that chronic sex offenders may
seek to enroll in a school so as to find candidates for sexual encounters. A
remarkable incident of that sort happened at an Arizona charter school.

An unusually young-looking 29-year-old sex offender tried to register in Mingus Springs Charter School in Chino on the pretense
that he was age 12. Sheriff department officials reported that the
ruse was an apparent attempt to lure children from the school
into sexual affairs. A 61-year-old man, who erroneously claimed
to be the offender's grandfather, had introduced the applicant to
school officials with papers that "appeared to be fake, and the 'boy'
looked much older than 12." Records revealed that the 29-year-
old had served time in an Oklahoma prison for sex crimes. The
bogus "grandfather" and "grandson," along with two accomplices,
were arrested for failing to register as sex offenders. (Sex offender,
2007)

Gang Members

The proportion of teenagers reporting gangs in their schools nearly doubled
between 1989 and 1995, rising to 37 percent of the youths surveyed near the
end of the 1990s (Howell & Lynch, 2000).

Gang members frequently consider the school to be special safe zone in
which rivalries are to be left behind. Hence, they leave the confrontations with
other gangs and their bullying to the streets so that their presence in school
does not jeopardize the conduct of the learning program. But whenever gang
antagonisms are played out on school property, school officials are obliged
to adopt remedies. One remedy is to expel gang members. However, this
has the effect of ending those teenagers' formal education, thereby reducing
their chance of finding legitimate employment and leading a law-abiding adult
life.

Schools' ways of dealing with gang-related fights are rather limited in scope
and potential effectiveness. There is nothing school authorities can do to dis-
band street gangs or to prevent them from recruiting new members. However,
administrators do have ways to curtail gang activity on campus. Those ways
include (a) employing security guards to patrol the campus and to disperse
groups that appear apt to instigate a fight, (b) requiring that visitors to the
campus obtain a pass from the office before they are allowed to move about
the campus, (c) outlawing the wearing of gang insignia at school, and (d) suspending or expelling gang members who attempt to intimidate schoolmates
or try to bring alcohol, drugs, or weapons to school. Teachers may help reduce
gang violence by getting to know gang members individually, treating them as
worthy persons, and offering them help and encouragement with their studies.

The Chronically Disrespectful

Schools can expel students who habitually insult staff members, fail to accept teachers or administrators' directives, and breach rules. The provision for banning such students is often described in student handbooks. For example, the Edina (Minnesota) schools' *Rights and Responsibilities for Student Management* handbook warns that high-school students guilty of a third verbal-abuse offense are subject to a ten-day suspension with a recommendation for expulsion (Edina Public Schools, 2007). The Manning High School (Clarendon County, South Carolina) handbook states that assaults or threats against a faculty or staff member can warrant suspension and possible expulsion (Manning High School, 2007). Students at Mount Miguel High School (Spring Valley, California) can be expelled for (a) excessive use of profanity, (b) repeated vulgarity or defiance, or (c) disruption of school activities (Mount Miguel High School, 2004). At Williamstown (New Jersey) High School, expulsion can result for (a) continued and wilful disobedience or (b) open defiance of the authority of any teacher or of other persons having authority over students (Williamstown High School, 2006).

Perpetually Unproductive Learners

The expression *flunking out* is perhaps the most familiar way to express the banning of students whose erratic attendance and failure to complete assignments causes school personnel to conclude that those individuals are such a waste of time and are such poor models for their classmates that they don't deserve to be in school. More often than not, unproductive learners aren't formally expelled but, instead, simply drop out of school, perhaps covertly encouraged to do so by school personnel who have found the laggards' continued presence burdensome. An increase in dropout rates since 2002 has been blamed on the federal government's No-Child-Left-Behind law that demands annual increases in schools' standardized-test scores in the fields of language and mathematics. Schools whose scores fail to improve are punished—forced to eliminate staff members, to send pupils to other schools, to turn over control to other agencies, or to close. Hence, schools can help avoid such punishment by getting rid of students who would do poorly on tests. The Illinois state superintendent of education testified at a legislative hearing that the No-Child-Left-Behind law produced a climate that "creates a disincentive [for schools] to hang on to students and help them go the extra mile to stay in school" (Grossman, 2004).

SUGGESTIONS FOR SCHOOL PRACTICE

The following proposals about coping with troublesome people are offered under five headings—troublesome intruders, staff and student sex offenders, thieves, student gang members, and staff and student religious proselytizers.

Troublesome Intruders

Methods suggested in Chapter 12 for protecting schools from wielders of weapons are also useful for fending off other unwelcome intruders, including bothersome venders, potential child molesters, nonstudent members of street gangs, and evangelists. Those methods include stationing security guards at school entrances to greet visitors, requiring visitors to provide evidence of their identity (driver's license, social-security card) and to sign a register, and locating video surveillance cameras at entrances and in corridors.

Staff and Student Sex Offenders

To help ensure that staff members and students understand exactly what actions qualify as offensive sex behavior, school officials can describe the prohibited acts and the consequences to be suffered by anyone guilty of such acts. This description can be included in a guidebook for staff members and in a handbook given to students and their parents.

Whenever a staff member or student has been accused of a sex offense, school officials are wise to already have in hand a written procedure for coping with such cases. The procedure can provide for (a) determining which individuals or agencies will investigate the accusation, (b) collecting witnesses' accounts of the incident, (c) protecting the identities of the alleged offender and alleged victim until there is secure evidence that a rule had, indeed, been breached (for example, was a sexual encounter consensual or forced), (d) which individuals or agencies will be responsible for adjudicating the case, and (e) if, how, and when parents, staff members, students, and the public press will be notified.

Thieves

Thieves can be intruders, school staff members, or students who steal funds or equipment.

To guard against the misappropriation of funds by people in positions of responsibility (administrators, club sponsors, and fund raisers), schools can (a) conduct periodic audits (quarterly, semiannually), (b) ensure that the auditors have no filial or social connections with the people in charge of funds ("don't put the fox in charge of the henhouse"), and (c) issue a statement of rules to be followed in the handling of funds.

To deter people from stealing equipment and supplies, schools can (a) apply a difficult-to-erase school ownership label to computers, printers, copiers, file cabinets, and similar items, (b) bolt or glue equipment to desks (computers, staplers, and typewriters), (c) lock doors to equipment storage areas when those rooms are not in use, and (d) activate building-security alarms when the school is not occupied.

The matter of what constitutes theft of school supplies or equipment is not always clear. Is a teacher a thief or an admirably diligent employee if she takes a school computer home to prepare lesson plans over the weekend? Does a student on the soccer team deserve censure for taking a school ball to a park after school in order to practice dribbling? Thus, school officials may find it useful to distribute a written statement to staff and students that illustrates the difference between stealing and legitimately borrowing school supplies and equipment.

Student Gang Members

As noted earlier, coping with student gang members confronts schools with two potentially incompatible responsibilities. First is the schools' responsibility to conduct a smoothly operating learning program and, in the process, to protect staff members and students from harm. Gang members who bring their hostile behavior to school can jeopardize the schools' ability to carry out that charge. Second is the responsibility to provide a suitable learning program for every student, a task that cannot be performed if gang members are either expelled or remain in school but are antagonistic and uncooperative.

In carrying out the first responsibility, schools often seek to reduce gang members' influence by outlawing the display of gang symbols. Lists of prohibited gang-membership indicators are often printed in student handbooks. For example, the Pawnee School District (Grover, Colorado) handbook states,

> [t]he Board [of Education] prohibits the presence on school premises, in school vehicles and at school-related activities of any

apparel, jewelry, accessory, notebook or manner of grooming which
by virtue of its color, arrangement, trademark or any other attribute
denotes membership in gangs which advocate drug use, violence,
or disruptive behavior. (Gang activity, 2005)

In pursuit of the second responsibility, teachers can seek to befriend gang
members by treating them in an affable manner, listening to their concerns
during counseling sessions, providing learning materials that might appeal to
their interests (books, articles, and computer programs), and assigning them
tasks that might warrant their schoolmates' respect (textbook monitor, leader
of a small-group project).

Staff and Student Religious Proselytizers

In both staff and student handbooks, schools can explain the kinds of religious activity legally allowed and the kinds prohibited in public schools. The
following passage illustrates what the explanation might include.

> [S]tudents have the right to engage in voluntary individual prayer
> that is not coercive and does not substantially disrupt the school's
> educational mission and activities. For example, all students have
> the right to say a blessing before eating a meal. However, school of-
> ficials must not promote or encourage a student's personal prayer.
> Students may engage with other students in religious activity dur-
> ing non-curricular periods as long as the activity is not coercive
> or disruptive. In addition, while students may speak about reli-
> gious topics with their peers, school officials should intercede if
> such discussions become religious harassment. . . . Personal reli-
> gious activity may not interfere with the rights or well-being of
> other students, and the threat of student harassment and pressure
> must be carefully monitored. It is also critical to ensure that the
> religious activity is actually student-initiated, and that no school
> employee supervises or participates in the activity. Any school pro-
> motion or endorsement of a student's private religious activity is
> unconstitutional. (Anti-Defamation League, 2004a)

Ceremonies and Performances

The term *ceremony* refers to a ritual that expresses a group or individual's beliefs. Examples of ceremonies are prayer sessions, customs that signify neophytes' initiation into a group, celebrations of significant events, or rites honoring revered people or deities. *Performances* are presentations before an audience in the form of drama, music, dance, speech, or pageantry.

Types of ceremonies and performances banned in schools include those of a religious, profane/vulgar, political, or criminal nature. An additional type is the abusive variety, especially in the form of hazing, as depicted in Chapter 8.

RELIGIOUS

As explained earlier, religion is the concern of two clauses in the first amendment to the U.S. Constitution. The establishment clause declares that the government cannot adopt or endorse any religion. The free-exercise clause asserts that every individual is free to follow whatever belief system he or she prefers. Whereas the establishment clause has generally been interpreted to mean that religion should be left out of public schools, the free-exercise clause implies that individuals can practice their religion how and where they wish— ostensibly even on school property. Furthermore, because religion is such an intimate part of American history and culture, will not schools be neglecting their educational duty if they entirely avoid teaching about religion? These contradictory demands face school personnel with the problem of deciding which, if any, religion-related ceremonies and performances can legally be included in public schools. Typical decision-making problems are illustrated in the following cases that involve cleansing presentations of religious elements, prayer, holiday traditions, and the nature of "reality."

Cleansing Presentations of Religion

Considerable confusion continues to accompany school authorities' attempts to avoid offending the first amendment's establishment clause—a confusion that leads to such events as the following:

> To transform a traditional religion-related character into an acceptable secular form, the superintendent of schools in Tiverton (Rhode Island) proposed that the name of the Easter Bunny who was scheduled to visit a craft fair at the town's middle school should be changed to Peter Rabbit in "an attempt to be conscious of other people's [non-Christian] backgrounds and traditions." In response, a member of Rhode Island's state legislature proposed a bill, nicknamed the *Easter Bunny Act*, to stop local municipalities from changing the names of traditional icons—"The Easter bunny is not a religious symbol. Why it's banned doesn't make sense." (School renames, 2007)

> When a girl planned to sing a Christian-themed song at the Winneconne High School (Winnebago County, Wisconsin) graduation ceremony, school officials insisted that she substitute the words "He," "Him" or "His" for the three lyric references to the word "God" in the song. The girl reacted by filing a lawsuit, charging that the ban violated her rights under the first amendment's free-exercise-of-religion clause. School officials relented when faced with the lawsuit, so the girl was allowed to include the song's references to God as long as she did not mention God in her spoken introduction to the song. (Morano, 2003)

Prayer

U.S. Supreme Court rulings have outlawed the mandatory recitation of standardized prayers in public schools (*Engel versus Vitale*, 1962), a required moment of silence "for meditation or voluntary prayer" (*Wallace versus Jaffree*, 1985), prayers as invocations and benedictions at graduation ceremonies (*Lee versus Weisman*, 1992), and school-endorsed public prayer at athletic events (*Santa Fe Independent School District versus Doe*, 2000). However, the courts have allowed students to pray on their own initiative, either individually or in a group, during their free time at school, such as during recess or lunch period. However, problems still arise about who should be allowed to pray and under what conditions.

Islamic doctrine requires that adherents pray toward the holy city of Mecca five times each day. For Islamic students, one obligatory prayer time occurs during school hours—around noon or some-what later. How, then, might schools accommodate such students' religious duty without breaching laws governing prayer in public schools?

At Carver Elementary School near San Diego (California), an early afternoon 15-minute recess period permitted nearly 100 Muslim pupils to use a special room for praying while their non-Islamic classmates went to the playground. In reaction to this provision, an attorney for a conservative Christian organization complained that the school's policy of accommodating Muslim's prayer practices "presumes that Christians are less religious and less inspired to worship and praise the Lord and come together." He asked the school district to set up another special room in which Christians could also gather to pray.

Observers of the Carver controversy suggested that "the whole matter may land in court. Potentially at issue is to what extent actions taken by a public school to accommodate special religious needs of some students might require similar allowances for other students." (Dotinga, 2007)

In October 2007, the Illinois state legislature passed a *Silent Reflection and Student Prayer Act* requiring that "In each public school classroom the teacher in charge shall observe a brief period of silence with the participation of all the pupils therein assembled at the opening of every school day. This period shall not be conducted as a religious exercise but shall be an opportunity for silent prayer or for silent reflection on the anticipated activities of the day." (Silent reflection, 2007)

An atheist and his school-age daughter reacted to the law by filing a suit in federal court, contending that the law mandated prayer in public schools in violation of the first amendment's establishment clause. Thereupon, the federal judge in mid-November issued a preliminary injunction barring the district in which the daughter was enrolled from holding the moment of silence while the lawsuit progressed through the court system. When issuing the injunction, the judge said the law was likely unconstitutional. Sponsors of the law in the state legislature said they did not mind removing the word *prayer* from the act, which would leave the law with its *silent meditation* intent that had been found constitutionally acceptable in others states' "moment-of-silence" laws. (Coen, 2007)

Holiday Traditions

Pageants and plays celebrating Christmas have a long history in American schools. However, ever since Christian performances came under judicial attack in the latter decades of the twentieth century, continuing debate has focused on the issue of what—if any—Christmas festivities can legally take place in public schools.

The cancellation of a performance of Charles Dickens' *Christmas Carol* at Lake Washington High School in Kirkland (Washington) raised the question of whether Dickens' creation was a literary classic that was properly studied in public schools or, instead, was a violation of the separation of church and state. The school principal said he had called off the production by a private theater group because it would have prompted a discussion about the connection between a public school and religion. An assistant superintendent explained that, according to school-district policy, "Teaching about religious holidays is permissible, but celebrating them is not. You can teach about a variety of religions, but should not emphasize a particular one." Whether the *Christmas Carol* could be considered an endorsement of Christianity was unclear, but the Washington Lake principal did not want to take a chance that it would be judged so. (Dickens classic, 2004)

Parents of pupils at a Colorado public charter school objected to the school's elaborate Christian festivities at Christmas time, with no recognition of other faiths that also held celebrations near the end of the year, such as Kwanzaa and as Judaism with its Hannukah days. The parents asked the principal to include celebrations of other faiths, and "According to the parents, the principal was willing to add a Hannukah song if they wanted, but only because Jesus was Jewish." When the parents' efforts failed, they appealed to the Jewish Anti-Defamation League (ADL) for help in pursuing their cause. The League responded by offering the school—as well as all public schools—a pamphlet titled *The December Dilemma— December Holiday Guidelines for Public Schools*. The intent of the guidelines was explained in the publication's introduction:

"Every December, public school students, parents, teachers and administrators face the difficult task of acknowledging the various religious and secular holiday traditions celebrated during that time of year. Teachers, administrators and parents should try to promote greater understanding and tolerance among students of different traditions by taking care to adhere to the requirements of the First Amendment [which] guarantees freedom of religion to all Americans—including young schoolchildren—by prohibiting the government from endorsing or promoting any particular religious point of view. This prohibition has led courts to ban such plainly coercive religious activities in public schools as organized prayer and the teaching of creationism. The law is less clear regarding the limits on holiday celebrations in public schools, but a number of guidelines should be followed in order to ensure that our public schools can best celebrate the religious freedom upon which our nation was founded." (Anti-Defamation League, 2004b)

The charter school reacted to the guidelines by employing an attorney to charge the ADL in the public press with "trying to censor Christmas." The Alliance Defense Fund (a conservative Christian organization) joined in support of the principal's holiday festivities, and the Catholic League for Religious and Civil Rights issued an alternative set of holiday guidelines which stated

"Public Schools cannot prohibit legitimate acknowledgment of Christmas as an important cultural and religious celebration. The First Amendment guarantees freedom of religion to all Americans, including young schoolchildren. It forbids the government or public school authorities from imposing arbitrary, coercive, and prohibitive regulations that directly threaten to interfere with the right of students to acknowledge the Christmas season." (Catholic League, 2007)

In summary, debates have continued over what sorts of festivities are constitutionally permitted in public schools at Christmas time, with each side in a debate basing its arguments on material suited to its particular interests.

In the charter-school case, the Jewish Anti-Defamation League founded its reasoning on the first amendment's establishment clause whereas the Catholic League based its claims on the free-exercise clause.

Not only can conflicts concern performances that appear to valorize a particular religion but also concern how accurately a religion is portrayed. Both of those matters—favoritism and accuracy—were at stake when a play titled *The Last Call* was performed during a mandatory assembly at Steele Middle School in Muskegon (Michigan).

> The drama had been written by members of the Shiloh Tabernacle Church in Muskegon, with the plot ostensibly based on the Bible's Book of Revelations. One scene portrayed a mother being reunited in heaven with the baby she aborted. Another scene pictured a lesbian dying of AIDS and being damned to an eternity of misery after killing the man who molested her. School authorities were distressed by the drama's apparently urging a religious message on the audience and for the play's questionable interpretation of the Bible. As a result, the superintendent sought to avoid similar problems in the future by scheduling an inservice workshop for administrators on the separation of church and state. (Edwards, 2006)

Performances that might appear to nearly everyone to have no bearing on religion can, in some people's opinion, be interpreted as promoting dangerous religious beliefs. Such was the case when the Noel Coward comedy *Blithe Spirit* was about to be performed by South Walton (Florida) High School's drama department.

> The play depicts a socialite, Charles Condomine, being haunted by the ghost of his first wife, Elvira, following a séance with a medium. The subsequent action features Elvira, in her spirit guise, desperately trying to disrupt Charles' current marriage. When the South Walton High drama department announced its plan to produce *Blithe Spirit*, members of the community who identified themselves as *Concerned Walton County Parents* requested that school officials not permit the performance, because "the play could teach children about the occult and influence them adversely." It turned out that none of the complainants had a child in the school system. However, according to school-district policy, any time a complaint was filed against a drama, preparations for the production had to stop until the problem was resolved. In the *Blithe Spirit* episode, the

superintendent of schools appointed a committee of teachers, parents, and students. When the committee unanimously approved of
Blithe Spirit, production resumed "with some minor adjustments
over some adult subject material."

The mother of a drama student said, "One of the biggest issues
I have is that anyone can just walk off the street and into the board
of education and shut down a production or remove a book. Under
this microscope, our kids won't be able to perform material from
Shakespeare to Disney. [My aim is] to be able to do this show at the
school and change the complaint process." (Leonard, 2007)

PROFANE/VULGAR

Different people's interpretations of what constitutes *profane* and *vulgar*
cause difficulty for school officials in deciding which performances to ban.
Part of the problem results from changes in public standards of decency over
the past half century. Another source of confusion is the disagreement among
subgroups of society (the elderly versus the young, fundamentalist Christians
versus nonbelievers, new immigrants versus long-term inhabitants) about
what sorts of performances are offensive enough to outlaw. Consider, first, an
objectionable style of dancing.

Several Los Angeles (California) high schools have banned the *Crip
Walk* or *Crip Walking* because of the dance style's gangland origin
and ties. The *Crip* dance consists of jittery stutter-steps accompanied by foot pivots and shuffles. The dance is named for its creators,
the Crips, a violent street gang that originated in Los Angeles in
the 1970s. Over the years, the Crips (in their blue attire) have been
bitter enemies of the rival Bloods (in red). A student at Crenshaw
High School explained, "If you go to a spot where the Bloods are
and you do the Crip walk, you are going to get shot." To reduce
gang violence in high schools, officials banned the dance and all
gang symbols. The principal of Manual Arts High School said, "We
don't allow any kind of gang stuff. In terms of dress codes at school,
we don't allow red or blue shoelaces. . . . We ban ball caps."

Over the past decade, as *Crip Walking* has grown increasingly
popular outside of gangs, some observers have objected to schools
outlawing the dance. One critic who studies gangs said, "It's a
little bit of paranoia. If it was called the boogie-woogie walk, nobody

would care." He compared the dance to other gang customs—such
as wearing low-riding baggy pants—that became popular among
teenagers. (Libaw, 2002)

The reason that performances are banned—or at least altered—is often
because they include phrases that someone believes are publicly offensive or
inappropriate for school-age children. Censored expressions include words
that refer to people's "private" parts and functions (asshole, penis, fart, shit),
are blasphemous (God damn-it, go to hell, for Christ's sake), or denigrate
ethnic groups (nigger, kike, wop).

> At an evening of "readings" sponsored by a literary magazine at
> John Jay High School (Cross River, New York), three honor stu-
> dents took turns reciting an excerpt from *The Vagina Monologues*, a
> popular feminist drama that expresses various women's thoughts
> about sexual subjects. Prior to the event, a John Jay faculty member
> had ordered the girls to delete the word "vagina" from the passage
> "My short skirt is a liberation flag in the women's army. I declare
> these streets, any streets, my vagina's country." But when the girls
> performed before the audience, they included the forbidden word,
> which resulted in their being suspended from school for a day by
> the high school principal.
>
> When the author of *The Vagina Monologues* heard of the incident,
> she protested that "The school's position is absurd, a throwback to
> the Dark Ages. So what if children were to hear the word? Would
> that be terrible? We're not talking about *plutonium* here or *acid
> rain* —words that destroy lives. It's a body part!"
>
> One girl's mother joined in defending the three monolgists—
> "To me, they were reciting literature in an educational forum and
> they did it with grace and dignity."
>
> The high school principal, in support of his suspension decision,
> said the school "recognizes and respects student freedom of ex-
> pression. That right, however, is not unfettered. When a student is
> told by faculty members not to present specified material because
> of the composition of the audience and they agree to do so, it is ex-
> pected that the commitment will be honored and the directive will
> be followed. When a student chooses not to follow the directive,
> consequences follow." (Girls suspended, 2007)

The question of how much the veracity of a drama is damaged by ridding
it of profanity is often the focus of conflicts over performances. Such was the

source of discord when members of Sleepy Hollow (New York) High School's Gay-Straight Alliance planned to stage *The Laramie Project*—a true-life drama that examines the killing of a gay student at the University of Wyoming. The youth had been beaten, tied to a fence, and left to die on the outskirts of the city of Laramie.

> When Sleepy Hollow school officials read *The Laramie Project* script, they informed the students that the dialogue's profanity breached the school's speech rules. The school superintendent explained, "We have a code of conduct, and it specifies language guidelines, It's ironic that, given the [homosexual] subject matter, the subject matter itself was never controversial. It was just the language. We are a school, and there are generally accepted standards."
>
> The student dramatists complained that their work was being unfairly censored. The co-president of the Alliance said, "The play is taken from interviews [with participants in the actual Wyoming episode], and we were very worried about maintaining the play's artistic integrity. [But] we decided the message was more important than keeping in the words, so we edited it and the principal approved it." (Lombardi, 2007)

POLITICAL

Schools invite trouble when they allow ceremonies or performances that deal with divisive political issues. So teachers are confronted with an ofttimes troublesome decision—(a) they are expected to enlighten students about social issues and how to cope with such issues in a democracy; but (b) if teachers sponsor performances that address controversial matters, they risk being attacked by critics who dislike having such matters exposed or who disagree with a performance's approach to an issue. One of the most contentious political matters generating public conflict in the twenty-first century has been the Iraq War.

> The principal of Wilton (Connecticut) High School canceled a drama class's production of *Voices in Conflict*—a play consisting of monologues based on interviews, blogs, and newspaper accounts of American soldiers' experiences in the current Iraq War. The monologues' depiction of violence, injury, death, and heartache appeared to cast doubt on the justness of the war. During rehearsals, one student and her mother complained that the script was unbalanced

and disrespectful to soldiers in Iraq, so the principal called off the performance because he felt it "would hurt families that had lost loved ones or had family members serving overseas."

News of the cancellation drew nationwide attention. In a letter signed by 33 prominent playwrights, the National Coalition Against Censorship and the Dramatists Guild urged the Wilton High administration to allow the students to perform the play unedited. When Wilton officials failed to permit the performance, several professional theater companies hosted the students' play, including the prestigious *Public Theater in Manhattan*. The New York agency that licenses most student productions awarded the Wilton drama group a "Courage in Theater" certificate. (Bruinius, 2007)

Another heated political issue that has been people's sexual preference or orientation—heterosexual, homosexual, and bisexual.

As a result of public controversy and threatening phone calls, the Philadelphia School District erased *Gay and Lesbian History Month* from its 2007-2008 school calendar. In an effort to treat all groups equally, the district also eliminated African-American, Hispanic-Heritage, and Asian-Pacific-American "recognition months" as well as the *International Day of Disabled Persons*. The *American Family Association of Pennsylvania* applauded the gay/lesbian ban, whereas the *Philadelphia Citizens for Children and Youth* criticized the decision. (Snyder, 2007)

As demonstrated in earlier chapters, perennial questions arise about schools' policies that bear on relationships between church and state. For example, before the 1950s the pledge of allegiance that students routinely recited in school read as follows: "I pledge allegiance to the flag of the United States of America, and to the republic for which it stands: one nation, indivisible, with liberty and justice for all." Then the Catholic laymen's society, Knights of Columbus, sponsored a successful campaign to insert the word *God* into the pledge as a means of contrasting a religion-based America with an atheistic Soviet Union. Thus, in 1954 President Dwight D. Eisenhower inserted God into the pledge to follow the words "one nation." Since that time the official pledge has included God. However, a federal court ruling (*West Virginia versus Barnette*) has permitted students to opt out of reciting the pledge if their religious or patriotism convictions warrant their not participating.

At Boulder (Colorado) High School, a dozen students walked out of class while the pledge was broadcast into classrooms. Not only did they refuse to say the pledge, they were unwilling to hear it. The protestors were members of the school's long-established social-protest group, *Student Worker*. Once outside the classroom, the twelve delivered their own pledge without reference to God, while nearly 100 of their schoolmates watched.

In their version of the oath, the dozen declared, "I pledge allegiance to the flag and my constitutional rights with which it comes. And to the diversity, in which our nation stands, one nation, part of one planet, with liberty, freedom, choice, and justice for all."

A spokesperson for the group explained that their objection to *God* in the official oath was "all about separation of church and state."

Critics of the students were due to be disappointed if they expected school officials to ban the protest group's pledge and punish the *Student Worker* activists. The principal said no punitive action would be taken because "We're proud of the kids. If they don't like something, they're following a democratic process of telling the community that they don't like it." And they do so without upsetting the instructional program. (Morson, 2007)

Finally, performances may be banned if they feature or pay tribute to a politically despised organization or individual.

On Halloween in 2006, after a student wore a Hitler-style mustache and Nazi uniform to Leon M. Goldstein High School (Brooklyn, New York), the principal outlawed students' wearing any sort of Halloween costume in 2007. The ban was imposed because, according to the principal, the Hitler outfit had caused such consternation among staff and students that it disrupted the educational process. (Halloween banned, 2007)

CRIMINAL

When a dramatic performance that includes criminal acts is intended to be a comedy mocking ridiculous portrayals of life, people may demand that the performance be banned for its potentially destructive influence on students. A case in point was the plan of dramatists at La Cañada (California)

High School to present the musical comedy *Bat Boy* as the school's spring play.

> *Bat Boy*—an award-winning dark comedy first performed on Halloween 1997 in New York City—is a spoof of a story in the sensationalist tabloid *Weekly World News* about a half-boy, half-bat found living in a West Virginia cave. In the musical, Bat Boy is adopted by a family in the town of Hope Falls, learns to speak English with a refined accent, and tries to be accepted by the townspeople but is met with fear, hatred, and violence.
>
> The elements of the fantasy that raised the ire of La Cañada parents were the scenes featuring what one mother described as onstage "rape, incest, bestiality, drug use, violence, animals copulating, and murder, murder, murder." The high school's drama teacher defended *Bat Boy*, saying that the redeeming quality of the play was that "it teaches to love your neighbor, to forgive and to be true to one's vows."
>
> The school's administrators agreed to accept *Bat Boy* if the teacher "toned down" the script a bit. Defenders of the musical pointed out that it had been performed without untoward consequences in other California schools, such as Victor Valley High (Victorville) and Jesuit High School (Sacramento). (Fleming, 2005; Justus, 2005)

SUGGESTIONS FOR SCHOOL PRACTICE

Schools officials can prepare for potential unacceptable behavior during ceremonies and performances by issuing a statement identifying (a) kinds of behavior that is forbidden, (b) why such behavior is banned, (c) sanctions to be imposed on students who violate the ban, (d) the process by which such bans are implemented (who enforces, how, by what authority), and (e) what opportunities accused students have to defend or explain their actions. The statement can be included in the student handbook and distributed to faculty members who sponsor student organizations. In addition, officials can require—or at least request—that the bylaws governing student clubs, teams, or societies include written rules identifying kinds of behavior forbidden in ceremonies and performances.

Displays

Displays can assume a variety of forms—banners, posters, plaques, pictures, exhibits, dioramas, signs, symbolic objects, logos, and more. Three kinds of displays that schools often ban are ones that (a) promote a religion, (b) foster illegal, immoral, or anti-social behavior, or (c) advocate a controversial political position.

PROMOTING A RELIGION

As noted earlier, the first amendment to the United States Constitution requires that "Congress shall make no law respecting an establishment of religion." This proscription has been interpreted by federal courts to mean that schools, as government-sponsored institutions, should respect the separation of church and state and therefore not foster any religion. Over recent decades, that ban has generated conflicts over public schools' displays of religious maxims, pictures, and symbols.

The most contentious religious object has been the Jewish and Christian guide to proper human behavior known as the Ten Commandments (the Decalogue) from Chapter 20 of the book of Exodus in the Jewish Torah and Christian Old Testament. The commandments include three ways people should act and seven ways they should not act. Thus, people should (1) worship only the one true God, (2) respect one's parents, and (3) respect the Sabbath day by not working. People should not (4) use God's name in an insulting fashion, (5) worship idols, (6) kill, (7) steal, (8) commit adultery, (9) tell lies about others, or (10) yearn for anyone else's property or spouse. Four of these directives are specific to the Judeo–Christian religious tradition (worship the one true God, respect the Sabbath, never use God's name in vain, and avoid worshiping idols or "graven images"). The remaining six are precepts common to many other belief systems, both religious and secular. Thus, schools' posting the four Judeo–Christian rules could be interpreted as violating the U.S. Constitution's establishment clause, whereas displaying the six general rules would not.

When lawsuits have been filed that prohibit exhibits of the Decalogue in public schools, the courts have not been consistent in their rulings. In 1980 the U.S. Supreme Court entertained a case referred from the Kentucky Supreme Court where state judges had upheld a 1978 Kentucky statute requiring that the Ten Commandments be posted in every classroom. Kentucky legislators, when voting for the bill, had asserted that the statute's purpose was secular—that of encouraging pupils to behave properly. In addition, the legislators buttressed their secularity claim by contending that the ten biblical precepts formed the foundation of American jurisprudence: "The secular application of the Ten Commandments is clearly seen in its adoption as the fundamental legal code of Western Civilization and the Common Law of the United States" (*Stone v. Graham*, 1980).

However, the U.S. Supreme Court, in a 5-4 vote, reversed the lower court's judgment by declaring that the statute (a) had a religious—not a secular— purpose (b) promoted the Judeo–Christian tradition, and (c) unduly entangled the government with religion. Kentucky's attorneys argued that the postings did not violate the Constitution's establishment clause because the cost of the classroom plaques had been paid by voluntary contributions. Furthermore, students were not required to read the plaques, so reading the commandments would be a voluntary act at each individual's discretion. In reply, the Court deemed those reasons insufficient to overcome the appearance that schools were promoting a sacred religious text.

The year 1999 marked continuing efforts to display the commandments in schools in the wake of the shooting spree that killed thirteen and wounded twenty-three at Columbine High School in Littleton (Colorado). The Jackson County (Kentucky) School Board allowed volunteers to post the Ten Commandments in all public-school classrooms in "an effort to start having good morals in school . . . because of all the violent issues that have been showing up." Protestant ministers in Adams County (Ohio) placed tablets containing the commandments in front of four high schools in an attempt to reverse "moral decline." The Glynn County (Georgia) School Board assigned their attorney to "come up with a display of non-religious documents" that would include the Ten Commandments, with the "non-religious" label intended as a ploy to circumvent the Constitution's establishment clause. In Val Verde (California), the school board initially approved the school superintendent's request to post the commandments in the district office, but the board withdrew its permission after being threatened with a lawsuit by the American Civil Liberties Union (Robinson, 1999). In each of those cases, postings of the Decalogue were declared unconstitutional. But curiously, the Supreme Court later allowed a display of the Ten Commandments on the grounds of the Texas state capital.

Religious maxims have not been the only religious paraphernalia involved in disputes over bans. In 1999, a kindergartener in Baldwinsville (New York) Central School District submitted a poster he had created—with considerable help from his mother—to fulfill an assignment about ways to save the environment. His poster showed children holding hands around the world, people picking up garbage and recycling trash, and Jesus kneeling with hands stretched toward the sky. School administrators rejected the poster on the ground that it violated a district rule against depicting recognizable religious personalities. In response to the rejection, the boy's parents filed a lawsuit, claiming that (a) the child's right to free expression had been breached and (b) school officials had displayed official discrimination against religion. A federal district court dismissed the case as without merit, but judges in an appeals court ruled that (a) the school district's censoring the poster suggested an antireligious "viewpoint discrimination" on the part of school officials and (b) such a viewpoint could only be justified if officials showed that their censorship served an "overriding" government interest. Thus, the appeals court sent the case back to the district court "for further examination of whether there was discrimination and, if so, whether it might be justified, for example by the need to avoid the appearance of religious endorsement" (Greenhouse, 2006). Some observers interpreted the appeals-court decision to mean that "public schools cannot censor the religious viewpoints of students in class assignments" (U. S. Supreme Court, 2006). However, other observers disagreed, charging that the matter had not been settled and the ruling was simply a way for the justices to dodge the knotty issue of church/state separation versus individuals' right of religious expression.

Pictures of religious figures have also been the target of quarrels about displays in schools. In March 2006, a lawyer for the American Civil Liberties Union (ACLU) asked the Harrison County (West Virginia) School Board to remove the picture of Jesus, which, for the past 40 years, had been displayed in a hallway next to the main office in Bridgeport High School. The lawyer said, "I have absolute respect for anyone who looks at the painting for comfort. This is just a pure constitutional issue" of the separation of church and state. In support of his request, the attorney cited a 1994 Michigan case in which a court had ruled that a picture of Jesus hanging in the hallway of a Michigan school violated the U.S. Constitution's first amendment. As a potential solution to the problem, the superintendent of schools suggested that Bridgeport High School could start an "inspirational wall" on which pictures of other influential historical figures could be displayed, with the picture of Jesus moved to that wall. Christ's portrait would then not appear to be favoring Christianity over other faiths. However, an ACLU representative questioned the feasibility of such an attempt: "Will they allow Wiccans to put up their displays? Jews, Muslims, Buddhists, Hindus? I think they would run into some problems" (J. D. Anderson, 2006).

The Christian nativity scene (a diorama portraying the scene of Jesus' birth in a stable) has been a frequent subject of controversy at Christmas time and has produced debatable court decisions. New York City's school authorities banned nativity scenes in schools while, at the same time, permitting displays of such cultural objects as the Jewish menorah (candelabrum) and the Islamic star and crescent. In 2007, the U.S. Supreme Court let stand an appeals' court ruling that, while the nativity scene was prohibited, other religions' regalia were permissible under the school system's policy of using "holiday celebrations to encourage respect for the city's diverse cultural traditions" (Supreme Court won't review, 2007).

In summary, it is apparent that the issue of religious displays in public schools has not been resolved to everyone's satisfaction—including jurists' satisfaction—and that disputes are bound to continue in years to come.

FOSTERING ILLEGAL, IMMORAL, OR ANTISOCIAL BEHAVIOR

The term *illegal* in the present context refers to any act that violates a law. The term *immoral* means behavior considered wrong by a society's dominant values, whether or not that behavior is illegal. The expression *antisocial* refers to acts that denigrate members of subgroups within a society, with those subgroups defined by members' age, gender, religious, ethnic, social-class status, or health condition. Some acts qualify under only one of these types. Other acts fall within two or all three types.

Unlawful Behavior

The case of the banner reading "Bong Hits 4 Jesus" in Chapter 7 is an example of a prohibition upheld by the U.S. Supreme Court on the grounds that schools can outlaw displays that encourage illegal acts.

> The "special characteristics of the school environment" ... and the governmental interest in stopping student drug abuse—reflected in the policies of Congress and myriad school boards, including [that of Juneau-Douglas High School]—allow schools to restrict student expression that they reasonably regard as promoting illegal drug use. (Less-than-banner, 2007)

Confederate Flags

Examples of bans intended to prevent antisocial behavior are two court cases involving rules prohibiting the display of the U.S. Civil War's battle flag of the Confederacy.

At Madison Central High School in Richmond (Kentucky), two students were ordered by the principal to change their "Southern-Thunder" T-shirts that were emblazoned with an image of the Rebel flag. The principal explained that the shirts violated the school dress code that prohibited anything with an "illegal, immoral, or racist implication." He noted that African-Americans considered the flag an insulting reminder of their ancestors' condition of slavery. The two students refused to change their shirts and were suspended from school. They and their parents responded with a lawsuit, claiming that their freedom-of-speech rights had been breached. The presiding judge dismissed the case because, he said, it did not concern speech. When the case was later reinstated, the plaintiffs and school district settled it out of court in an undisclosed manner (Lawyers: Settlement, 2002).

In the second case, a federal judge dismissed a lawsuit against the Blount County (Kentucky) school system that had been filed by three students after a ban on displaying the Confederate flag was enforced by the principal of William Blount High School. The three plaintiffs contended that the Confederate flag represented their southern heritage and that the ban violated their constitutional rights to free speech. In reply, the school board's attorney argued that the school was suffering a period of racial unrest during which a death threat against blacks on a bathroom wall was accompanied by a drawing of the Confederate flag. Other threats mentioned the Ku Klux Klan and named six black students who would die. The court ruled that school officials could issue a ban if the banned material interferes with discipline or the school's operation. The appeals court that received the case decided that the flag was a "controversial, racial, and political symbol" (Millard, 2007).

Moral and Social Issues

A display that combined moral and social-equality issues involved T-shirts whose printed message read, "Free the Jena 6." The shirts were worn at Jena (Louisiana) High School after six black students had been arrested for beating up a white schoolmate. The beating had occurred some weeks after racial tensions intensified in Jena—a town of 2,900 with about 350 black residents—as the result of three nooses found hanging from a tree on the high-school campus. For the nooses prank, three white students were suspended, but no criminal charges were filed. In contrast, the six black youths involved in the beating incident were cited for attempted murder. The charge prompted members of the black community—backed by equal-rights activists from around the nation—to accuse the Jena district attorney of blatant racial prejudice. The T-shirts were part of that protest movement. The superintendent of schools said he imposed the T-shirt ban because the message on the shirts unduly disrupted the school's learning program (School bans shirts, 2007). The right of authorities to forbid displays that led to a "substantial disruption of school activities" had already been established in a Michigan case and was reasserted in the 2006 appeals' court ruling for the antigay T-shirt case of *Harper versus Poway* (see Chapter 7). The murder charge against the six Jena defendants was subsequently reduced to aggravated second-degree battery and conspiracy to commit aggravated second-degree battery. The defendants finally pled guilty to a lesser misdemeanor count.

ADVOCATING A POLITICAL POSITION

School policies often prohibit displays that support one side in political controversies or that favor one candidate over another in elections.

Illegal immigration became the subject of increasingly vitriolic political debate as America moved into the twenty-first century, with conflicts particularly intense in such western states as Arizona, California, and Colorado that were the recipients of millions of foreigners who had illicitly entered the United States from Mexico. Tensions among students over the immigration issue prompted school administrators to ban flags and clothing that heightened hostilities between native-born Americans and recent immigrants. In Westminster (Colorado), the principal of Shaw Heights Middle School forbade "clothing that makes a political statement [and] banners, flags, bandanas of all types." The principal of Skyline High School in Longmont (Colorado) temporarily banned the display of Mexican and U.S. flags by students. In Oceanside (California), following a walkout by 650 students over immigration legislation in Congress, the school superintendent barred middle- and high-school students from wearing "items that could be disruptive" and banned flags, placards, and signs (Kenworthy, 2006).

The issue of schools backing candidates for political office drew public attention in the Cherokee County (South Carolina) School District when the superintendent of schools stopped publication of Gaffney Middle School's student newspaper—*The Chief's Chronicle*—because it contained three political advertisements purchased by candidates for the upcoming school-board elections. In support of his ban, the superintendent cited a district policy stating that "schools will not display or distribute advertising materials of a commercial, political, or religious nature in the schools or on school grounds" (Student press, 2002).

However, it is also the case that schools sometimes do endorse displays intended to further a political agenda. An example is the mandated classroom exhibit of political documents ordered by the Kern County (California) High School District trustees. The documents included the motto "In God we trust" along with posters containing the U. S. Constitution, Declaration of Independence, and Bill of Rights. The posters would be placed in the district's 2,300 high-school classrooms and in boardrooms, libraries, and administrative offices. The project was first suggested by the president of the organization *In God We Trust—America Inc.*, who identified herself as a Republican and Christian but said her proposal was "not political. It's not religious. It's patriotism. American patriotism is love of God and love of country. It's pride in our country" (California school district, 2007).

SUGGESTIONS FOR SCHOOL PRACTICE

Two steps that school authorities can usefully take are those of (a) publicizing policies which govern displays that are banned and (b) anticipating future problems involving displays.

Student handbooks are convenient sites for information about ban policy. The policy statement can include a description of the sorts of displays prohibited, why such a ban is desirable, and the kinds of sanctions imposed on individuals who violate the ban. However, student handbooks now available rarely mention limitations on displays. Moreover, when they do address the issue of permissible displays, the statements are typically too brief to help readers judge exactly what sorts of material are forbidden. Such is true of the statement in the Omak High School (Washington) manual: "The high school principal (or designee) must approve all postings or displays on the high school campus." A similar brief mention of displays appears in the North High School (Waukesha, Wisconsin) student guidebook: "Any signs must be approved by the administration before being put in the hallways. Any sign or poster put up without permission will be removed. Signs may be placed only in approved areas."

A second step in coping with displays consists of officials anticipating potential future conditions that would warrant a new ban. For example, an apparent need for a new ban arose in the Mexican-versus-American-flags dispute and in the Jena T-shirt episode. Whereas the precise nature of such conditions may be difficult or impossible to predict, school authorities can at least prepare by outlining the elements of an explanation to be offered to students, parents, and the public press when the need arises for a new ban. For example, administrators can predict the general contents of a letter that will be sent to parents on such occasions. The letter can explain (a) what incidents have precipitated the need for a ban, (b) the exact kinds of displays that are prohibited, (c) the reasons that such a prohibition is desirable, (d) the legal foundation for the ban, (e) the kinds of sanctions to be applied to people who breach the ban, and (f) ways in which parents and students might constructively react to the ban, either in supporting it or in opposing it.

A Likely Future

As illustrated in chapters 1 through 15, schools may ban a host of things, including

- Books and other reading material
- Computers, Internet Web sites, computer games, and such electronic personal assistants as camera cell phones
- Movies, videos, television programs, pictures, and photographs
- Types of clothing
- Kinds of food and drink
- Bullying and harassment
- Musical selections
- Vandalism and graffiti
- Illicit drugs, harmful household inhalants, alcohol, and tobacco
- Weapons, explosives, pocket knives, fingernail files, and similar objects
- People who potentially pose a threat to the welfare of students, school personnel, and the learning program. Such people include

  troublesome intruders (child molesters, sex offenders, street-gang members, religious proselytizers, vendors), troublesome school staff members (thieves, sex offenders, religious zealots, incompetent workers), and

troublesome students (sex offenders, gang members, the chronically disrespectful, perpetually unproductive learners).

- Ceremonies and performances—religious, profane/vulgar, political, criminal, abusive
- Displays—religious, socially offensive, political

Schools ban things for a variety of reasons: (a) to avoid violating the U.S. Constitution's passage that prohibits the government from establishing a preferred religion and that protects freedom of speech and access to information, (b) to promote the teaching of values that influential individuals or groups cherish, (c) to protect students and school personnel from physical and psychological harm and from theft, (d) to shield the young from experiences that they are too immature to cope with constructively, (e) to foster the efficient operation of schools' learning programs, and (f) to preserve school equipment, buildings, and grounds.

The sorts of things that are forbidden, and the reasons they are prohibited, can differ from one era to another, as a result of changes in the kinds of people that make up the society and in the prevailing standards of acceptable behavior. Consequently, changes have appeared in reasons that books are banned, in the drugs and drinks prohibited, the kinds hazing outlawed, the types of vandalism condemned, the forms of speech censored, the varieties of music and dance proscribed, the weapons barred, and more.

So, against such a historical background, what might be expected in the future? That question is addressed in the following final pages.

SPECULATION ABOUT THE YEARS AHEAD

My estimate of what schools are likely to ban in the future is based on trends in recent years and on conditions that either accelerate or retard the pace of those trends. In the following discussion I propose six such conditions, and I estimate how they might influence the future of banning in schools. The conditions include (a) technological innovation, (b) office holders' religious convictions, (c) minorities' political skills, (d) social sensitivity, (e) shifting behavior standards, and (f) the state of the economy. I am not suggesting that these are the only conditions affecting trends. Rather, the six have been chosen merely to illustrate ways that various conditions might influence bans in years to come.

Technological Innovation

The most spectacular, widespread technological advance affecting both the general society and schools over the past three decades has been the development of electronic computers and their associated devices and facilities. Computers have hastened the world into what has been dubbed "the information age." A second innovation—television—has joined computers in reducing the popularity of books and other print media. Book sales, library patrons, and newspaper circulation declined as millions of people turned to the Internet and television as their primary sources of information and entertainment. I imagine that this trend will continue in the future at an accelerating pace and will significantly affect the nature of schools' bans.

I expect that socially conservative individuals will continue to urge the banning of books and periodicals in schools, but their activity will be dwarfed by people's concern about banning students' access to Internet Web sites and prohibiting students from the in-school use of such personal –digital assistants (PDAs) as camera cell phones and music players. As digital gadgets become more elaborate and miniaturized, banning rules are likely to become more complex. Furthermore, conflicts will likely increase about students' freedom of access to information in contrast to school officials' rights to control that access. And regulating students' digital devices will become more difficult, particularly in controlling students' use of the Internet outside of school hours, such as in cyber-bullying that involves malicious attacks on schoolmates and teachers.

Office Holders' Religious Convictions

From the 1960s into the early 1990s, a series of U.S. Supreme Court decisions eliminated—or at least reduced—the Christian religious practices that had been part of public schooling since colonial times. Those practices included school-sponsored prayer, Bible reading, religious lessons, Christmas celebrations, public funds paid to private religious schools, permanent religious displays (Ten Commandments, portrait of Jesus, Christian proverbs, crosses), and released time from school for religious instructions. But after the U.S. Congress passed the Equal Access Act (EAA) in 1984, the trend of legislation began to turn in favor of more religion in public schools. Over the 1985–2000 era, legislation banning religion in public schools overlapped legislation promoting religion in schools. Then the trend definitely shifted in favor of more religion in schools when President George W. Bush's administration took office in 2001. The principal force behind the change was the Religious Right, a coalition of evangelical Christian political groups that played a key role in President Bush's election and his subsequent policies. Republicans dominated both houses of Congress and held nearly all significant political offices in the federal administration. From the viewpoint of deciding what schools could ban and could not ban, the most powerful government division was the court system, and particularly federal courts, with the U.S. Supreme Court at the pinnacle of the system. By 2007, eight of the nine jurists on the Supreme Court were appointees of Republican presidents. The most recent pair of judges were chosen by President George W. Bush—Chief Justice John G. Roberts and Justice Samuel A. Alito, both Catholics, who advanced the Court's religious composition to 57 percent Catholic.

It is apparent that the Bush administration interpreted the Constitution's religious-establishment and religious-free-choice clauses to mean that the government can, indeed, promote religion in schools—and especially Christianity—by such means as (a) using public moneys for vouchers to pay children's fees in religious schools, (b) funding conservative Christian groups' "abstinence-only" sex education in public schools, and (c) President Bush's endorsing the teaching of biblical creationism in science classes.

In effect, as historical evidence clearly demonstrates, the religious convictions of people who hold public office can be powerful determinants of what religious beliefs and practices are banned in schools. This is true at all levels of the political-power hierarchy, ranging from the nation's presidency, federal administrative hierarchy (such as the U.S. Office of Education), Congress, and the court system down to state governors' offices, state legislatures, state and local courts, county commissioners, city mayors, and school boards.

So what do such recent trends foretell for future school bans? The answer depends on whom the voters choose to put in office in the years ahead. If Republicans dominate, the role of religion in schools is likely to increase. If Democrats dominate, existing bans on religion in schools are apt to remain in effect, and funds for such federal programs as abstinence-only sex education and vouchers for children to attend religious schools will be eliminated.

Minorities' Political Skills

As America's ethnic minorities have rapidly increased in size and diversity over the past half-century, the monopoly previously held by white, European-heritage Americans in determining the conduct of schooling has increasingly been challenged. A growing array of organizations representing ethnic interests has spread across the nation, with those groups increasingly led by politically astute leaders who press their demands on politicians and on the general public through legislative lobbyists, election campaigns, rallies, and news media—television, radio, newspapers, and Internet blogs.

During the closing decades of the twentieth century and into the twenty-first century, the efforts of those organizations have contributed to schools' paying greater attention to the needs of socially disadvantaged minority students, especially blacks, Hispanics, American Indians, Southeast Asians, and non-English-speaking immigrants. That attention has contributed to bans on speech that denigrates ethnic groups, on bullying members of such groups, and on traditions—such as school clubs' unwritten rules—that deny opportunities to minority students. I believe that such bans will increase in the future.

Social Sensitivity

The ban on behaviors that impair minority students' chance to succeed in school is part of a more general social-sensitivity trend affecting schools' treatment of students who are different in some significant way from the traditionally favored majority. By *significant* I mean in terms of physical skills, gender, or sex-role preference. Thus, until recent times, rarely did schools provide accommodations for physically handicapped students, such as ramps (in lieu of stairs) and easy-to-reach drinking fountains. Boys' athletics were traditionally supported by far greater funds than were girls' sports, and homosexual students were not allowed to form school clubs. Those past practices functioned as unwritten bans imposed by custom. Hence, the spread of social sensitivity resulted in the lifting of such informal bans, with that trend likely to continue in the future. Or, when the trend is cast in its reverse form, it becomes "Banning unequal treatment of social groups will probably accelerate in the years ahead."

Shifting Behavior Standards

The 1960s marked a loosening of traditional restrictions on people's sexual behavior and on their use of such mind-altering substances as marijuana and LSD (lysergic acid diethylamide). The change was part of a broader resistance-to-authority movement by a host of teenagers and young adults who objected to the Vietnam war, to the military draft, to the banning of premarital sex, to rules and laws set by the middle-aged and the elderly, to the ill-treatment of minorities, and more. The slogan "Make love, not war" became a watchword along with "If it feels good, do it."

Some elements of the 1960s' "hippy movement" lost their appeal and dissipated—or at least declined—over subsequent decades (such as the acceptability of using illicit drugs), but relaxed sexual standards would continue in the form of more unmarried couples living together, more sexually provocative movies on television, more people openly living as homosexuals, and modes of dress that expose more of the body. The uncensored Internet has contributed to this trend by giving people access to sexual material that would, by nearly anyone's standard, qualify as pornography.

These changes have confronted school personnel with problems of deciding what kinds of sex-related behavior should be permitted in schools. In effect, what forms of dancing should be banned? What Internet Web sites should be blocked? What styles clothing should be outlawed? What sexually provocative books, photos, videos, songs, and speech should be prohibited?

I expect that these problems will not only continue into the future, but they will become even more challenging than in the past as technological innovations expand youths' access to sexually stimulating stimuli and as parents' control over children's and adolescents' behavior continues to diminish, especially when both parents work outside the home, the high divorce rate continues to climb, and one-parent families increase.

State of the Economy

Economic conditions can affect bans by influencing how effectively the schools can implement bans. For example, successfully applying bans on weapons, vandalism, and illicit drugs can be expensive, especially in communities with high crime rates. During good economic times, schools can more readily afford the security devices that increase the safety of students, staff, and property—such devices as metal detectors, surveillance cameras, security guards, alarm systems, special door locks, night lights, break-resistant windows, and drug-testing procedures. Schools located in depressed economies cannot afford these "luxuries." It is also the case that schools with high teacher/student ratios because of inadequate financial support suffer more problems of implementing bans than do schools with low teacher/student ratios. Thus, an instructor in charge of a class of forty-five students faces a greater challenge in monitoring students' speech, vandalism, bullying, cell phones, and drug use than does an instructor with a class of twenty-five.

Hence, it seems apparent that economic conditions will continue to influence how effectively schools apply bans, with implementation easier in healthy economies than in ailing ones.

References

89 Grams of Crack Cocaine Found at Elementary School. (2007, April 18). *The News Press.* http://tallahassee.com/legacy/special/blogs/2007/04/89-grams-of-crack-cocaine-found-at.html.

About Speech Codes. (2007). *Spotlight.* www.thefire.org/index.php/article/5822.html?PHPSESSID=.

Acton-Boxborough Regional High School. (2007). *Student Handbook.* www.ab.mec.edu/abrhs/pdffiles/handbook.pdf.

Actual Hazing Cases. (2005). *Respect the Game—RTG.* http://www.ohsaa.org/RTG/Resources/hazing/Cases.htm.

Addiction Health Services. (2007, February 28). What Is the Worst Illegal Drug to Take? *AHS Views.* http://www.addictionhelpservices.com/blog/2007/02/what-is-worst-illegal-drug-to-take.html.

Alward, M. M. (2001, January 13). Banned Books: Should Huckleberry Finn be Banned? *Suite 101.* http://www.suite101.com/article.cfm/canadian_tourism/49239.

American Academy of Pediatrics. (2004, January 1). Soft drinks in Schools. *Pediatrics,* 113 (1), 152–154. http://aappolicy.aappublications.org/cgi/content/full/pediatrics;113/1/152.

American Library Association. (2007). *The 1000 Most Frequently Challenged Books of 1990–2000.* http://www.ala.org/ala/oif/bannedbooksweek/bbwlinks/100most frequent ly.htm.

Andersen, A. A. (2005, March 21). Benchmarking School Security of the District of Columbia Public Schools. *DCWatch.* http://www.dcwatch.com/govern/ig050321.htm.

Anderson, J. (2006, August 25). Portland Schools Junk the Junk Food. *Portland Tribune.* http://www.portlandtribune.com/news/story.php?story_id=1156474468 68597100.

Anderson, J. D. (2006, April 21). ACLU Enters Jesus Picture Dispute. *Wren's Nest News.* http://www.witchvox.com/wren/wn_detaila.html?id=15354.

Andreatta, D. (2007, Mary 24). Google Expels Cheat Sites. *New York Post.* http://www.nypost.com/seven/05242007/news/nationalnews/google_expels_cheat_sites_nationalnews_david_andreatta.htm.

Anti-Defamation League. (2004a). *Prayer in Public School.* http://www.adl.org/religion_ps_2004/prayer.asp.

Anti-Defamation League. (2004b). *The December Dilemma—December Holiday Guidelines for Public Schools.* http://www.adl.org/issue_education/december_dilemma_2004/default.asp.

Appropriate Attire Policy. (2006). *Redwood Middle School.* http://www.rm.nvusd.k12.ca.us/Dress_code/Dress_code_2006-07.htm.

Arizona School Suspends Boy for Sketching Gun. (2007, August 22). *USA Today.* http://www.usatoday.com/news/nation/2007-08-22-ariz-suspension_N.htm.

Austin, D. (2007, July 11). Vernonia Principal in Hot Water Over Pot. *Oregonian.* http://www.oregonlive.com/news/oregonian/index.ssf?/base/news/1184126109316030.xml&coll=7.

Bags of Cocaine Brought to Class by Second-Grader. (2006, February 28). *NBC-10.* http://www.nbc10.com/news/7550102/detail.html.

Bahrampour, T. & Shapira, I. (2005, November 6). Sex at School Increasing, Some Educators Say. *Washington Post,* p. C01.

Ban on 'The Passion of the Christ' Continues as New Double Standards Are Revealed. (2005, January 19). *FIRE Press Release.* http://www.thefire.org/index.php/article/5128.html?PHPSESSID=.

Ban the Christmas Music, Ban the Christian Band. (2004, December 21). *Zerointelligence.* http://www.zerointelligence.net/archives/000491.php.

Barbarian. (2006, September 27). Debunking the MySpace Myth of 100 Million Users. *Forevergeek.* http://forevergeek.com/articles/debunking_the_myspace_myth_of_100_million_users.php.

Barge, C., & Moreno, I. (2007, December 7). Third Teacher Sex Scandal Rocks Brighton Charter School. *Rocky Mountain News.* http://www.rockymountainnews.com/news/2007/dec/07/brighton-schoolteacher-arrested-sex-assault/.

Barnard, N. (1993, July 27). *Witness Statement.* http://www.mcspotlight.org/people/witnesses/nutrition/barnard_neal.html.

Barnes, R. (2007, March 20). Justices Consider Rights Issue. *Washington Post,* p. A03. http://www.washingtonpost.com/wpdyn/content/article/2007/03/19/AR2007031901648_2.html.

Beckwith, M. (2007, September 25). Ruling Backs High School's Decision to Bar Band from Playing 'Ave Maria.' *Student Press Law Center.* http://www.splc.org/newsflash. asp?id=1613.

Beito, D.T., Luker, R.E., & Johnson, R.D. (2005, May). Consulting All Sides on "Speech Codes." *Organization of American Historians.* http://www.oah.org/pubs/nl/2005may/beito.html.

Belden, D. (2007, July 12). Burnett County, Wis. / Ex-St. Paul Teacher Gets Six Months for Porn. *Pioneer Press.* http://www.twincities.com/wisconsin/ci_6353263.

Belgrade School Board to Allow Convicted Sex Offender to Get GED. (2007, November 11). *KBZK.* http://www.montanasnewsstation.com/global/story.asp?s=7276796.

Bell, A. (2006, January 4). New Jersey Tests High School Athletes for Steroids. *PBS News Hour*. http://www.pbs.org/newshour/extra/features/jan-june06/steroids_1-04.html.

Bertin, J.E. (2002, July 26). *NCAC Letter to the Cromwell Board of Education About the Removal of 2 Books*. http://www.ncac.org/literature/20020726~CT-Cromwell~Cromwell_CT_BOE_Considers_Removing_2_Books_from_Middle_School.cfm.

Better Safe Than Sorry? School Weapons Policies. (2001, March 23). *BNET Research Center*. http://findarticles.com/p/articles/mi_m0EPF/is_22_100/ai_72607596.

Bickford, J. (2002). Turning Adversity into Opportunity. *American Dreams*. http://www.usdreams.com/Alger12.html.

Black, H. (1969, February 14). Dissenting Opinion. *Tinker et al. v. Des Moines Independent Community School District et al.* http://www.law.cornell.edu/supct/html/historics/USSC_CR_0393_0503_ZD.html.

Bloom, A., (2003, August 12). High School Hazing. *Teen Wire*. http://www.teenwire.com/infocus/2003/if-20030812p247-hazing.php.

Bomb-Making Manuals: Explosive Content. (2007). *Anti-Defamation League*. http://www.adl.org/poisoning_web/bomb_making.asp.

Bomb Survey. (2000). *Jefferson County Sheriff's Department*. http://www.cnn.com/SPECIALS/2000/Columbine.cd/Pag es/BOMBS_TEXT.htm.

Bombs and School Security. (2005). http://www.schoolsecurity.org/trends/school-bombs.html.

Bonisteel, S. (2007, November 8). Students Feel the Squeeze as Schools Ban Hugs. *Fox News*. http://www.foxnews.com/story/0,2933,309296,00.html.

Brennan, W. (1982, June 25). *Board of Education v. Pico*. http://caselaw.lp.findlaw.com/scripts/getcase.pl?court=US&vol=457&invol=853.

Breslow, M. (2007, August 31). Judge Shocked by Teacher's Stash of Porn. *Hartford Courant*. http://www.courant.com/news/education/hc-sa-held2aug31,0,6239823.story.

Brorby, W. (1997). *Bauchman v. West High School*. http://caselaw.lp.findlaw.com/scripts/getcase.pl?court=10th&navby=case&no=954084.

Brown, M.D. (2005, May 3). National Arson Awareness Week Begins. *U.S. Department of Homeland Security*. http://firechief.com/awareness/arson-awareness-week050205/.

Bruinius, H. (2007, June 12). Canceled School Play about Iraq Brings Out Real Drama. *Christian Science Monitor*. http://www.csmonitor.com/2007/0612/p20s01-woam.html.

Bryson, K.L. (2007). *Bridge to Terabithia Rationale*. http://www.ncte.org/about/issues/censorship/resources/113744.htm (retrieved October 20, 2007).

Buchanan, W. (2004, December 17). Teacher Is Arrested in Child Porn Probe. *San Francisco Chronicle*. http://www.sfgate.com/cgi-bin/article.cgi?f=/c/a/2004/12/17/BAGA6ACKUJ1.DTL&hw=Buchanan+teacher+porn&sn=001&sc=1000.

Bullying: What Is Bullying? (2005). *About*. http://homeworktips.about.com/library/weekly/aa011999.htm.

Bullying Officially Illegal Under Schools Act. (2007, June 4). *Toronto Star*. http://www.thestar.com/article/221375.

Bulwa, D. & Egelko, B. (2007, March 21). Fighting for the Right to Wear Tigger. *San Francisco Chronicle*. http://www.sfgate.com/cgi-bin/article.cgi?file=/c/a/2007/03/21/MNGRUOOVAD1.DTL.

Burger, C.J. (1973, June 21). *Miller v. California*. http://caselaw.lp.findlaw.com/scripts/getcase.pl?court=us&vol=413&invol=15.

Cain, B. (2005, May 7). Soda Pop Industry Helps Kill Oregon Junk-Food-Ban Bill. *Seattlepi.com*. http://seattlepi.nwsource.com/local/223382_junkfood07ww.html.

California Education Code. (2007). *Section 48907*. Sacramento, CA: State of California.

California School District Approves 'In God We Trust' Classroom Displays. (2007, November 6). *Fox News*. http://www.foxnews.com/story/0,2933,308405,00.html.

Carr, C. (2004, June 23). Valley Center: A Stunned Community Reacts to School Vandalism. *North County Times*. http://www.nctimes.com/articles/2004/06/24/news/columnists/carr/22_14_306_23_04.txt.

Carter, S. (2003, November 7). School Officials Use Tools to Halt Violence, Threats. *Oregonian*. http://www.oregonlive.com/news/oregonian/index.ssf?/base/news/1068124 14083310.xml.

Casino, C. (2007, May 8). Ban or Censor Words in Rap and Hip Hop? *Mefeedia*. http://mefeedia.com/entry/2538127/.

Cassidy, P. (2007, May 24). Graffiti Leads to Backpack Ban at Barnstable High School. *Cape Cod Times*. http://www.capecodonline.com/apps/pbcs.dll/article?AID=/20070524/NEWS11/70524003.

Catholic League. (2007, October 3). *The December Celebration*. http://www.catholicleague.org/rer.php?topic=Church+and+State&id=78.

Cauchon, D. (1999, April 13). Zero-Tolerance Policies Lack Flexibility. *USA Today*. http://www.usatoday.com/educate/ednews3.htm.

Cauvin, H.E. & Haynes, V.D. (2005, March 1). Second Teen Charged in Spreading Mercury. *Washington Post*. http://www.washingtonpost.com/wp-dyn/articles/A61802-2005Feb28.html.

Cavanagh, S. (2005, December 20). U.S. Judge Rules Intelligent Design Has No Place in Science Classrooms. *Education Week*. http://www.edweek.org/ew/articles/2005/12/20/16dover_web.h25.html.

Cavoukian, A. (2003, December 16). Strict Controls Needed if Video Surveillance Used in Schools. *Information and Privacy Commission*. http://www.ipc.on.ca/scripts/index.asp?action=31&P_ID=14823 &N_ID=1&PT_ID=13169&U_ID=0.

Center for Safe and Responsible Internet Use. (2005). *Mobilizing Educators, Parents, Students, and Others to Combat Online Social Cruelty*. http://www.cyberbully.org/.

Center on Alcohol Marketing and Youth. (2007, April). *Alcohol Advertising and Youth*. http://camy.org/factsheets/index.php?FactsheetID=1.

Centers for Disease Control. (1991, November 15). Alcohol and Other Drug Use Among High School Students. *MMWR—Morbidity and Mortality Weekly Report*. http://www.cdc.gov/mmwr/preview/mmwrhtml/00015573.htm.

Centers for Disease Control. (2006, July 7). Cigarette Use Among High School Students—United States, 1991–2005. http://www.cdc.gov/MMWR/preview/mmwrhtml/mm5526a2.htm.

Champaco, B. (2007, December 8). Sex Offenders in School: What Are the Rules? *News Tribune*. http://www.thenewstribune.com/news/local/story/223929.html.

Chapman, S. (2007, June 11). Forrester: Worldwide PC Numbers to Hit 1Bn Next Year. *Computer World UK*. http://www.computerworlduk.com/technology/hardware/processors/news/index.cfm?newsid=3409.

Charter School Chief Charged with Theft. (2007, September 5). *San Diego Union-Tribune.* http://www.signonsandiego.com/uniontrib/20070905/news_1n5region.html.

Chavez, S.M. (2007, October 19). Schools Take Hard Line Against Public Displays of Affection. *Dallas Morning News.* http://www.dallasnews.com/sharedcontent/dws/dn/latestnews/stories/101907dnmetsexharass.516c6.html.

Cheerleaders Disciplined for Putting Feces on Pizza. (2005, June 16). *Houston Chronicle.* http://www.chron.com/cs/CDA/ssistory.mpl/metropolitan/3227978.

Chellappa, V. (2004, February 19). Sherwood High School Vandalized. *Silver Chips.* http://silverchips.mbhs.edu/inside.php?sid=2990.

Childhood Obesity—Do You Have an Overweight Child? (2007). *My Overweight Child.* http://www.myoverweightchild.com/?gclid=COH21O314Y4CFQe1YAodzV1CUQ (retrieved September 27, 2007).

Child Pornography. (2005). *Wikipedia.* http://en.wikipedia.org/ wiki/Child_pornography.

Chocolate War. (2007). *Spark Notes.* http://www.sparknotes.com/lit/chocolatewar/.

Chocolate War Author Battles Effort to Ban Book. (2000, June 14). *Freedom Forum.* http://www.freedomforum.org/templates/document.asp?documentID=12693.

Citizens for Literary Standards in Schools. (2007). *I Know Why the Caged Bird Sings.* http://www.abffe.com/bbw-classkc-angelou.htm(retrieved August 17, 2007).

Clinton Announces New Tools to Crack Down on Internet Gun Criminals and Reduce Gun Violence. (2000, October 3). *White House.* http://clinton4.nara.gov/WH/new/html/ Tue_Oct_3_123009_2000.html.

Cocaine Use Related to Level of Education Achieved. (2007, August 29). *Public Health News Center.* http://www.jhsph.edu/publichealthnews/press_releases/2007/harder_cocaine.html.

Coen, J. (2007, November 16). 'Silence' on Hold for Now. *Chicago Tibune.* http://www.chicagotribune.com/news/local/northwest/chisilence_16nov16,0,4578697.story.

Cohen, C. (2006, July 9). "Ave Maria" Controversy. *Seattle Times.* http://seattletimes.nwsource.com/html/opinion/2003116424_webmonletsio.html?syndication=rss.

Colgate, B. (2003, August). *Sports Medicine: High School Drug-Testing Programs.* http://www.nfhs.org/web/2003/11/sports_medicine_high_school_drugtesting_programs_august_2003.aspx.

Colo. Prep Yearbook Shows Alcohol, Pot. (2007, May 29). *Boston Globe.* http://www.boston.com/news/education/k_12/articles/2007/05/29/colo_prep_yearbook_shows_alcohol_pot/.

Columbine High School Massacre. (2005). *Wikipedia.* http://en.wikipedia.org/wiki/Columbine_High_School_massacre.

Constitutional Rights Foundation. (2005). *The Challenge of School Violence.* http://www.crf-usa.org/violence/school.html.

Controversy at Cherry Hill. (2007). *PBS—Culture Shock.* http://www.pbs.org/wgbh/cultureshock/teachers/huck/controversy.html.

Corcoran, K. (2005, September 22). Fired Teacher Gets 1 Year in Sex Case. *Indianapolis Star.* http://www.indystar.com/apps/pbcs.dll/article?AID=/20050922/NEWS01/509220438.

Cortenbach, K.E. (2007). *A High School's Unofficial Social Structure.* Personal Communication.

Court Rejects 'Intelligent Design' in Science Class. (2005, December 20). *CNN.* http://www.cnn.com/2005/LAW/12/20/intelligent.design.ap/index.html.

Cox, A. (2005, August 31). Custom-Made Fit for School. *CNN.* http://www.cnn.com/2005/US/08/12/style.rules/.

Crane, J.P. (2005, June 30). Internet Bullying Hits Home for Teen. *Boston Globe.* http://www.boston.com/news/education/k12/articles/2005/06/30/internet_bullying_hits_home_for_teen/?page=2.

Currie, C.M. (1999, July 16). Unlocked Doors Lead to School Vandalism. *Craig Daily Press.* http://www.craigdailypress.com/extra/archives/0712arc/no716.html.

Dean, M. M. (2005, December 14). 4th-Grader Is Arrested for Trying to Poison Her Teacher. *Philadelphia Daily News.* http://www.philly.com/mld/dailynews/13402699.htm.

Definition of Hacking. (2007). DocDoppers. http://www.docdroppers.org/wiki/index.php?title=Definition_of_hacking.

Definitions of Hazing. (2007). *Student Handbook, Edina Senior High School.* www.edina.k12.mn.us/edinahigh/students/handbook.htm.

Delgado, R. (2003, January 15). S.F. Schools Join War on Obesity, Ban Junk Food. *San Francisco Chronicle.* http://www.sfgate.com/cgi-bin/article.cgi?file=/chronicle/archive/2003/01/15/BA220952.DTL.

de Vise, D. (2007, July 13). Montgomery Finds Racial Slur Offends, No Matter the Context. *Washington Post.* http://www.washingtonpost.com/wp-dyn/content/article/2007/07/12/AR2007071202370.html.

Dickens Classic Too Religious for School. (2004, December 9). *WorldNetDaily.* http://www.worldnetdaily.com/news/article.asp?ARTICLE_ID=41826.

Dirk, T. (2007). Sex in Cinema: The Greatest and Most Influential Erotic/Sexual Films and Scenes. http://www.filmsite.org/sexinfilms.html.

Dotinga, R. (2007, July 12). Public Schools Grapple With Muslim Prayer. *Christian Science Monitor.* http://www.csmonitor.com/2007/0712/p01s03-ussc.html.

Douglas, J. (2005, February 14). Sword-Wielding Student Cuts Classmate. *WFAA-TV.* http://www.wfaa.com/sharedcontent/dws/wfaa/jdouglas/stories/wfaa050214_wz_lamarsword.a991d738.html.

Eagan, M. & Gonzalez, R. (2005, Mary 19). Attack on Coach Resonates. *Hartford Courant.* http://www.courant.com/news/local/hc-coachattack0519.artmay19,0,6741239.story?coll=hc-headlines-local.

East Central High School. (2007). *Student Handbook.* http://www.east-central.k12.ia.us/vnews/display.v/ART/46ddbdd836870.

Edina Public Schools. (2007). *Rights and Responsibilities for Student Management.* http://www.edina.k12.mn.us/parents/rights.htm.

Edwards, B. (2006, June 5). School Play Causes 'First Amendment' Issues. *WOOD-TV Broadcasting.* http://www.jewsonfirst.org/06b/public093.html.

Ellickson, P. (1998). Teenage Alcohol Misuse. *Rand Health.* http://www.rand.org/pubs/research briefs/RB6004-1/index1.html.

Eriksen, H. (2007, July 11). Katy ISD Rethinks Girl's Graffiti Punishment. *Houston Chronicle.* http://www.chron.com/disp/story.mpl/front/4958410.html.

ESRB. (2007). *Game Ratings and Desciptor Guide.* http://www.esrb.org/ratings/ratings_guide.jsp (retrieved November 29, 1007).

Evans, M. (2007, September 17). Crackdown! *MSNBC.* http://www.msnbc.msn.com/id/20817735/.

Ex-D.C. Charter School Executive Sentenced for Theft, Tax Evasion. (2007, December 5). *Education Week*, 27 (14), 3.

Facts About Bullying. (2007). *Safer Schools News* (Vol. 22). http://www.keystosaferschools.com/Newsletter_Vol.22.htm (retrieved November 2, 2007).

Farrell, N. (2002, June 7). High School Hackers Make the Grade. *VNU Net*. http://www.vnunet.com/vnunet/news/2119010/school-hackers-grade.

Farris, J. (2005, February 8). *Blau v. Fort Thomas Public School District*. http://caselaw.lp.findlaw.com/data2/circs/6th/036337p.pdf.

Fast Food Nutrition Links. (2007). *About.com*. http://southernfood.about.com/library/weekly/aa081402a.htm.

Fat Calories. (2007). *Fast Food Nutrition Fact Explorer*. http://www.fatcalories.com/.

Fielder, D. (2007, September 20). Student Arrested After Mushrooms Found in Car. *Dallas Morning News*. http://www.dallasnews.com/sharedcontent/dws/dn/latestnews/stories/092007dnmetmushrooms.foeacb07.html.

Fischer, H. (2007, May 25). Horne Pressuring Districts to Ban High School Junk Food. *Arizona Daily Star*. http://www.azstarnet.com/metro/184670.

Fleming, B. (2005, April 19). Bat Boy Banned Again? *Brian Fleming's Weblog*. http://www.slumdance.com/blogs/brian_flemming/archives/001571.html.

Fletcher, B.B. (1994, October 4). *Peloza v. Capistrano Unified School District*. http://www.talkorigins.org/faqs/peloza.html.

Fong, T. (2007, May 30). 4 Evergreen Students OD on Sleeping Pills. *Rocky Mountain News*. http://www.rockymountainnews.com/drmn/local/article/0,1299,DRMN_15_5561464,00.html.

Former KC Teacher Indicted in Child Porn Case. (2007, March 29). *Kansas City Star*. http://www.kansascity.com/115/story/128215.html.

Fortas, A. (1969, February 24). *Tinker et al. v. Des Moines Independent Community School District et al.* http://www.bc.edu/bc_org/avp/cas/comm/free_speech/tinker.html.

Four Juveniles Accused of Damaging School Portable. *St. Petersburg Times*. http://www.sptimes.com/2004/07/25/Southpinellas/Four_juveniles_accuse.shtml.

Freeh, L.J. (2005). *A Parent's Guide to Internet Safety*. Washington, DC: Federal Bureau of Investigation. http://www.fbi.gov/publications/pguide/pguidee.htm.

Gallessich, G. (2006, February 24). UCSB Develops Portable Cocaine Sensor; High School Students, Nobel Laureate Contributed. *UC Newsroom*. http://www.universityofcalifornia.edu/news/article/7901.

Gang Activity. (2005). *Pawnee School—Student Handbook*. http://www.pawneeschool.com/handbook/gang_activity.

Gara, R. (2005, August). Students Increasingly Exposed to Drugs at School. *Daily News Central*. http://health.dailynewscentral.com/content/view/1536/0.

Gavin, M.L. (2005, August). Overweight and Obesity. *Kids Health*. http://www.kidshealth.org/parent/general/body/overweight_obesity.html.

Geiger, C. (2006, July 9). "Ave Maria" Controversy. *Seattle Times*. http://seattletimes.nwsource.com/html/opinion/2003116424_webmonlets10.html?syndication=rss.

Gilbert, A. & Olsen, S. (2006, January 24). Do Web Filters Protect Your Child? *CNET News.com*. http://news.com.com/Do+Web+filters+protect+your+child/2100-1032_3-6030200.html.

Gilbert, H. (2005, October 14). Teacher Takes Plea in Child Abuse Case. *Oregonian*. http://www.oregonlive.com/metronorth/oregnian/index.ssf?/.

Girls Suspended Over 'Vagina Monologues.' (2007, March 6). *CTV.* http://www. ctv.ca/servlet/ArticleNews/story/CTVNews/20070306/monologues_070306/20.

Girls Trash Kansas School Art Room. (2005, November 22). *Raleigh News & Observer.* http://dwb.newsobserver.com/24hour/weird/story/2924139p-11590587c.html.

Glaucoma Foundation. (2007). *Medical Marijuana.* http://www.glaucoma.org/ treating/medical_marijua.php (retrieved November 19, 2007).

Grant, D.G. (2004, August 4). Police Arrest 4 in School Vandalism. *Detroit News.* http://www.detnews.com/2004/schools/0408/06/b08d-231904.htm.

Green, M.W. (1999, September). *The Appropriate and Effective Use of Security Technologies in Schools.* Washington, DC: National Institute of Justice Research. http://www.ncjrs.org/school/home.html.

Greenhouse, L. (2006, April 25). Justices Decline Church-State Case Involving a Kindergarten Poster of Jesus. *New York Times.* http://www.nytimes.com/2006/ 04/25/washington/25.

Grogan, D. (2002, July 29). Connecticut Residents Seek to Ban Two Newbury Medal Winners From School. *Bookselling this week.* http://news.bookweb.org/ freeexpression/ 677.html.

Grossman, K.N. (2004, January 9). Schools Pressured to Dump Bad Students, Critics Say. *Chicago Sun-Times.* http://www.suntimes.com/output/education/cst-news-drop09.html.

Guadagni, R.A. (2007, July 2). *Scott v. Napa Valley Unified School District* (case 26-37082, Superior Court for the State of California, County of Napa).

Halloween Banned at Brooklyn High School, Hitler to Blame. (2007, October 8). *Digital Journal.* http://www.digitaljournal.com/article/238306/Halloween_ Banned_at_Brooklyn_High_School_Hitler_to_blame.

Halls, K.M. (2005). *Crutcher and Banned Book Week 2005.* http://www. chriscrutcher.com/content/blogcategory/4/3/.

Hallucinogens. (2007, March 2). *Drug Facts.* http://www.whitehousedrugpolicy. gov/drugfact/hallucinogens/index.html.

Harden, B. (2007, January 25). Gore Film Sparks Parents' Anger. *Washington Post.* http://www.washingtonpost.com/wp-dyn/content/article/2007/01/25/ AR2007012501387_2.html.

Harris, R. (2004, November 17). Anti-Plagiarism Strategies for Research Papers. *Virtual Salt.* http://www.virtualsalt.com/antiplag.htm.

Harry Potter Can Stay in School, Georgia Judge Rules. (2007, May 29). *Minnesota Star Tribune.* http://www.startribune.com/484/ story/1212 614.html.

Hartsock, T. (2006, July 9). "Ave Maria" Controversy. *Seattle Times.* http://seattle times.nwsource.com/html/opinion/2003116424_webmonlets10.html? syndication=rss.

Hatcher, C.G. (2001). *So You Wanna be a Hacker?* http://www.safetyed.org/help/ hacker.html.

Hate Speech. (2007, September). *Wikipedia.* http://en.wikipedia.org/wiki/Hate_ speech.

Haynes, C.C. (2003, November 16). December Dilemma: What Should Schools do About Christmas? *First Amendment Center.* http://www.firstamendmentcenter. org/commentary.aspx?id=12217.

Heaney, R. (1980, April 22). *Florey v. Sioux Falls School District.* http://www. belcherfoundation.org/florey_v_sioux_falls_ scho ol_district.htm.

Heins, M. (2003, June 24). Ignoring the Irrationality of Internet Filters, the Supreme Court Upholds CIPA. *Free Expression Policy Project.* http://www fepproject.org/commentaries/cipa decision.html.

Hernandez, C. (2007, August 16). Study Finds Millions of Students Attend 'Drug-Infested' Schools. *Detroit News.* http://www.detnews.com/apps/pbcs.dll/article? AID=/20070816/SCHOOLS/708160422/1026.

Honawar, V. (2007, November 7). Cellphones in Classrooms Land Teacher on Online Video Sites. *Education Week,* 27 (10), 1, 12.

Hoover, N.C. & Pollard, N.J. (2000, August). *High School Hazing.* Alfred, NY: Alfred University. http://www.alfred.edu/hshazing/executive_summary.html.

Howell, J.C. & Lynch, J.P. (2000). *Youth Gangs in Schools.* Washington, DC: Office of Juvenile Justice and Delinquency Prevention. http://www/neijrs.org/htmlojjdp/ jjbul200082/contents.html.

Howell Students Protest Classmates' Suspensions. (2005, May 11). *Detroit News.* http:// hosted.ap.org/dynamic/stories/M/MI_PAINTED_PHRASEPROTEST_MIOL? SITE=MIDTN&SECTION=HOME&TEMPLATE=DEFAULT.

Huck Finn—Teachers Guide. (2007). *PBS—Culture Shock.* http://www.pbs.org/ wgbh/cultureshock/teachers/huck/aboutbook.html.

Hui, T.K. (2005, September 14). Five charged in Wake schools fraud case. *Raleigh News & Observer.* http://www.nswsobserver.com/news/crime_safety/wakefraud/story/ 2794916p-9235803c.html.

Hume, E. (2005, September 27). Racist Graffiti Found in Franklin High Restroom. *Sacramento Bee.* http://www.sacbee.com.content/news/story/13631858p-14474248c.html.

I Know Why the Caged Bird Sings. (2007). *Spark Notes.* http://www.sparknotes. com/lit/cagedbird/.

Internet Boosts Sale of Illegal Drugs, Study Shows. (2007). *About.* http://alcoholism. about.com/cs/coke/a/blduke030822.htm.

Internet Filter Report. (2007). *Internet Filter Review.* http://internet-filter-review. toptenreviews.com/?ttreng=1&ttrkey=internet+filter&gclid=CLOsqbXKk40CF QEyYQodZy7pkA.

Isaacson, L.A. (1998, January). Student Dress Codes. *ERIC Digest.* http://eric. uoregon.edu/publications/digests/digest117. html.

Is There a Potential Criminal Case Here? (2007). *Answers.* http://answers.yahoo.com/ question/index?qid=20071008121120AAkNBC0 (retrieved November 6, 2007).

Jacks, S. (2007, June 20). New School Junk Food Bill Signed. *KGW.* http://www. kgw.com/education/localeducation/stories/kgw_062007_news_junk_food.216f aee4.html.

Jacksonville Police Suspend Taser Use. (2005, February 24). *St. Petersburg Times.* http:// www.sptimes.com/2005/02/24/State/Jacksonville_police_s.shtml.

Jacques, S. (2005, June 9). Student Must Pay $5K for School Vandalism. *Portsmouth Herald.* http://www.seacoast.com/news/06092005/news/46623.htm.

James, A. (2007, March 20). Teachers Stew Over Movie Ban in Schools. *Times Herald-Record.* http://recordonline.com/apps/pbcs.dll/article?AID=/20070320/NEWS/ 703200318.

Johnson, K.D. (2005, August). *School Vandalism and Break-ins.* http://www.cops. usdoj.gov/files/ric/Publications/SchoolVandalismBreakIns.pdf.

Johnston, L.D., O'Malley, P.M., Bachman, J.G., & Schulenberg, J.E. (2006, December 21). *Teen Drug Use Continues Down in 2006, Particularly Among Older Teens; but Use of Prescription-Type Drugs Remains High.* University of Michigan News and Information Services: Ann Arbor, MI. http://www.monitoringthefuture.org.

Jones, A. (2007, July 19). Study: Anti-Smoking Ads Have Opposite Effect on Teens. *Atlanta Journal-Constitution.* http://www.ajc.com/metro/content/news/stories/2007/07/19/smoking_0720.html.

Junk Food Ban? (2007, April 27). *Science Daily.* http://www.sciencedaily.com/ releases/2007/04/070426222511.htm.

Justus, M. (2005, November 17). "Bat Boy: the Musical—Presented by the HLS Drama Society. *The Record.* http://media.www.hlrecord.org/media/storage/paper609/news/2005/11/17/Opinion/bat-Boy.The.Musical.Presented.By.The.Hls.Drama. Society-1109992.shtml.

Kanfer, S. (2000). Horatio Alger: The Moral of the Story. *City.* http://www.city-journal.org/html/104urbanities-thmoral.html.

Karl & Associates. (2005). *Youth Related Computer Crime.* http://www.karisable. com/crpcyouth.htm.

Kelley, T. (2006, December 18). Talk in Class Turns to God, Setting Off Public Debate on Rights. *New York Times.* http://www.nytimes.com/2006/12/18/nyregion/18kearny.html?_r=2&oref=slogin&pagewanted=all&oref=slogin.

Kennedy, R. (2007). Hazing—What Three Private School Students Experienced. *Private Schools.* http://privateschool.about.com/cs/students/a/hazing1_2.htm (retrieved November 1, 2007).

Kenworthy, T. (2006, April 6). Schools Ban Flags as Immigration Debate Gets Tense. *USA Today.* http://www.usatoday.com/news/nation/2006-04-06-immigration-flags_x.htm.

Knich, D. (2005, October 15). County to Hold Parents Responsible for School Vandalism. *The Island Packet.* http://wwwislandpacket.com/news/local/story/5256408p-4771601c.html.

Koch, W. (2005, November 30). More Women Charged in Sex Cases. *USA Today.* http://www.usatoday.com/printedition/news/20051130/a_femalesexcrimes30.art.htm.

Koppel, N. (2007, August 30). Are Your Jeans Sagging? Go Directly to Jail. *New York Times.* http://www.nytimes.com/2007/08/30/fashion/30baggy.html?_r=1&oref=slogin.

Kovach, G.C. (2004, February 26). Officials: Students had Gun, Porn. *Dallas Morning News.* http://www.dallasnews.com/sharedcontent/dws/news/localnews/stories/022704dnmetnaughtytape.580d4.html.

Kovacs, J. (2004, December 9). Christmas Music Banned From Bus. *World Net Daily.* http://www.worldnetdaily.com/news/article.asp?ARTICLE_ID=41837.

Kozinski, A. (2006, April 20). *Dissenting Opinion: Harper v. Poway Unified School District.* http://www.ca9.uscourts.gov/ca9/newopinions.nsf/3BC4CBC4E3F50F4 1882571560022D4D/$file/0457037d.pdf.

Lamont, L. (2007, May 14). Bullied Teen Awarded Income for Life. *Sydney Morning Hearld.* http://www.smh.com.au/articles/2007/05/14/1178995042035.html.

Lawyers: Settlement Near in Challenge to School's Rebel Flag Ban. (2002, September 12). *Freedom Forum.* http://www.freedomforum.org/templates/document. asp?documentID=16950.

Legon, J. (2002, December 18). Student Gets 'A' for Hacking School Computer. *CNN.* http://archives.cnn.com/2002/TECH/internet/12/17/ student.hack/index. html.

Leinwand, D. (2007, June 19). Study: Drug Chat Pervasive Online. *USA Today.* http:// www.usatoday.com/printedition/news/20070619/a_online19.art.htm?loc= interstitialskip.

Leonard, A. (2007). Drama Surrounds Stage Production. *Happenings and Thoughts on all of Walton County.* http://www.southwalton.com/?p=831(retrieved December 19, 2007).

Less-Than-Banner Ruling. (2007, June 27). *Washington Post.* http://www.washington post.com/wpdyn/content/article/2007/06/26/AR2007062601864.html.

Libaw, O. (2002, June 14). The New Forbidden Dance. *ABC News.* http://www. streetgangs.com/topics/2002/061402dance.html.

Livingstone, S. (2005, June 8). Fight Against Steroids Gaining Muscle in High School Athletics. *USA Today.* http://www.usatoday.com/sports/preps/2005-06-08-sports-weekly-steroids-report_x.htm.

Lombardi, F. (2004, November 9). A Snapshot of Cameras at Schools. *New York Daily News.* http://www.nydailynews.com/11-09-2004/news/story/250961p-214899c.html.

Lombardi, K.S. (2007, June 3). A High School Drama Over Artistic Freedom. *New York Times.* http://www.nytimes.com/2007/06/03/nyregion/nyregionspecial2/ 03colwe.html.

Lopez, L. (2005, March 25). Shootings spur school building design changes. The Oregonian. http://www.oregonlive.com/news/oregonian/index.ssf?/base/front_ page/1111748652291610.xml.

LSD Sickens Three Children at Elementary School. (1998, September 25). *CNN.* http://www.cnn.com/US/9809/25/children.sickened.

Lueck, T.J. (2007, May 2). Judge Rules Against New York City Ban on 'Graffiti Instruments.' *New York Times.* http://www.woostercollective.com/2006/05/ judgeoverturns_new_york_citys_ban_on_gr.html.

Lyznicki, J.M., McCaffree, M.A., & Robinowitz, C.B. (2004, November 1). Childhood Bullying: Implications for Physicians. *American Family Physician.* http://www. ama-assn.org/ama/pub/category/print/14312.html.

Mahoney, D. & Faulker, M. (1997, December 1). *A brief Overview of Pedophiles on the Web.* http://www.prevent-abuse-now.com/pedoweb,htm.

Manning High School. (2007). *Student Handbook.* http://www.clarendon2.k12.sc.us/ mhs/handbook.htm.

Marech, R. (2005, March 8). Reward Offered for Information on Racist Graffiti at Middle School. *San Francisco Chronicle.* http://www.sfgate.com/cgibin/article.cgi? f=/c/a/2005/03/08/BAGBMBLTE81.DTL.

Marijuana Lyrics. (2007). *Drugs Plaza.* http://www.drugs-plaza.com/musiclyrics_ marijuana.htm.

Marin Institute. (2007). Alcohol Advertising and Youth. http://www.marininstitute. org/Youth/alcohol_ads.htm. (Retrieved November 25, 2007.)

Mauro, T. (2007, March 6). Court Vacates 9th Circuit Ruling Against Anti-Gay T-Shirt. *First Amendment Center.* http://www.firstamendmentcenter.org/analysis. aspx?id=18251.

McDonald's Salad Has 18.4 Grams of Fat, Cheeseburger Has 11.5 Grams. (2004, March 9). *Medical News Today.* http://www.medicalnewstoday.com/articles/6435.php.

McElhatton, J. (2004, May 14). 'Too Much Money' Being Spent on School Security, Cafritz Says. *Washington Times.* http://www.washtimes.com/metro/20040514-105900-5226r.htm.

Medical Marijuana. (2007). *Drug War Facts.* http://www.drugwarfacts.org/medicalm.htm.

Menard, J. & Martindale, M. (2005, March 25). Bullying Can Push Students Over Edge. *Detroit News.* http://www.detnews.com/2005/schools/0503/25/A01-128962.htm.

Mendoza, M. (2007, July 5). Nutrition Education Efforts Failing. *Chicago Tribune.* http://www.chicagotribune.com/services/newspaper/premium/printedition/Thursday/chi-fatfight_05jul05,1,3525130.story?ctrack=2&cset=true.

Methamphetamine. (2007, November 25). *The Partnership for a Drug Free America.* http://www.drugfree.org/Parent/Drug Guide/Methamphetamine.

Meyer, K. (2003, June 14). Bill Ensures Vandals Pay Restitution. *Anchorage Daily News.* http://www.akrepublicans.org/meyer/23/info/meye20030614011.php.

Millard, B.C. (2007, May 25). Confederate Flag Lawsuit Dismissed. *Daily Times.* http://www.thedailytimes.com/apps/pbcs.dll/article?AID=/20070525/NEWS/705250317.

Mistrial Declared in Case Against Former Md. Local Superintendent. (2007, December 5). *Education Week,* 27 (14), 3.

Molotov Cocktail. (2005). *Wikipedia.* http://en.wikipedia.org/wiki/Molotov_cocktail (retrieved December 6, 2005).

Monk-Turner, E., Ciba, P., Cunningham, M., McIntire, P.G., Pollard, M., & Turner, R. (2004, December). A Content Analysis of Violence in American War Movies. *Analyses of Social Issues and Public Policy,* 4 (1), 1–11.

Morano, M, (2003, June 3). School Reverses Ban on Use of 'God' at Graduation Ceremony. *Cybercast News Service.* http://www.conservativenews.org/ViewCulture.asp?Page=%5CCulture%5Carchive%5C200306%5CCUL20030603b.html.

Morson, B. (2007, September 28). Dozen Boulder High Students Walk Out Over Pledge. *Rocky Mountain News.* http://www.rockymountainnews.com/drmn/local/article/0,1299,DRMN_15_5709185,00.html.

Mount Miguel High School. (2004). *Student Handbook.* http://mmhs.guhsd.net/MMStudentHandbook.htm#behavior.

Mullally, C. (2007, January 4). Banned Books. *First Amendment Center.* http://www.firstamendmentcenter.org/speech/libraries/topic.aspx?topic=banned_books.

Murray County (Georgia) High School. (2004). *Student Handbook.* http://www.murray.k12.ga.us/handbooks/FINAL%20high%20school%202004-2005.htm.

Napolitano, J. (2005, November 10). Oak Lawn High Suspends Hackers. *Chicago Tribune.* http://www.chicagotribune.com/technology/chi-051110computerhacking,1,1706537.story?coll= chi-news-hed.

National Clearing House for Alcohol and Drug Information. (2007). *Tips for Teens: The Truth About Cocaine.* http://ncadi.samhsa.gov/govpubs/phd640/(retrieved November 21, 2007).

National Institute on Drug Abuse. (2006, December). *NIDA InfoFacts: High School and Youth Trends.* http://www.nida.nih.gov/Infofacts/HSYouthtrends.html.

National Institute on Drug Abuse. (2007, March). *NIDA InfoFacts: Steroids.* http://www.nida.nih.gov/Infofacts/Steroids.html.

National School Safety and Security Services. (2007). *School-Related Deaths, School Shooting, and School Violence Incidents—2005–2006.* http://www.schoolsecurity.org/trends/school_violence05-06.html.

National Television Violence Study. (1997). Thousand Oaks, CA: Sage.

National Television Violence Study, Year Three: 1996–97. (1997). Media Awareness Network. http://www.media-awareness.ca/english/resources/research_documents/reports/violence/nat_tv_violence.cfm.

Nearly 800 Plagiarism Web Sites Make School Cheating Easier than Ever, Secure Computing Reports. (2005, September 7). *Business Wire.* http://findarticles.com/p/articles/mi_m0EIN/is_2005_Sept_7/ai_n15346376.

Newman, M. (1995, October 27). Some Progress is Seen on Federal Initiative for Gun-Free Schools. *New York Times.* http://query.nytimes.com/gst/fullpage.html?res=9B01E4DD1F39F934A15753C1A963958260.

New Mark Twain Letters Reveal He Poked Fun at Huck Finn Ban. (1935, November 2). *New York Times.* http://www.twainquotes.com/19351102.html.

New Silly Reasons to Ban Books. (1999, May/June). *Teacher Librarian,* 26 (5).

Noll, K. (2001, March). Advice for Parents and Teachers. *Teachers Net Gazette.* http://teachers.net/gazette/MAR01/noll.html.

NORML. (2007a). *About Marijuana.* http://norml.org/index.cfm?Group_ID=7305 (retrieved November 18, 2007).

NORML. (2007b). *Principles of Responsible Cannabis Use.* http://norml.org/index.cfm?Group_ID=3417 (retrieved November 18, 2007).

North Carolina Battling Sexual Predators on MySpace. (2007, May 24). *Vindy.com.* http://www.vindy.com/content/national_world/333331756220859.php.

Nyhan, P. (2007, August 15). More Kids are Seeing More Drugs in School. *Seattle PI.* http://seattlepi.nwsource.com/local/327815_teensdrugs16.html.

Office of Intellectual Freedom, American Library Association. (2007). *Initiator of Challenge.* http://www.ala.org/Template.cfm?Section=bbwlinks&Template=/ContentManagement/ContentDisplay.cfm&ContentID=40912.

Ogawa, J. (2007, October 1). Report Says Arrested Scott Athlete Was Delivering Cocaine at School. *Lexington Herald-Leader.* http://www.kentucky.com/181/story/191287.html.

Olentangy High School. (2007). *Student Handbook.* http://www.olentangy.k12.oh.us/district/board/policy/handbooks/high/14conduct.html.

O'Malley, M. (2004, January 7). Vandals Slash Tires on 25 Buses; Classes Go On In North Royalton. *Cleveland Plain Dealer.* http://www.cleveland.com/education/index.ssf?/base/isedu/1073480105167150.xml.

O'Neal, K. (2003, November 11). Two Boys Charged With Shouting Bomb Alert. *Indianapolis Star.* http://www.indystar.com/articles/0/091706-3970-103.html.

Opinion: What Have Other People Thought About Bridge to Terabithia? (2007). *Scholastic.* http://www.scholastic.com/kids/homework/pdfs/Bridge_to_pt4.pdf.

Ovalle, D. (2007, July 25). Dade Teacher is Arrested on Drug Charges. *Miami Herald.* http://www.miamiherald.com/460/story/182335.html.

Overweight and Obesity. (2007). Centers for Disease Control and Prevention. http://www.cdc.gov/nccdphp/dnpa/obesity/index.htm.

Passion of the Christ. (2007). *Wikipedia.* http://en.wikipedia.org/wiki/The_Passion_of_the_Christ.

Patchin, J.W. & Hinduja, S. (2005, October 11). *Cyberbullying Study.* http://www.cyberbullying.us/.

Paul, K. (2002, April 30). Bus Hijacker's Plan 'Rudimental.' *Las Vegas Sun.* http://www.lasvegassun.com/sunbin/stories/ sun/2002/apr/30/513381592.html.

Paulson, A. (2003, December 30). Internet Bullying. *Christian Science Monitor.* http://www.csmonitor.com/2003/1230/p11s01-legn.html.

Peacefire. (2007). *Wikipedia.* http://en.wikipedia.org/wiki/Peacefire.

Pearlman, L. (2007, February 22). Mormon Family Sues Santa Rosa Schools Over Pro-Gay Policies. *Bay Area Reporter.* http://www.ebar.com/news/article.php?sec=news&article=1581.

Perry, J.L. (2001, August 8). School Vandalism Beyond Belief. *NewsMax.* http://www.newsmax.com/archives/articles/2001/8/7/190918.shtml.

Petersen, E. (2000). *Bridge to Terabithia: A Timeless Tale of Friendship.* http://www.ulster.net/~petersne/essay.htm.

Petress, K. (2007). *Noble Causes and Disastrous Effects of Campus Speech Codes.* http://www.umpi.maine.edu/~petress/essay20.pdf.

Police Say Seventh Graders Sold Cocaine at School. (2007). *WLTX-19.* http://www.wltx.com/news/story.aspx?storyid=55455 (retrieved November 18, 2007).

Principal Arrested After Buying Cocaine at School. (2007, February 23). *The News Press.* http://tallahassee.com/legacy/special/blogs/2007/02/principal-arrested-after-buyin-cocaine.html.

Quan, H. (2007, April 16). SSF High School Blanketed with Graffiti. *KCBS.* http://www.kcbs.com/pages/358004.php?contentType=4&contentId=414907.

Radke, J. (2003, March 7). Schools Sued Over Refusal to Ban Prayers. *Las Vegas Sun.* http://www.lasvegassun.com/sunbin/stories/lv-ed/2003/mar/07/514764190.html.

Raghunathan, A. (2007, July 25). Pinellas Teacher Accused of Growing Marijuana in His House. *St. Petersburg Times.* http://www.sptimes.com/2007/07/25/Northpinellas/Pinellas teacher accu.shtml.

Railton, S. (Ed.). (1998). *Mark Twain in His Times.* Charlottesville: University of Virginia. http://etext.lib.virginia.edu/railton/index2.html.

Real Life Cases of Bullying. (2005). *Teacher Net.* http://www.teachernet.gov.uk/wholeschool/behaviour/tacklingbullying/examplesofbullying/.

Reinhardt, S. (2006, April 20). *Harper v. Poway Unified School District.* http://www.ca9.uscourts.gov/ca9/newopinions.nsf/D2D4CBF690CD61A6882571560001FEBD/$file/0457037.pdf?openelement.

Rendon, R. (2007, August 14). In Sugar Land, Perry Signs Religion-in-Schools Bill. *Houston Chronicle.* http://www.chron.com/disp/story.mpl/metropolitan/5054636.html.

Report: Fewer Soft Drinks in School. (2007, September 17). *MSNBC.* http://www.msnbc.msn.com/id/20820091/.

Risinger, C. F. (1993, August). Religion in the Social Studies Curriculum. *ERIC Digest.* http://www.ericdigests.org/1994/religion.htm.

Roberts, G. (2003, November 26). 'Huck Finn' A Masterpiece or An Insult. *Seattle Post-Intelligencer*—http://seattlepi.nwsource.com/local/1499 79_huck26.html.

Roberts, J. G. (2007, June 25). *Morse v. Frederick.* www.scotusblog.com/movabletype/archives/06-278_All.pdf.

Robinson, B.A. (1999, July). Ten Commandments Legal Developments 1999. *Religious Tolerance.* http://www.religioustolerance.org/equ_acce.htm.

Robinson, B.A. (2003, April 18). The Federal Equal Access Act. *Religious Tolerance.* http://www.religioustolerance.org/equacce.htm.

Rolfe, D. (1997, April). Movie Violence Then and Now. *The Dove Foundation.* http://www.dove.org/columns/1997/column9704.htm.

Rubenstein, S. (2001, May 18). 2 Teens Suspended in School Vandalism. *San Francisco Chronicle.* http://www.sfgate.com/cgi-bin/article.cgi?f=/c/a/2001/05/18/MNL227495.DTL.

Russell, R. (1998, May 19). The Champ. *Suite 101.* http://www.suite101.com/article.cfm/censorship_books/7468.

Ryman, A. (2005, December 7). Schools Wrestling with Holiday Concerts. *Arizona Republic.* http://www.azcentral.com/arizonarepublic/news/articles/1207nocarols.html.

Saltman, J. (1998, January/February). Censoring the Imagination: Challenges to Children's Books. *Emergency Librarian,* 25 (8–12).

Santos, F. (2005, September 21). Protest Over Metal Detectors Gains Legs as Students Walk Out. *New York Times.* http://www.nytimes.com/2005/09/21/nyregion/21walkout.html?oref=login.

Scanner Alerts School to Sex-Offenders. (2007, December 2). *KABC.* http://abclocal.go.com/kabc/story?section=news/local&id=5809598.

Schemo, D.J. (2006, February 11). In Small Town, 'Grease' Ignites A Culture War. *New York Times.* http://www.nytimes.com/2006/02/11/national/11fulton.html&?ei=5088 &en=6ff393ff4112b535&ex=1297314000&partner=rssnyt&emc=rss&pagewanted=all.

Schoepf, M. (2004, November 9). Fake Pistol Causes Two Suspensions. *Pioneer Press.* http://www.twincities.com/mld/twincities/news/local/10131967.htm.

School Bans 5 from Grad Ceremony. (2005, May 27). *Star Bulletin.* http://starbulletin.com/2005/05/27/news/story4.html.

School Bans Shirts Supporting Beating Suspects. (2007, August 29). *MSNBC.* http://www.msnbc.msn.com/id/20500790/.

School Renames Easter Bunny 'Peter Rabbit.' (2007, April 7). *ABC News.* http://abcnews.go.com/GMA/story?id=3018390.

School Won't Erase 'Beautiful' Vandalism. (2005, June 2). *Houston Chronicle.* http://www.chron.com/cs/CDA/ssistory.mpl/nation/3208158.

School's Ban on Christmas Carols Sparks Debate. (2004, December 22). *MSNBC.* http://www.msnbc.msn.com/id/6745305/#storyContinued.

Schumacher, C. et al. (1997). *YRBS High School Results: Grades 9–12.* http://www.epi.hss.state.ak.us/pubs/yrbs/yrbs_toc.htm.

Sex Offender Applies to School—as 12-Year-Old. (2007, January 20). *MSNBC.* http://www.msnbc.msn.com/id/16716644/.

Sexual Harassment at School: Know Your Rights. (2007). *Equal Rights Advocates.* http://www.equalrights.org/publications/kyr/shschool.asp (retrieved November 7, 2007).

Shapira, I. (2007, November 2). Knives, Not Guns, Have Been Weapon of Choice in Campus Crimes, Study Finds. *Washington Post.* http://www.washingtonpost.com/wp-dyn/content/article/2007/11/01/AR2007110102260.html.

'Silent Night' Secularized. (2005, December 7). *World Net Daily.* http://www.wnd.com/news/article.asp?ARTICLE_ID=47784.

Silent Reflection and Student Prayer Act. (2007, October 11). *Illinois Compiled Statutes.* http://www.ilga.gov/legislation/ilcs/ilcs3.asp?ActID=1008&ChapAct=105

ILCS 20/&ChapterID=17&ChapterName=SCHOOLS&ActName=Silent+Reflection+and+Student+Prayer+Act.

Sjohon, H. (2007, June 4). Cracker. *Search Security Definitions.* http://searchsecurity.techtarget.com/sDefinition/0,,sid14_gci211852,00.html.

Smith, B. (2007, May 29). Next Installment of Mom vs. Potter Set for Gwinnett Court. *Atlanta Journal-Constitution.* http://www.ajc.com/metro/content/metro/gwinnett/stories/2007/05/28/0529metPOTTER.html.

Snider, J. (2007, August 15). More Drugs in Schools? *USA Today.* http://www.usatoday.com/news/nation/2007-08-15-drugs-school_N.htm.

Snyder, S. (2007, August 10). Schools Drop Recognition Months. *Philadelphia Inquirer.* http://www.philly.com/inquirer/local/20070810_Schools_drop_recognition_months.html.

Sofsian, D. (2005, August 16). The Rise of High School Drug Testing. *Ezine Articles.* http://ezinearticles.com/?The-Rise-of-High-School-Drug-Testing&id=74369.

Spitzer, E. (2007, April 28). *Healthy Schools Act to Implement Nutritional Standards for Schools.* http://www.ny.gov/governor/press/0428071.html.

Stacom, D. (2005, September 1). Schools Closed After Bus Vandalism. *Hartford Courant.* http://www.courant.com/news/local/hc-thombus0901.artsep01,0,320909.story?coll=hc-headlines-local.

Stearns, J. (2003, December 12). Threat Puts Vineyard High School on Alert. *Boston Globe.* http://www.boston.com/news/education/k_12/articles/2003/12/12/threat_puts_vineyard_high_school_on_alert/.

Stelzer, A. (2005, February 17). Taser Concerns Grow as Death, Injuries Mount. *The New Standard.* http://newstandardnews.net/content/?action=show_item&itemid=1486.

Stone v. Graham. (1980, November 17). http://caselaw.lp.findlaw.com/cgibin/getcase.pl?court=US&vol=449&invol=39.

Stossel, J. (2006, October). How to Fire an Incompetent Teacher. *Reason Magazine.* http://www.reason.com/news/show/36802.html.

Stowe, S. (2006, February 2). Citing Obesity Rates, Harford Plans to Ban School Sales of Sugary Drinks. *New York Times.* http://www.nytimes.com/2006/02/02/nyregion/02food.html?ex=1180670400&en=cbbcb7ff29a2e5cc&ei=5070.

Student Dress Code. (2005, July). *Stafford County Public Schools.* http://www.pen.k12.va.us/Div/Stafford/dresscode.html.

Student Press Law Center. (2002, October 29). *Middle School Paper Withheld for Printing Political Ads.* http://www.splc.org/newsflash_archives.asp?id=503&year=2002.

Students Use Cedarbug High School Computer to Get Private Data. (2007, June 7). *Pioneer Press.* http://www.twincities.com/wisconsin/ci_6083019?nclick_check=1.

Substitute Teacher Convicted in School Computer Porn Case. (2007, January 2007). *Boston Globe.* http://www.boston.com/news/local/connecticut/articles/2007/01/09/substitute_teacher_convicted_in_school_computer_porn_case/.

Sullivan, T. (2007, October 24). Belgrade High School Bans Sex Offender from Regular High School. http://bozemandailychronicle.com/articles/2007/10/24/news/10expulsion.txt.

Supreme Court Won't Review New York City Ban on Nativity Scenes in Public Schools. (2007, February 20). *Fox News.* http://www.foxnews.com/story/0,2933,253143,00.html.

Teen Punished for Saying 'That's so Gay' Loses Lawsuit. (2007, May 16). *First Amendment Center*. http://www.firstamendmentcenter.org/news.aspx?id=18563.

Teen Says He Brought Gun to School to End Taunts. (2007, August 2). *CNN*. http://www.cnn.com/2007/US/law/08/02/principal.shot.ap/index.html#cnnSTCText.

Thermos, W. (2005, December 9). Boy, 17, Admits He Booby-Trapped Pens. *Los Angeles Times*. http://www.latimes.com/news/local/la-me-pens9dec09,1,3510118.story?coll=laheadline s-california.

Thomas, R.M. (2003). New Frontiers in Cheating. *Encyclopaedia Britannica Book of the Year*, pp. 206–207. Chicago: Encyclopaedia Britannica.

Thomas, R.M. (2006). *Violence in America's Schools*. Westport, CT: Praeger.

Thomas, R.M. (2007). *God in the Classroom: Religion and American Public Schools*. Westport, CT: Praeger.

Thompson, C. (2005, April 1). Student Jailed in Bomb Plot. *Arizona Republic*. http://www.azcentral.com/arizonarepublic/news/articles/0401schoolplot01.html.

Tobacco Use. (2007, August). *BHS Student Handbook*. http://www.tipton-county.com/bhs/handbook.htm.

Torres, K. (2003, December 10). Hacking Gets Teen 10-Day School Time-Out. *Atlanta Journal-Constitution*. http://www.ajc.com/wednesday/content/epaper/editions/wednesday/metrof36dac50329afobf0003. Html.

Trashy and Vicious. (1885, March 19). *New York Times*.

Trotter, J. (2007, June 16). Perry Signs UIL Steroid-Testing Law. *Austin American Statesman*. http://www.statesman.com/news/content/region/legislature/stories/06/16/0616steroids.

Tryon, C. (2004, November 1). Fahrenheit 9/11 in the Classroom. *The Chutry Experiment*. http://chutry.wordherders.net/archives/002933.html.

Two Juveniles Arrested for JLS Middle School Vandalism and Hamster Killing. (2004, March 1). *City of Palo Alto*. http://www.cityofpaloalto.org/press/New%20Releases/20040301.htm.

Understanding Plagiarism. (2007). *Prentice Hall Tutorial*. http://wps.prenhall.com/hss_understand_plagiarism_1/0,6622,427064-main,00. html.

U.S. Census Bureau Facts for Feature: Back to School—2007-2008. (2007, June 14). *PR Newswire*. http://www.prnewswire.com/cgi-bin/stories.pl?ACCT=ind_focus.story&STORY=/www/story/06-142007/0004608454&EDATE=THU+Jun+14+2007,+11:58+AM.

U.S. School Food Standards to Tackle Obesity. (2007, April 26). *Medical News Today*. http://www.medicalnewstoday.com/articles/69021.php.

U.S. Supreme Court: Public Schools Can't Censor Religious Views of Students in Class Assignments. (2006, April 24). *Charleston Gazette*. http://wvgazettemail.com/forums/viewtopic.php?t=7525&sid=52f5bb44f34a9e1515f0d05d5f73d168.

Vallance, J. (2007, February 20). What Every American Can Do to Prevent Misuse of Prescription Drugs. *Whitehouse Drug Policy*. http://www.whitehousedrugpolicy.gov/news/press07/022007.html.

Vandalism. (2005). *BT Police*. http://www.btpolice.com/vandalism.htm.

Vandals at Conant High do $100,000 in Damage. (2005, June 2). *Chicago Tribune*. http://www.chicagotribune.com/business/content/education/chi0506020297jun02,1,536964.story?coll=chi-education-hed&ctrack=2&cset=true.

Vanderford, J. (2005). School Vandalism Investigated. *Kolnkgin*. http://www.kolnkgin.com/news/features/1/1830967.html (retrieved November 4, 2005).

Van Sant, P. (2004, April 13). Dangerous Minds. *48 Hours—Investigtive.* http://www.cbsnews.com/stories/2004/04/12/48hours/main611479.shtml.

Violence. (2007). *Common Sense.* http://www.commonsensemedia.org/resources/violence.php.

Violence in Our Schools. (2005, March 21). www.columbine_angels.com/Shootings-2005-2009.htm.

Vitello, P. (2005, September 27). Ex-Schools Chief Pleads Guilty to Huge Theft. *New York Times.* http://www.nytimes.com/2005/09/27/nyregion/27roslyn.html.

Wagner, A. (2005, November 15). School Evacuated After Boy, 10, Sets Fire in Bathroom. *Washington Times.* http://www.washtimes.com/metro/20051114-112156-8258r.htm.

Walsh, M. (2007, October 10). Teacher's Appeal on "Peace" Speech Denied. *Education Week,* 27 (7), 18.

Walton, E.R. (2003, September 9). Judge Says School System Erred in Expulsion. *Greenville News.* http://greenvilleonline.com/news/2003/09/09/2003090913949.htm.

Washington State Legislature. (2007). Possessing Dangerous Weapons on School Facilities. http://apps.leg.wa.gov/RCW/default.aspx?cite=9.41.280(retrieved December 4, 2007).

Washington Township High School. (1999). *Student Handbook.* http://www.wtps.org/wths/handbook/conduct.html#alcohol%20drugs.

Weigl, A. (2007, May 23). State Senate Approves MySpace Bill. *Raleigh News & Observer.* http://www.newsobserver.com/news/story/577639.html.

Welles, K. (2005, April 28). Beating, Kicking, Bullying Ongoing at Local Schools. *WPIX-TV.* http://www.wpxi.com/target11/4426745/deta il.html.

Westley, M.N. (2005, April 28). Assault Allegation Probed at School. *Salt Lake Tribune.* http://www.sltrib.com/utah/ci_2692538.

White, B. (1988, January 13). *Hazelwood School District v. Kuhlmeier.* http://caselaw.lp.findlaw.com/scripts/getcase.pl?court=US&vol=484&invol=260.

Who Is Doing the Banning? (2007). *Banned Books.* http://www.banned-books.com/bborgs.html.

Wilbur, D.Q. (2005, April 22). 15-Year-Old Charged in Charter School Arson. *Washington Post.* http://www.washingtonpost.com/wp-dyn/articles/A7958-2005Apr21.html.

Williams, A. (2006, May 4). School Board Bans Junk Food. *Register-Guard.* http://www.registerguard.com/news/2006/05/04/d1.cr.4jboard.0504.p1.php?section=cityregion.

Williamstown High School. (2006). *Student Handbook.* http://www.monroetwp.k12.nj.us/hs/main%20links/hs%20handbook/hs%20student%20handbook.htm.

Witsil, F. (2007, March 26). Parents Back School's MySpace Ban. *Detroit Free Press.* http://www.wzzm13.com/news/specials/online_article.aspx?storyid=73091.

Woolf, M. (2004, August 4). No-Blame Approach to Bullies Comes Under Attack. *Independent.* http://news.independent.co.uk/uk/politics/story.isp?story=547700.

Yee, T. (2005, April 5). Do You Think "The Adventures of Huckleberry Finn" Should be Banned From Schools? *Silver Chips.* http://silverchips.mbhs.edu/inside.php?sid=5187.

Index

About the Author

R. MURRAY THOMAS is Professor Emeritus, University of California, Santa Barbara, and the author of several books, including *Religion in Schools—Controversies Around the World* (Praeger, 2006), *Violence in America's Schools* (Praeger, 2006), *God in the Classroom* (Praeger, 2007), and *Manitou and God* (Praeger, 2007), among other titles.